# Archaeologies of the Contemporary Past

*Archaeologies of the Contemporary Past* turns what is usually seen as a method for investigating the distant past onto the present. In doing so, it reveals fresh ways of looking at both ourselves and modern society, as well as the discipline of archaeology.

The contributions to this volume represent the most recent research in this area. From different theoretical perspectives a variety of contexts are examined: Art Deco and landfills, miner strikes and college fraternities, an abandoned council house, as well as mass graves. In the light of developments since the 1980s, the authors variously engage the positive insights an archaeology of the contemporary past provides. This new archaeology gives a crucial understanding of the experience of modernity and the communities it continues to affect.

Such approaches challenge the decisions and boundaries of archaeological practice where the distinction between the subject and object of study is unsettled. Moreover they challenge the 'taken for granteds' of recent experience, bringing to light that which has been left hidden and unsaid, thereby serving as a critical intervention for re-describing and contesting the exclusions and inclusions of experience that shape modern life.

**Victor Buchli** is Lecturer in the Department of Anthropology at University College London. He is the author of *An Archaeology of Socialism* (1999). **Gavin Lucas** is currently directing excavation and post-excavation programmes for the Cambridge Archaeological Unit. He is the author of *Critical Approaches to Fieldwork* (2000).

# Archaeologies of the Contemporary Past

## Victor Buchli and Gavin Lucas

With contributions from:

Margaret Cox, Mercedes Doretti, Luis Fondebrider, David Hart, Ian Hodder, Jean-Pierre Legendre, Teresita Majewski, Laurent Olivier, William Rathje, Michael Brian Schiffer, Greg Stevenson, Laurie Wilkie, Sarah Winter and the Ludlow Collective (Donna L. Bryant, Phil Duke, Jason Lapham, Randall McGuire, Paul Reckner, Dean Saitta, Mark Walker and Margaret Wood).

London and New York

First published 2001 by Routledge
11 New Fetter Lane, London EC4P 4EE

Simultaneously published in the USA and Canada
by Routledge
29 West 35th Street, New York, NY 10001

*Routledge is an imprint of the Taylor & Francis Group*

Typeset in Goudy by
MHL Typesetting Limited, Coventry
Printed and bound in Great Britain by
St Edmundsbury Press, Bury St Edmunds, Suffolk

*British Library Cataloguing in Publication Data*
A catalogue record for this book is available from the British Library

*Library of Congress Cataloging in Publication Data*

Buchli, Victor
    Archaeologies of the contemporary past/Victor Buchli and Gavin Lucas; with
    contributions from Margaret Cox ... [et al.].
        p. cm.
    Includes bibliographical references and index.
    1. Archaeology–Methodology. 2. Archaeology–Philosophy. 3. Archaeology–Case
studies. 4. Civilization, Modern–20th century. I. Lucas, Gavin, 1965– II. Cox, Margaret.
III. Title.
CC75 .B825 2001                                                     00-044651
930.1′01–dc21

ISBN 0-415-23278-3 (hbk)
        0-415-23279-1 (pbk)

For Jenny and Mitchell

# Contents

# Figures

# Contributors

**Victor Buchli**, Dept of Anthropology, University College London, England.

**Margaret Cox**, School of Conservation Sciences, Bournemouth University, England.

**Mercedes Doretti**, Argentine Forensic Anthropology Team (EAAF), Buenos Aires, Argentina.

**Luis Fondebrider**, Argentine Forensic Anthropology Team (EAAF), Buenos Aires, Argentina.

**David Hart**, South African Heritage Resources Agency (SAHRA), Cape Town, South Africa.

**Ian Hodder**, Dept of Anthropology, Stanford University, Palo Alto, USA.

**Jean-Pierre Legendre**, Conservateur au Service Régional de l'Archéologie de Lorraine, France.

**Gavin Lucas**, Cambridge Archaeological Unit, University of Cambridge, England.

**The Ludlow Collective** (Donna L. Bryant, Phil Duke, Jason Lapham, Randall McGuire, Paul Reckner, Dean Saitta, Mark Walker and Margaret Wood), c/o Randall McGuire, Dept of Anthropology, Binghamton University, New York, USA.

**Teresita Majewski**, Statistical Research Inc., Tucson, USA.

**Laurent Olivier**, Musée des Antiquités Nationales, Saint-Germain-en-Laye, France.

**William Rathje**, Dept of Anthropology & BARA, University of Arizona, Tucson, USA and Stanford University Archaeology Center, Palo Alto, USA.

**Michael Brian Schiffer**, Dept of Anthropology, University of Arizona, Tucson, USA.

**Greg Stevenson**, Dept of Archaeology, University of Wales, Lampeter, Wales.

**Laurie Wilkie**, Dept of Anthropology, University of California, Berkeley, USA.

**Sarah Winter**, Henshilwood, Yates & Winter, Cape Town, South Africa.

# Acknowledgements

We would like to thank several people for their encouragement and critical advice during various stages of the production of this book. Needless to say our first debt is to the contributors, scattered across the globe, who were extremely generous with their time and professionalism in order to create this work. Mike Rowlands strongly supported its inception while Mike Shanks has provided continued encouragement of the project and the topic. The book started as a session at TAG in 1997 and the responses from there, and presentations at the Third Annual Heritage Seminar at Clare Hall, Cambridge (1998) and the EAA at the University of Bournemouth (1999), have provided much needed critical reflections on many key themes addressed in this book. In addition, thanks must go to two anonymous referees at Routledge for further comment and advice. Finally, deepest thanks go to our original commissioning editor at Routledge, Vicky Peters, who pushed the work through with complete confidence and commitment, a task completed latterly by her assistant, Polly Osborn. Similarly a number of institutions were key to the realisation of this project: the Cambridge Archaeological Unit, Sidney Sussex College, Cambridge and the Department of Anthropology, University College, London.

The cover illustration is a photograph of Rachel Whiteread's work, 'House', erected in 1993 in the East End of London (R. Whiteread, *House*, 1995, London: Phaidon Press). The work is a monumental plaster cast of the interior of an abandoned Victorian terrace house with all the minutiae of lived experience preserved in the plaster mould like a death mask. The local community subsequently insisted on its demolition in 1994. This work and others by her embody many of the complex, difficult and at times irreconcilable issues involved in the 'presencing of absence' in the recent past and we are very grateful to her for permission to reproduce her work here.

# Introduction

# Chapter 1

# The absent present
## Archaeologies of the contemporary past

*Victor Buchli and Gavin Lucas*

## Development of the archaeology of the contemporary past

Archaeology developed as a discipline concerned with the distant past, not only helping to establish the antiquity of humankind but unravelling ancient histories long buried and previously undreamt of. Throughout most of the history of archaeology, these early times remained the prime foci of the discipline, the more recent past receiving much less attention and something presumed best left to historians. Even when archaeologists did work in historic periods such as Medieval and early Modern Europe or Colonial America, these were, until recently, marginal fields in the discipline and frequently seen as ancillary to History. Since the 1960s, this attitude has been slowly changing and as we enter the new millennium, we no longer regard archaeology as a discipline defined by a particular time period – indeed the theoretical upheavals initiated during the 1960s can be seen as largely responsible for this. By focusing attention on the nature of archaeological methods and data, in particular on the fact that, as archaeologists, we deal primarily with material culture, the whole issue of how recent the subject matter of archaeology should be, becomes irrelevant.

The archaeology of modern or contemporary material culture arose during this upheaval, manifesting itself during the 1970s with projects on the university campuses of Tucson, Arizona led by Michael Schiffer and at Honolulu, Hawaii by Richard Gould. One of the most famous projects to emerge from the former campus was Rathje's Garbage project set up in 1973 and still going strong. These projects reached a wider audience and acclaim with the publication in 1981 of *Modern Material Culture: The Archaeology of Us*, edited by Gould and Schiffer, stemming from a symposium at the American Anthropological Association meetings in 1978. Indeed, it was in this volume that Rathje explicitly stated that archaeology can no longer be defined either by digging or a concern for old data, but is '... a focus on the interaction between material culture and human behaviour, regardless of time or space' (Rathje 1979: 2; Rathje 1981: 52). But what was the agenda of the 'archaeology of us' – was it really a concern with contemporary/modern material culture or were they after something else?

The answer is rather ambivalent; on the one hand, there is no doubt that many of the authors saw the archaeology of contemporary society as an important theme, in particular as part of the larger project of the archaeology of the historic and/or recent past. Nevertheless, Rathje, Schiffer and Gould all gave equal, if not more, prominence to the ethno-archaeological and pedagogic value of such studies. A primary concern of the volume lay in trying to understand the relation between material culture and human behaviour in terms of generalising statements, even laws, as befitted the spirit of the time which could then inform more conventional archaeological research. As Schiffer and Gould state in their preface to the volume mentioned above, '... anyone looking for direct applications of the recent findings to past human behaviour presented by the chapters in this book will be disappointed. The archaeological payoff of this book can only be realised indirectly, first by positing relationships of a general nature and then by deriving predictions or tests of each relationship with respect to particular prehistoric- or historic-archaeological cases' (Gould and Schiffer 1981: xvi).

The studies in that volume and subsequent research on contemporary material culture have tended to reproduce this dual characteristic – indeed, perhaps one can examine the subsequent history of archaeological work on our own material culture according to the prime concerns driving it. Two main strands of modern material culture studies in archaeology may be identified: first are those that are explicitly ethno-archaeological and concern themselves with more general issues of material culture which are supposed to feed back into research in traditional archaeological periods. Second though, are those that deal explicitly with the present as an archaeology of us, sometimes enfolding their study within a longer-term, historical perspective. Of course not all studies fall exclusively into these categories and nor should they – one can be equally concerned to elucidate aspects of our everyday material life and draw more general inferences on the nature of material culture. But it is important to characterise the primary agenda behind any study of modern material culture, for the concern of this book is to distinguish the archaeology of contemporary or modern material culture from its function as ethno-archaeology.

Ethno-archaeological approaches to contemporary material culture in archaeology have a long pedigree – Kidder excavated a town dump back in the 1920s, although he did not publish it, probably because he saw it only as a heuristic exercise for his own edification (Rathje 1979: 3). Such studies though have been occasional and rarely published. The real impetus came in the 1970s in the wake of the New Archaeology. Work already mentioned on the university campus in the States focused on a range of contexts, most of which were intended both to instruct students in the principles of archaeological reasoning and develop critical understanding of how the archaeological record formed. Much of Schiffer's career has been devoted to exploring processes involved in the formation of the archaeological record and much of this was based on studies of the material culture of his own society. Indeed many of the papers in the Schiffer and Gould volume are explicitly ethno-archaeological. Such middle-range research has continued into the present, but another strand of ethno-archaeological studies of modern material culture emerged with the rise of post-processualism, particularly from Ian Hodder and his students.

Hodder's own study of a pet-food factory and the role of bow ties worn by the workers was quite clearly an attempt to understand more general issues surrounding material culture and, in his conclusion, he raises the question of its implications for archaeologists dealing with the past (Hodder 1987: 19). While Hodder's study is firmly within his contextual archaeology and his own perspectives on the nature of material culture, on the whole it differs little in intent from Schiffer and Gould's work, namely the elucidation of the relation between material culture and human actions or behaviour. Regardless of the markedly different views on this relation, both processual and post-processual ethno-archaeological studies of modern material culture share this perspective: whatever the similarities or differences, such studies are not primarily interested in the archaeology of modern material culture but use it as a means to an end.

The second thread, and the subject of this volume, is with the archaeology of us, and it is also the least developed. Rathje identified three phases in the development of the archaeology of us, which he saw as part of a multi-disciplinary interest in modern material culture (Rathje 1979). The first phase is defined by an interest in popular culture, which manifests itself archaeologically in 'what if?' games – such as, what if archaeologists were to dig our remains in a thousand years, what would that tell them about us? The second phase is more reflexive and links material culture to behaviour, but does so in a very passive way so that it becomes purely a search for material correlates of social or ideological aspects of society – 'studies in search of stereotypes' as Rathje aptly describes them (Rathje 1979: 20). The third phase is defined by the awareness that material culture is not passive and reflective but can act back upon us in unexpected ways, which has particular resonance in popular mythologies of technology. Thus one of the first concerns is for studies on the social context of technology, one example being resource management issues and consumerism. Rathje's phases are useful although in many ways the 'archaeology of us' as more than an occasional project only really emerged in his third phase and is still not a major area of research within archaeology. Indeed, the best known contemporary research project remains Rathje's Garbology, which has focused its investigation on 'fresh' garbage and, since 1987, landfills. Rathje has identified what he sees as the unique element of this kind of archaeology in that:

> … all of its studies have been grounded in the hands-on sorting of quantifiable bits and pieces of garbage in place of collecting data through interview-surveys, government documents, or industry records. In other words, the Garbage Project is studying consumer behaviours directly from the material realities they leave behind rather than from self-conscious self-reports.
>
> (Rathje 1996)

This quote also highlights the major focus of the project – consumerism – and some very revealing interpretations have emerged. For example, studies on fresh garbage highlight themes revolving around differences in what people said or thought they did and what they actually did, while the study of landfills had wider implications for recycling and source reduction of waste (ibid.). Rathje clearly sees the project as helping to change current practices and, as such, reinforces an important element of the archaeology of us. Another recent study is by Schiffer; his *The Portable Radio in American Life* is explicitly situated within the tradition of behavioural archaeology and serves as 'an alternative to personal histories, narrow technological and social histories and cryptohistories dished out by corporations' (Schiffer 1991: 4). As such it acknowledges the sheer overabundance of information that characterises twentieth-century experiences. But this excess – as surely as any dearth of information – obscures other understandings and voices and, in this respect, raises another significant side to an archaeological approach.

Schiffer's study deconstructs corporate 'cryptohistories' of products established by dominant multi-national electronics manufacturers to reveal a very different story, one that also has far-reaching impacts on the development of twentieth-century societies. As Schiffer states: 'Because ignorance of real product history is so widespread, cryptohistory has a way of insinuating itself into serious discussions of industrial and economic policy' (Schiffer 1991: 226). A dependence on received discourses about 'taken for granted' objects such as the portable radio seems to provide banal and trivial information enforcing an obfuscation of the origins of everyday things. Schiffer's archaeological approach serves to make connections and reveal hidden narratives unavailable to the researcher employing the traditional data and methodologies of design, social or cultural history. At the crux of Schiffer's argument is the waning of American industry and the loss of jobs and ensuing social costs that are naturalised and obscured by such dominant corporate 'cryptohistories' which structure our understandings of industry, national policy and the material world around us.

Comparable post-processual studies explicitly focusing on modern material culture include Shanks and Tilley's study of British and Swedish beer cans where they affirm the importance of an archaeology of the present (Shanks and Tilley 1987: 172). However, they criticised the projects spawned by the University of Arizona as being too 'empiricist and functionalistic' and limiting insights, but most significantly, failing 'to realise the potential of the study of modern material culture as a critical intervention in contemporary society, an intervention with transformative intent' (ibid.). This is certainly true of the more ethno-archaeological type of projects, but perhaps less true of Rathje's Garbology. Their own study of beer cans showed how the differing designs in Britain and Sweden can be seen as different ideological resolutions of a major contradiction in Western society over the consumption of alcohol – as a lifestyle activity associated with pleasure and as a potential poison to the healthy body. However, they reiterate a point of Rathje's, thereby echoing the concerns of other commentators on modern experience which focus on daily practice and the quotidian as important sites of analysis:

> If we are to demonstrate that archaeology really can make a distinctive contribution towards an understanding and critique of the present then, we feel, reference must not only be made to discourses but must pay detailed attention to the material culture-patterning as well.
>
> (Shanks and Tilley 1987: 172–3)

This point was directed specifically at the structuralist studies of material culture such as by Barthes (see below), and also aimed at Daniel Miller's earlier study of state housing (1984a, 1984b). To be fair to Miller, however, he also makes the same point in his conclusion (Miller 1984b: 47), and more significantly, it is Miller who has done more than anyone in Britain to advance the subject of modern material culture studies. It is to this subject that we now turn and ask what relation an archaeology of the contemporary past might have with it.

## Archaeology and modern material culture studies

While having grown out of Hodder's post-processual archaeology with Shanks and Tilley, Miller has since gone on to develop a new 'discipline' of material culture studies, although Miller would question whether it actually is, or should constitute a distinct discipline in the sense of, say, archaeology (Miller 1998). Miller takes up many of Hodder's points about the nature of material culture – he does not espouse any general theory (as for example Schiffer and Miller 1999) but rather seeks to focus attention on the materiality of culture and the specific way it operates in contemporary society. Arguing against the simplistic structuralist uses of material culture which portray it as merely reflecting or reproducing structures evident in other arenas (e.g. ethnicity, gender and race), Miller argues for the active role of material culture and consumption in social relations. This very trait also makes it able to transcend disciplinary boundaries and draw different connections and ways of seeing (Miller 1998).

The burgeoning field of material culture serves as a forum for these preoccupations with the human interaction with the artefactual world (Miller 1998, Editorial 1996). As Daniel Miller has stated, modern material culture is an inherently multidisciplinary space where a number of disciplines converge: 'Material culture studies is not then constituted by ethnography, but remains eclectic in methods. Approaches from history, archaeology, geography, design and literature are all equally acceptable contributions' (Miller 1998: 19). Most mainstream design history for example is more concerned with design *per se* and not with use/consumption or indeed other aspects of the material world which are more marginal to the discipline such as the vast majority of ordinary everyday objects and the contexts of their uses. However, more recent studies (Atfield 1999, Sparke 1986, Crowley and Ried 2000, Glassie 1999) have attempted to work along similar holistic lines; some design/art historians have ventured outside the confines of traditional boundaries to engage issues similar to those engaged by specialists in material culture trained in anthropological and archaeological traditions.

Many archaeologists have argued for a similar role for anthropological archaeology as a holistic enterprise concerned with the totality of human social and cultural experience (Rathje 1981, Schiffer and Miller 1999). In that sense it has the advantage of synthesis across a wide range of concerns that other disciplines such as design history, art history and cultural geography are not as well equipped to deal with. This point is constantly reiterated by the archaeologists represented in this book who are not distinguished methodologically by exclusive work in the non-discursive realm and the use of trowels and the like. So is archaeology the same as material culture studies? Perhaps the issue is not about re-defining the boundaries of archaeology as a material culture science irrespective of time or place – in fact such disciplinary circumscription is largely irrelevant if it were not perhaps arrogant. Rather, what counts is that archaeologists can bring unique contributions to the study of modern material culture because of their methods and theoretical perspectives – disciplinary divisions really do not matter. This volume therefore does not pretend to define the field of the 'archaeology of us'; what it does however show, is what happens when archaeology works with contemporary material culture and the themes and issues that such studies raise. We believe that on the whole, only archaeological approaches could have uncovered these themes and it is important therefore that we discuss why we think this.

## Absent presences

### Temporal proximity

We began by saying that archaeology developed precisely because it was concerned with the distant past, and a past with no written sources. An archaeology of the present, of us, would seem to be a perverse exercise in terms of a traditional archaeology – in the first instance, it deals with the present, not the past and in the second, it deals with contexts that are textually and discursively rich. While we no longer have to justify the extension of archaeology into recent historic or even modern periods which have rich textual evidence, there is a sense in which the theme of temporal distance remains largely unaddressed. One of the issues arising from an archaeology of the present for example is the justification for distinguishing it from historical archaeology. On the one hand, there is no doubt that themes and issues of today can be elucidated by an historical perspective and linking the present to the past is an important exercise. But equally there is something to be gained by focusing explicitly on an archaeology of the present, on an archaeology that engages with the here and now. The idea of the 'contemporary past' suitably sums this up compared with an historical approach which might be said to be concerned with the 'recent past'. 'Recent' implies close in time to us, 'contemporary' implies now; the difference is between proximity and identity.

The difference is more than semantic – there is a deep sense in which the 'archaeology of now' engages ourselves in a way much more intimately than any historical approach. With the latter, the object of study remains at some distance, there is still some gap, no matter how small, between the archaeologist and what is studied. With the archaeology of us, any gap is constantly being contested and collapsed because we are implicated in what we do to an extent much more immediate than with any other kind of archaeology. If anything, this is an archaeology of the future, if we take such an oxymoron seriously. Not so much in the sense of 'doing the job' for archaeologists of the future which Rathje describes, but in the sense of creating the future by being actively engaged in the materialisation of the present – as much as designers, for example. Caught in the double hermeneutic whereby we cannot study without changing the object of our study is perhaps nowhere more true than in the archaeology of the present. In this light, the question of the alterity or otherness, of the object of study becomes sharply focused.

### Archaeology as alienation

Traditional epistemology asserts the gap between past and present, between archaeologists and the society they study; if this epistemological distanciation has a temporal implication, what does it mean when this temporal distance collapses? To a large extent, the archaeological method (as science) can sustain the distance – as it does in ethno-archaeology or more generally sociological and ethnographic work, where the epistemological issues remain much the same. However, there is a sense in which turning our methods back onto ourselves creates a strange, reversed situation – a case of making the familiar unfamiliar. For example, the archaeological method applied to objects of the distant past serves to familiarise something inherently alien and unfamiliar. This is a domesticating strategy, and one essentially aimed at knowledge and control over something over which we have no control (Lowenthal 1985, pp. 252–5). But consider what happens when the same methodology is applied to the contemporary past – when we classify objects in the home for example by material categories such as ceramic, metal or plastic, or when we quadrant a bedroom floor for spatial control of artefact distribution (see Chapter 14). This is almost a perverse exercise in making familiar categorisations and spatial perceptions unfamiliar – a translation from an everyday perceptual language into an archaeological one (consider for example the conceptual artist Mark Dion's project/installation *Tate Thames Dig* 1999).

The archaeological method takes us further away, distances us from any attachment to the objects and the material world we encounter. In the same move it makes those objects of archaeological inquiry palatable and sanitised by its distancing effects, enabling us adequately to cope with any distress we might feel in the situation – the distress of invading someone's privacy for example or uncovering a mass grave. We take two examples: the first is that of corporeal decay. Most of us are disturbed by images of corpses, especially ones that are in a state of decomposition; yet people have to deal with such corpses all the time, from forensic teams to medics. Through training, they become desensitised to such sights, the bodies become objectified into forensic or medical cases requiring autopsy and diagnosis. As archaeologists, we are trained exactly the same way when excavating prehistoric burials. We might think this is not the same, because there is rarely flesh surviving on archaeological bodies, although archaeologists still deal with such situations (e.g. mummies), but perhaps more significantly, we still feel distressed about viewing the bones from mass graves but do not think twice about bones from a prehistoric cemetery.

Clearly context is critical to our reactions to a corpse, exceeding any 'universal' distinction between fleshed and unfleshed, in particular the sense that perhaps the corpse is in the *wrong* place. A transgression has occurred which elicits feelings of disgust around the corpse, which gives forensics its 'edge' over the routine excavation of prehistoric or historic burials. It is a transgression to which we can only be sensitive because it is something with which we can emotionally identify, something that draws on our self-image. It is very difficult to imagine a comparable sense of transgression in a traditional archaeological context – while we might be able to perceive its possibility, this is not the same as *feeling* it. This is because, as archaeologists, we are trained to distance ourselves from what we study – the alienation of our subject lies at the heart of archaeological methodology. To demonstrate this further, let us give another example. In a public presentation of our study of a council house, one of the more severe responses we received concerned the invasion of privacy. The ensuing debate spun the issue out much further to ask, for example, why is it acceptable to conduct this study in, say, an African village or even for that matter, a prehistoric one, and not in our home country? It raised into relief precisely the point being discussed now. We do not question the invasion of privacy in other countries or other times, because it is *other*; that is what archaeology studies – the other. Other corpses, other homes. Moreover, they are not simply already other, but are inscribed as other, or sustained as other, *because* of archaeological methodology. It is not upsetting that council cleaners went in after us, saw all that we saw, touched all that we touched; what was upsetting is that we objectified one of our own (despite obvious asymmetries), made them 'other', doing precisely what all archaeologists do everywhere, every day. Perhaps the real issue is that we never question this.

### Transgression

This operation of a familiar subject/object made unfamiliar creates profound anxieties and, as such, functions as a diagnostic tool for relevant and socially engaged cultural work. It coincides with Kristeva's notion of the abject:

*L'abjection* is something that disgusts you. For example you see something rotting and you want to vomit. It's 'abject' on the level of matter. It can also be a notion that concerns moral matters – an abjection in the face of crime, for example. But it is an extremely strong feeling which is at once somatic and symbolic, and which is above all a revolt of the person against an external menace from which one wants to keep oneself at a distance, but of which one has the impression that it is not only an external menace but that it may menace us from the inside. So it is a desire for separation, for becoming autonomous and also the feeling of an impossibility of doing so – whence the element of crisis which the notion of abjection carries within it. Taken to its logical consequences, it is an impossible assemblage of elements, with a connotation of a 'fragile limit'.

(Kristeva 1997: 372)

The issue of nausea is something that appears very often in the archaeology of the contemporary past, the somatic response to the archaeological act and the 'fragile limits' it negotiates. This is the nausea of decomposing bodies familiar to forensic archaeologists and the aversion to rotting waste of the garbologist and the issues of putrid excess addressed by these archaeologists as well as the 'instinctive' aversion to the object of study, whether repulsion at perceived violations of privacy or the stench of rotting corpses. Such studies highlight areas of unconstituted discourse and most of the papers in this volume illustrate this point through the highly charged emotional, ethical and political themes that they evoke. Michael Shanks has discussed this theme in relation to the conservation work of traditional archaeology: 'Conservation stems loss and decay, and I would connect it with a series of drives: ridding oneself of nausea, of decay; there is a sense of illness and holding off death' (Shanks 1992: 73). Shanks comments further that 'The excremental culture of archaeology, which may wish to avoid the nausea of loss and an absent past, finds gratification in a purifying perhaps neurotic desire to hold on and to order. It is allied with the marginalization of feeling and of heterogeneity, the irreducible otherness of the past' (Shanks 1992: 75).

Comparable with the abject is the idea of the uncanny or *unheimlich* in Schelling and Freud which has been explored by Anthony Vidler in his book *The Architectural Uncanny* (1992). Vidler relies heavily upon archaeological analogies to sustain his discussion of architectural interpretation and while for the most part such musings on archaeology outside the discipline seem irrelevant, in the case of the contemporary past, the architectural historian/ theoretician and the archaeologist of the contemporary past are working in similar territory. It might be useful here to re-appropriate this archaeological analogy when considering the archaeology of the contemporary past. According to Vidler, archaeology and the archaeological act is by definition an 'uncanny' act which reveals that which should have remained invisible (Vidler 1992: 48). The *unheimlich* is also often intimately related to the idea of 'haunting'. The idea of ghosts is very close to the archaeological imagination: the disappeared, the past and how such spectres enthral us, at once horrifying and comforting. Vidler's discussion of Pompeii as an uncanny experience is instructive. The sight of the quotidian frozen in time by a catastrophe and revealed many centuries later induces this sense of the *unheimlich*. The 'uncanny' effect seems to be the result of repetition, a doubling through a simultaneous process of presencing and distancing. This 'doubling' creates a residue, a ghost that is uncanny and disturbing, which is unassimilable, there but not there. An absent present. This occurs with profound consequences when considering the archaeology of the disappeared for example and the implications of a romantic preoccupation with the uncanny is stripped of its aesthetic qualities and becomes a profound therapeutic act.

Archaeologies of the contemporary past expose just such realms of the abject and the uncanny; because of their approach focusing on the material, the non-discursive, they frequently engage with the unconstituted. This is not simply the unsaid, but the unsayable – it lies outside the said, outside discourse. This does not mean it is not visible, not experienced, but all too often the experience is crowded out by other, hegemonic discourses. The feelings of abjection and the uncanny arise precisely because we are suddenly faced with no words to articulate the experience.

### Non-discursivity and the unconstituted

The issue of text is raised by both Rathje and Schiffer in their recent work – for Rathje, contemporary texts often do not have the same kind of information about consumer behaviour which he can glean from garbology, while for Schiffer, the texts such as corporate cryptohistories are, if anything, giving too much information. There is a sense in which text can be both deficient and excessive with regard to material culture and, in either sense, unbalanced. There is always an element that remains outside discourse, unconstituted.

A recurrent theme of this book is the absent present. As a theme, it resonates with a growing body of literature on post-modernity and post-colonialism, particularly those dealing with issues around national and individual identity, issues of ethnicity/race and gender where subaltern identities and discourses are relegated to the margins, mute and silent (Bhabha 1994; Butler 1993). The realm of the disenfranchised, the subaltern, while usually outside the realm of discourse, is precariously near and as such it is not an unknown object of discourse but rather a non-object, forming the boundaries of the social and enfranchised. Homi Bhabha's writings on post-colonialism and issues of nationalism and identity argue that the location of important cultural work in the late twentieth century is not through the articulation of national identities or established bodies of knowledge, but interstitial, being created in the spaces between such bodies. In the process of translation and the articulation of the untranslatable and inarticulable, incommensurable elements emerge, 'stubborn chunks' (Bhabha 1994: 219). Moreover, the crossing of these boundaries creates 'blasphemies' which often result in violent, visceral reactions – such as occurred with the writing, translation and articulation of Salman Rushdie's *Satanic Verses* (Bhabha 1994: 225). Bhabha quotes Judith Butler on similar effects on the generation of 'queer' identities (Bhabha 1994: 219); Butler's work considers how categories such as the 'feminine' and 'queer' fall outside the dominant heterosexual matrix, not in the sense of a 'beyond' but as marginal, forming the boundaries of the dominant discourse; they are a constitutive outside. Moreover, she introduces the notion of 'matter' as those things that are brought into the realm of discourse which are viable, as in 'mattering' and as a consequence of their social worth, materialised (Butler 1993).

We argue that an archaeology of the contemporary past can perform the same kind of operation – it can materialise the material in the sense of making it matter, it can bring Bhabha's 'stubborn chunks' to the fore – but along with all the painful associations this carries such as ambivalence and nausea. This sort of work suggests a different sphere of activity. Rather than 'discovery' it can be characterised as an opening up, occupying an 'intermediate' space or an iterative time: an archaeology of the future and social possibility rather than of the past and social facticity; one that is constitutive of the present as much as any other contemporary materialising practice such as architecture or design among others (Buchli 2000 and Stevenson, this volume).

### Archaeology as constituting the unconstituted

The popular image of archaeological investigations into the present – that is popular views on garbology – are deliberate ways of taking the familiar to make it distant and with a certain social effect in mind. When people put into play such an archaeological operation, the purpose is to create a distance from the familiar, to make the familiar unfamiliar and ironically by defamiliarising taken for granteds, making what is too well known almost less known, one attempts to establish some sort of truth about what is being observed, the analytical distance that defamiliarises curiously enough establishes truthfulness about who we are. The same effect is achieved with the time capsule which, ostensibly an attempt to prevent archaeologists of the future from misinterpreting, misrepresenting us, in actual fact serves to underline a sense of our own material identity in the present. Individuals and organisations constitute their own material record of their experiences as a way of constituting the present, giving it a monumental quality (often it is fragile ephemera that is saved) and coming to terms with their experience through the exercise of attempting to preserve artefacts for future generations to look at. Thus this conceit is an epistemological claim and argument with which to establish certain truth claims, turning something discursive into a non-discursive, materialising discourse.

Archaeology clearly has a significant role to play in mediating these extremes, but ultimately, archaeology too is most often about producing texts – making the undiscursive discursive, making 'the mute stones speak'. What might be hazarded as unique as argued above is that the archaeology of the contemporary past addresses those aspects of experience that are non-discursive; inarticulate and otherwise unconstituted practices (either through suppression or otherwise). Though other disciplinary forays into the realm of twentieth-century material culture studies generally tend to be at the discursive level, archaeology penetrates even more into the non-discursive levels of experience to address tensions, contradictions, exclusions, pains, etc. The traditional lack or limited extent of textual/discursive analysis within archaeology makes it well equipped to deal with non-discursive realms of experience and with particular poignancy when the subject is the contemporary past.

Recent theoretical works on the subaltern and dispossessed have shown that the realm of discourse is the realm of the enfranchised. It is usually through the examination of the quotidian, the overlooked and 'taken for granted' that the traces of subaltern voices and experience can be constituted. It has been one of the great methodological feats of literary and cultural historians to attempt to constitute these voices in various projects concerned with, for example, slave narratives, women's narratives, queer narratives, etc. In addressing the issue of the non-discursive realm the archaeological act comes directly into contact with the subaltern, the dispossessed and the abject. This is not simply in terms of the usual archaeological preoccupation with remains, but the practical and social act of uncovering that which has once been hidden. The two converge here both literally and figuratively.

If prehistory is often characterised by a dearth of material with which to understand past social processes, the experience of the twentieth century and the recent past is confronted with an equally obscuring excess of information. The archaeological act traditionally has attempted to tease information out of the apparent poverty of information, allowing the artefacts to speak. The inverse becomes true when archaeology addresses the recent past. Within so many voices, which are almost universally dominant competing ones, other voices are silenced and do not speak, or more accurately, are not able to be heard. Thus the archaeological act, as the case studies in this volume show, attempt to constitute and articulate these voices. Beyond just performing the scholarly duty of constituting more and more information with which to understand the circumstances of our existence, the result has acute social effects enabling a critical empiricism that works on the contradictions of contemporary experience.

Such subaltern and 'silent' and abject voices are disturbing indicators of the contradictions and painful effects of twentieth-century experience. The archaeologist in this respect performs a very painful therapeutic operation that at times helps individuals and communities address these unconstituted painful and obscured silences. At times such a constitution of these experiences by the archaeologist is not permitted or is contested (as in Argentina or Britain) or is too painful to be addressed until a later, more appropriate time when such issues can be addressed more safely (World War Two, Auschwitz, Stalinism). Thus the archaeology of the contemporary past can happen only at certain times and in certain contexts in different parts of the world. At this point one might question when and why an archaeology of a contemporary past appears. What are the social and historical circumstances that permit such cultural work or not? What is clear is that the archaeological act, in addressing the absent present, addresses the silent and painful lacunae in our understanding of recent experience. As these case studies show, it almost invariably goes to the heart, or more accurately, the painful nerves and tensions of experience that would disrupt and/or challenge the dominant voices structuring our experiences. That is why it is often the case that the archaeological act is an extremely delicate and painful operation which elicits considerable emotion and at times objection.

In this respect the traditional operation of 'archaeological uncovering' serves a different purpose in the recent past, one that is more immediate, socially relevant, and as a consequence tense and often painful which addresses the painful ridges (or scars) delineating the contours of experience. In this respect the age-old methodological distinction of 'excavation' and 'uncovering' that which has been hidden from view through the analysis of artefacts yields considerable power in addressing the issues of recent experience. The diagnostic properties originally attributed to material culture as evolutionary indices by nineteenth-century ethnographers and archaeologists, function in other vital ways when confronted with the recent past. Orvar Löfgren has commented on Swedish material culture studies' greater concern with 'back-door research entrances to general problems' (Löfgren 1997: 110) which focus on the 'micro-physics' and 'micro-sociology' of consumption by focusing on specific artefact types and in-depth 'thick descriptions' of people's interactions with otherwise mundane objects and activities. Löfgren suggests a more critical return to the empiricism that characterised ethnology and archaeology in the last half of the nineteenth century when material culture as a concept emerged and what could or could not be constituted as material culture was determined, entered into museum collections and became national cultural history. As such, archaeology has never really given up these ancient techniques and has always been eminently suited to such 'back-door' techniques in its traditional methodologies and, as we can see here in this collection of studies, archaeology very much continues to do so through its critically empirical work. However, other disciplines that share a concern for the material culture of twentieth-century and recent experience do not perform this operation as effectively, rarely performing the act of making the invisible visible, presencing that which is absent or creatively constituting that which previously was inconstitutable, literally bringing into being and constituting a material culture when there had been none before and thereby expanding the scope of discursive culture.

### Redemption

Shanks draws an analogy between the archaeological act and psychotherapy. He notes that psychotherapy '. . . is to help patients reflect about themselves and sort out the relation between their past experience and present behaviour' (Shanks 1992: 78). Thus the psychotherapeutic encounter, just as the archaeological one, '. . . is to bring about a release of meanings of the past which will prove to be of use. This is practical reasoning.' It is also the pragmatic turn as evinced by various neo-pragmatist philosophers indebted to the tradition established by Michel Foucault, which sees the purpose of the intellectual, cultural worker as someone who enables her audience to 'cope' more adequately with changing contingencies (Rorty 1991). Rorty sees philosophy's role in exposing them as continuous with that of literature and the social sciences. Rorty's pragmatist '. . . thinks contemporary democratic societies are *already* organised around the need for continual exposure of suffering and injustice, and that no "radical critique" is required, but just attention to detail' (Rorty 1991: 25). It is precisely this attention to detail, this critical empiricism, that assists much of the archaeology of the contemporary past in its therapeutic endeavours.

The archaeological act works towards constituting that which has fallen outside the realm of discourse for a wide variety of reasons (all of which are usually symptomatic of the contradictions of modern experience). It also serves as a critique of other discourse-dependent disciplines such as design history, as Greg Stevenson's and Majewski and Schiffer's papers in this volume demonstrate, as well as broader issues including nutritional policy and environmental sustainability, as William Rathje shows in his contribution. Thus the old bugbear of traditional archaeology 'suffering' from the lack of discursive/textual evidence has, on the contrary, served it well by forcing it to develop techniques to understand human behaviour enabling a critical empiricism where discursive evidence is lacking. This has certainly been the case of historical archaeology which has demonstrated the importance of its work to supplement and more importantly challenge discursive historical evidence. Along the continuum of this framework we can see how valuable the archaeology of the absent present is towards approaching those issues that fall outside the realm of discourse in modern experience.

So what is unique about archaeology's role in this? Beyond its overt emphasis on material culture, it moves away from the interests of design, art and architectural history and attempts to make that which is *absent* present through the effects of the archaeological act. This is an inherently creative act which constitutes objects for the formation of discourses that did not exist before. More than ever the troublesome romantic notion of 'discovery' affecting archaeology becomes supplanted by 'creativity' instead. Stevenson has suggested that archaeologists are as much 'designers' of the material world as any others. The constitution of these objects of discourse and their political implications are more emphatically deliberate and willed into being than what is suggested by the serendipitous and somewhat passive notion of discovery. Rather than saying that 'we are only uncovering what has always been there', we propose that archaeologists constitute things in the present, not only conceptually but materially as well. This is a creative materialising intervention, which has redemptive and therapeutic powers which help individuals and communities cope with painful contradictions that otherwise would remain unarticulated.

## References

Atfield, Judy (ed.) (1999) *Utility Reassessed*, Manchester: Manchester University Press.

Bhabha, Homi (1994) *The Location of Culture*, London: Routledge.

Buchli, Victor (2000) 'Constructing Utopian Sexualities: Bolshevik Archaeology and Architecture' in R. Schmidt and B. Voss (eds), *The Archaeology of Sexuality*, New York: Routledge.

Butler, Judith (1993) *Bodies that Matter*, London: Routledge.

Crowley, David and Susan Ried (eds) (2000) *Style and Socialism*, London: Berg.

Editorial (1996) *Journal of Material Culture* 1: 5–14.

Glassie, Henry (1999) *Material Culture*, Indiana University Press.

Gould, Richard A. and Michael B. Schiffer (eds) (1981) *Modern Material Culture Studies: The Archaeology of Us*, New York: Academic Press.

Hodder, Ian (1987) 'Bow Ties and Pet Foods: Material Culture and the Negotiation of Change in British Industry', in Ian Hodder (ed.) *The Archaeology of Contextual Meanings*, Cambridge: Cambridge University Press.

Kristeva, Julia (1997) *The Portable Kristeva*, K. Oliver (ed.), New York: Columbia University Press.

Löfgren, Orvar (1997) 'Scenes from a Troubled Marriage: Swedish Ethnology and Material Culture Studies', *Journal of Material Culture*, 2(1): 95–113.

Lowenthal, David (1985) *The Past is a Foreign Country*, Cambridge: Cambridge University Press.

Miller, Daniel (ed.) (1998) *Material Cultures*, London: University College London Press.

Miller, Daniel (1984a) 'Appropriating the State from the Council Estate', *Man*, vol. 23, pp. 353–72.

Miller, D. (1984b) 'Modernism and Suburbia as Material Ideology', in D. Miller and C. Tilley (eds) *Ideology, Power and Prehistory*, Cambridge: Cambridge University Press.

Rathje, William (1979) 'Modern Material Culture Studies', *Advances in Archaeological Method and Theory*, 2: 1–27

Rathje, W. (1981) 'A Manifesto for Modern Material Culture Studies', in Schiffer and Gould (eds) *Modern Material Culture Studies: The Archaeology of Us*, New York: Academic Press.

Rathje, W. (1996) 'The archaeology of us', in C. Ciegelski (ed.) *Encyclopaedia Britannica's Yearbook of Science and the Future – 1997*, New York: Encyclopaedia Britannica Inc.

Rorty, Richard (1991) *Essays on Heidegger and Others*, Cambridge: Cambridge University Press.

Schiffer, Michael B. (1991) *The Portable Radio in American Life*, Tucson and London: The University of Arizona Press.

Schiffer, Michael B. and A. R. Miller (1999) *The Material Life of Human Beings*, London: Routledge.

Shanks, Michael (1992) *Experiencing the Past*, London: Routledge.

Shanks, Michael and Christopher Tilley (1987) *Re-constructing Archaeology*, Cambridge: Cambridge University Press.

Sparke, Penny (1986) *An Introduction to Design and Culture in the Twentieth Century*, London: Allen & Unwin.

Vidler, Anthony (1992) *The Architectural Uncanny*, Cambridge, Mass.: MIT Press.

# Part I

# Production and consumption

# Chapter 2

# Models of production and consumption

*Victor Buchli and Gavin Lucas*

Production and consumption arguably form the central poles of contemporary material life, indeed the material basis of social existence in capitalist and socialist industrialised societies. Much of modern social theory can be caught in the extremes of Marx's definition of production as the objectification of labour and Baudrillard's inversion of this formula in an anti-utilitarian conception of consumption. Marx argued that because value in human life came through productive labour, under capitalism neither labourer or capitalist are ultimately content – the labourer because they are alienated from the fruits of that labour, the capitalist because they enjoy what they did not produce. This model, after Hegel's master and slave relationship, may be over-simplistic, but more importantly it focuses everything around the pole of production which serves as the basis of social and historical existence. The flipside to this perspective, which has tended to dominate the way we see modern society until recently (see the recent works of Miller 1986, 1995, 1998) whether from a Marxist viewpoint or not, is that consumption is unproblematic. Consumption as merely the acquisition of goods on the basis of their utility value – i.e. the provision of basic human needs, and the consumer as the 'rational man', making 'rational' decisions on the basis of these given needs.

Despite various forays into issues of consumption throughout this century from writers such as Veblen, Simmel and Weber, the study of consumption as a problematic field emerged only in the 1970s and 1980s. Perhaps the earliest critic of consumption was Georges Bataille, who was heavily influenced by earlier anthropological work (e.g. Mauss). Bataille attacked the whole orthodoxy of political economy in his major work *The Accursed Share*, by challenging the notion that economies worked on a basis of finite or limited resources. Rather he saw this as a restricted conception of the economy and argued that in a more general view, there was always an excess of resources – social and historical structures are not defined on the basis of scarcity therefore, but *excess*. Cultural life is ultimately characterised by how societies deal with this problem of excess. The notion that consumption, as a means of dealing with excess rather than defined by utility and need was taken up by Baudrillard who has pushed the idea to its limit, questioning both the 'natural' basis of human needs and the 'natural' uses of objects – needs are not given but socially and culturally created, objects are not inherently useful for anything but can indeed become whatever we want them to be.

In terms of mainstream cultural studies of the 1970s and 1980s, two different strands are identifiable. One, coming out of the same post-modern context as Bataille and Baudrillard, has focused on consumption as a symbolic and semiotic rather than strictly utilitarian activity – the works of Baudrillard but also Barthes exemplifying this strand (Barthes 1973; 1977; Baudrillard 1981; 1996). The other falls more within an empirical and sociological framework and has studied the way consumption is not merely a passive but a creative activity which different groups within society use as a means of self-expression – works by Hebdige (1993) and others on sub-cultures and Bourdieu on class (Bourdieu 1984). Today, both these strands feed into a dynamic and increasingly significant area of research which cross-cuts disciplinary boundaries (Miller 1995; 1998). Indeed, Miller has made a key point about consumption, which in a way takes us back to Marx and the emphasis on production; Miller argues that in contemporary society, precisely because we are alienated from production (most of us do not produce what we consume), consumption, not production, has become the prime means of forging a relationship with the world (Miller 1995: 17). It is moreover within consumption and not production that some of the major social contradictions confront us, epitomised in the figure of the housewife. This has been especially apparent in feminist works. Miller argues that the housewife can metaphorically stand in for the contradictions of the modern consumer, being both of low social status and yet at the same time wielding huge power through choice in a global market economy, 'the consumer as global dictator'.

Despite the shift though towards consumption as a key category of analysis in modern material culture studies, is there a sense in which the relation between production and consumption has not been properly deconstructed? There is no doubt that there is a disjunction between producers and consumers in terms of both class and geography – but this has probably always been a component of life, even in pre-industrial societies. There is a lurking myth behind the Marxist critique of alienation, the myth of the pre-industrial lifestyle as one of near self-sufficiency so that people lived directly off the products of their own labour. This of course ignores the processes of specialisation and exchange that occur and have occurred in most pre-industrial societies (Sahlins 1974). More generally, the notion of producing in order to give away, in order not to enjoy the product of one's own labour, is a theme resonant in sacrifice and gift-exchange; Bataille's point is in fact that people have always been defining themselves more through such acts than everyday production for one's own consumption. The converse is also the case – we do not just consume for ourselves but also for others – and here Danny Miller's recent work on shopping and sacrifice, drawing explicitly on Bataille, is a good example (Bataille 1991 and Miller 1998).

Perhaps we should compare this basically Marxist model of the relation between humans and artefacts with the conventional archaeological model. The

Marxist model, constructed from the human viewpoint, articulates the relation in terms of objectification/externalisation and appropriation/internalisation – a kind of cyclical model whereby the production and consumption of material culture is articulated through the externalisation of ideas into things, and then re-internalised into ideas again. In contrast, the archaeological model is more from the viewpoint of the object and expresses the same relation in terms of culturation/c-transforms and naturalisation/n-transforms whereby the production and consumption of material culture is articulated through the synthesis and construction of raw materials into artefacts and their subsequent breaking down and decay back into the natural system. Conjoining the two models in a single diagram, we obtain that shown in Figure 2.1.

The diagram shows two axes, one marking the processes of externalisation and internalisation, the other, those of creation and dissipation, together making up a grid of production and consumption. In each of the four cells delimited by this grid is a term that sustains both the social and physical models of the production–consumption cycle. Starting clockwise in the top left-hand side, the concept of materialisation articulates the process of creative externalisation – that which incorporates both the idea of objectification and production/manufacture. Moving on, dissipative externalisation is characterised by the term 'waste', in the sense of both ejecta and decay, that which is thrown out (of the body, of the house, of society) and which decomposes, breaks down. Dissipative internalisation can be understood through a dual definition of usage, as both 'using up' and 'using for', to consume an object so it is taken out of circulation or the economy, and to consume it for some purpose. Finally, creative internalisation is appropriation, the attachment of an object to the self or group so it becomes part of its identity and at the same time transforms or shapes that identity.

The chapters that follow can all be seen to investigate different aspects of this grid. All three share in common a commitment to the role of archaeology in investigating these aspects, indeed argue that it can provide something that most other disciplines lack – a strong and long tradition of dealing with material

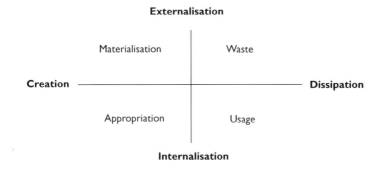

Figure 2.1 Production and consumption.

culture. More particularly, Majewski and Schiffer's and Stevenson's chapters primarily deal with the creative, left-hand side of the grid, with the issues of materialisation and appropriation. For example, in distinguishing the processes of invention, commercialisation and adoption, Majewski and Schiffer provide a framework for understanding how commodities are materialised, both as part of social and technological processes. Furthermore, in arguing for consumerism as a key term, as something that goes beyond consumption, they are stressing the importance of active consumption or appropriation, the fact that the consumption of goods can be used creatively to alter identities, the economy and more generally the material world, as in the case of the 'Japan Craze' in the late nineteenth century. Similarly, Stevenson argues for the active nature of consumption and in the context of design and art history, critiques generic terms such as Art Deco as masking the everyday processes of materialisation and appropriation within which most everyday objects such as ceramics are implicated.

Significantly, there are a number of similarities in these two chapters – for example, as well as both using case studies of ceramics, both raise the issue of the distinction between high/fashionable style and traditional style as being an important dynamic. Stevenson's paper in particular brings this out most forcefully in discussing the contradictions in Clarice Cliff's 'Art Deco' ceramics, which were 'domesticated' translations of high Modernism as expressed by leading artists of the period. Not only do her ceramics exhibit this duality in design or materialisation through the conflation of Modernist forms with traditional decoration, but also in their consumption or appropriation whereby these modern ceramics were often placed in very traditional, non-modern settings of the contemporary home. The tension between the 'high' and 'traditional' is thus one good example of how to understand the creative processes of production and consumption.

It seems fitting to start off the book with archaeological case studies of ceramics. They are more traditionally recognisable as archaeological and provide an opening through which we can approach archaeological studies on more recent subjects and their particular emphasis on consumption. It also provides a self-reflexive approach to archaeology's methodological beginnings as well as earlier forms of modern consumption, for the rise of consumerism and material culture studies along with ethnology and archaeology occur together in the second half of the nineteenth century (Löfgren 1997: 111). Additionally, the role of pottery as the archetypal, traditional waste debris of archaeological contexts is an appropriate way into the aesthetics of waste that Lupton and Miller argue characterises the experience of Modernism in the late nineteenth and early twentieth centuries (Lupton and Miller 1992). Such quotidian waste has traditionally been the empirical basis of archaeology.

Rathje's chapter thus takes us to the other side of the grid, to dissipation, both as consumption and waste. While his main point is to emphasise the importance of an integrated archaeology, the strength of Rathje's garbology can be said to lie in its investigation into the dissipative nature of contemporary society. Through identifying major discrepancies between reported and actual behaviour, the relation between waste and consumption has been painstakingly studied through investigations of fresh and landfill garbage over three decades and produced a wealth of information, his 'First Principle of Waste' being a good example. The less consumption behaviour varies, the less waste is generated; such a principle can be seen as a different perspective on the tension between traditional and popular styles elaborated by Schiffer, Majewski and Stevenson. Insofar as the dynamic of old-fashioned and in-fashion articulates processes of materialisation and appropriation, the very speed and variability of this dynamic can be said to articulate processes of usage and waste.

To summarise, the overall social effects of the archaeological act – whereby absence is presenced – can be seen here in terms of the critical insights that Majewski and Schiffer and Stevenson bring to the genealogies of consumer practices and product design that are too often concealed in dominant crypto-histories (Schiffer 1991). Similarly, Rathje's work offers a more direct critical intervention into our understanding of consumer practices, literally examining the consequences of our excesses – critically presencing what has been dissipated, buried and wasted in order to support our dominant myths buttressing modern consumerist societies.

## References

Barthes, Roland (1973) *Mythologies*, London: Paladin.

Barthes, R. (1977) *Image, Music, Text*, Glasgow: Fontana/Collins.

Bataille, George (1991) *The Accursed Share vol 1*, New York: Zone Books.

Baudrillard, Jean (1981) *For a Critique of the Political Economy of the Sign*, St Louis: Telos Press.

Baudrillard, J. (1996) *The System of Objects*, London: Verso.

Bourdieu, Pierre (1984) *Distinction*, Cambridge, Mass.: Harvard University Press.

Hebdige, Dick (1993) *Subculture: The Meaning of Style*, London: Routledge.

Löfgren, Orvar (1997) 'Scenes from a troubled marriage', *Journal of Material Culture*, 2(1): 95–113.

Lupton, Ellen and Miller (1992) *The Bathroom and the Kitchen and the Aesthetics of Waste*, Cambridge, Mass.: MIT Visual Arts Center.

Miller, Daniel (1986) *Material Culture and Mass Consumption*, Oxford: Basil Blackwell.

Miller, D. (1995) 'Consumption as the vanguard of history' in D. Miller (ed.) *Acknowledging Consumption*, London: Routledge.

Miller, D. (1998) *A Theory of Shopping*, Cambridge: Polity.

Sahlins, Marshal (1974) *Stone Age Economics*, London: Tavistock.

Schiffer, Michael (1991) *The Portable Radio in American Life*, Tucson and London: The University of Arizona Press.

# Chapter 3

# Beyond consumption

## Toward an archaeology of consumerism

*Teresita Majewski and Michael Brian Schiffer*

In 1982, Kent V. Flannery ridiculed archaeologists – garbologists in particular – who had taken up the analysis of modern American artifacts. Despite Flannery's denunciation, Rathje's 'Projet du Garbage' and other modern material culture studies have survived and prospered. As a genre of archaeology, however, modern material culture studies have low visibility because, we suggest, they lack a thematic focus. In this paper, we attempt to remedy this situation by redefining modern material culture studies as the archaeology of consumerism, following scholars such as Martin (1993), Schiffer (1991), and Spencer-Wood (1987a).

Modern material culture studies are usually taken to be research on the artifacts of industrial societies that can furnish information about those societies (e.g., Gould and Schiffer 1981; Rathje 1979; Rathje and Schiffer 1982). But, in light of current research in ethno-archaeology and historical archaeology, this definition seems too limiting. For example, in the ethno-archaeology of traditional communities, many investigators, including Lewis Binford (1976), Susan Kent (1984), James Skibo (1994), and Brian Hayden (1987; Hayden and Cannon 1984), have recorded and analyzed imported artifacts of industrial manufacture. These projects suggest that ethno-archaeology in traditional societies, and modern material culture studies in industrial societies, merge seamlessly. Evidently, the 'us' in the 'archaeology of us' is becoming more inclusive, taking in all peoples who participate, even marginally, in the modern world system.

The boundary between historical archaeology and modern material culture studies is also blurring as the temporal reach of historical archaeology, particularly in 'rescue' and 'cultural resource management' contexts, comes ever closer to the present (e.g., Adams 1973; Carlson 1990; Claassen 1994; Delgado 1992; Orser and Babson 1990; Wood 1991). If, as Leland Ferguson observed in 1977 in his introduction to *Historical Archaeology and the Importance of Material Things*, the 'historic' period goes from 'the seventeenth century through the present day,' then modern material culture studies and historical archaeology may be indistinguishable.

As historical archaeology, ethno-archaeology, and modern material culture studies continue to coalesce (e.g., Gould 1990), the latter term is liable to disappear as the label for a distinct genre of archaeology. For pragmatic and intellectual reasons, however, we do not believe that this should happen. In the pragmatic realm, 'material culture studies' is a term now widely employed in other disciplines. Thus, by retaining 'material culture' and the modifier 'modern', archaeologists signal some commonality of subject matter with sociologists, historians, folklorists, cultural anthropologists, etc. Examples of these multidisciplinary studies include Berger (1992), Ingersoll and Bronitsky (1987), Kingery (1996a, 1996b), Lubar and Kingery (1993), Miller (1995), and Poicus (1991).

The intellectual reason for retaining the term 'modern material culture' relates to the growing realization that archaeologists studying 'modern' societies are concerned with phenomena of modernity – specifically consumerism. Although investigators might define modernity in different ways, most would recognize that one of its major features is consumerism. We suggest that modern material culture studies, which interdigitate with ethno-archaeology and historical archaeology, can be defined thematically as the archaeology of consumerism or, simply, consumerist archaeology.

Consumerism is the complex of technologies, organizations, and ideologies that facilitate the mass production, mass distribution, and mass consumption of goods. A consumer society is one organized around the provisioning of its members – particularly those of the middle and working classes – with a seemingly limitless array of ever-changing products serving diverse utilitarian and symbolic functions (Miller 1987, 1994, 1995; Schiffer 1991). Consumerism also extends to behavioral components of societies, such as households, corporations, religious and social institutions, and governmental agencies (Rathje and Schiffer 1982).

We emphasize that the study of consumerism goes well beyond consumption itself, taking in all aspects of consumer societies – political, religious, educational, legal, leisure, economic, aesthetic, and so on – including the infrastructure for transport, energy, and communication. Consumerism research also studies services, whether provisioned by the state or by private enterprise (Miller 1995), because the delivery and use of services involves artifacts. Although consumerism seems to thrive best under conditions of corporate capitalism and 'free' markets, attempts to create consumer societies on socialist and communist foundations are also of interest.

## The roots of consumerism

The aim of consumerist archaeology is to explain, through comparative studies, differences and similarities in consumer societies and in their developmental trajectories. Conceived in this way, consumerist archaeology has no fixed temporal boundaries – one could, after all, investigate the stirrings of consumerism in the Italian Renaissance, as has David Kingery (1993; also Goldthwaite 1993; McCray 1996), but most studies will concern the eighteenth century to the present. Moreover, consumerist archaeology also lacks arbitrary spatial boundaries. Many studies would treat Western and Westernized industrial societies, but also encompassed are Second and Third World peoples who (1) make products in the factories of multinational corporations, (2) consume such products made elsewhere, (3) make craft items for mass markets in industrial societies, and (4) participate in 'development' projects. Because studies of consumer behavior, *per se*, are nothing new in archaeology (e.g., see papers in Spencer-Wood 1987a), much previous work – theoretical, methodological, and empirical – can be folded into a broadly conceived consumerist archaeology.

A consumerist archaeology implies no *a priori* commitments to a particular paradigm, conceptual scheme, or theoretical program. Not only are theoretically diverse archaeologists – behavioralists, systems theorists, structuralists, Marxists, and so on – developing the archaeology of consumerism, but their empirical studies exhibit surprising convergences in subject matter, problem definition, methods, and in the commensurability of results. This suggests that research on consumerism can integrate archaeologists across major theoretical cleavages, perhaps by fostering the growth of appropriate theory for linking consumer choice with large-scale processes of market societies (Spencer-Wood 1987a: 9– 10). A consumerist archaeology also countenances, and gains strength from, asking both historical (particularistic) and scientific (general) questions.

## The contribution of archaeology to consumerist studies

With so many researchers in so many disciplines now studying material culture, consumerism, and consumer societies, it is appropriate to ask what practitioners of archaeology can contribute to this multidisciplinary enterprise. We suggest that archaeologists have much to offer; at the very least, we can introduce a modicum of methodological sophistication. Although investigators in countless disciplines have at last discovered material culture, the studies carried out are usually 'material culture' in name only. The actual artifacts examined and analyzed are often limited to documents, including texts about other texts and questionnaires; and the discourses tend to omit a discussion of people actually making, distributing, using, and reusing the material culture at issue (Schiffer and Miller 1999: 5–6). Thus, an archaeological perspective, developed from nearly two centuries of hands-on experience with every sort of artifact, can, at the very least, furnish instruction on how studies of consumerism and consumer societies can be empirically grounded.

In particular, we suggest that a consumerist archaeology is built on the following methodological commitments:

1   A concern to describe and explain the time–space parameters of events and processes, such as manufacture and use, in the life histories of artifacts and artifact types;

2   an appreciation for the involvement of people in the entire suite of activities making up the life history of an artifact or artifact type;

3 the recognition that artifacts carry out diverse utilitarian and symbolic functions;

4 employment of a comparative perspective, both diachronic and cross-cultural, but one that also acknowledges contingent, contextual factors in specific cases;

5 a commitment to achieving an understanding of the operating principles of technologies and artifacts and then using that knowledge when constructing explanations of variability; and

6 use of a hands-on approach for recording the formal, spatial, quantitative, and relational properties of artifacts themselves.

Building on these foundations, archaeologists – perhaps uniquely – can obtain *comparable* evidence on consumption patterns that spans decades, even centuries. Thus, our storied 'time depth' can furnish long-term databases for evaluating the abundant hypotheses, served up by investigators in many disciplines but seldom tested, that purport to explain the development of consumer societies. And, in striving to explain long-term patterns, archaeologists can formulate their own theories and models. Drawing on modern material culture studies, historical archaeology, and ethno-archaeology, we identify the kinds of long-term research programs that establish a framework for building an archaeology of consumerism.

First, we call attention to 'foundational studies.' These contribute two major kinds of information: (1) basic parameters of an artifact type or types – that is, when, where, and by whom it was manufactured; and (2) specific inferences about behavioral processes in the life history of artifacts, including materials procurement, manufacture, distribution, use, maintenance and repair, reuse, discard, and postdepositional processes. Although foundational studies themselves yield research products that can stand alone, as the name implies they are also building blocks for higher-level inferences and explanations. Examples include Noël Hume's (1970) work on British artifacts in Colonial America, Toulouse's (1971) classic work on glass manufacturers' marks, and Godden's (1964) universally referenced compendium of makers' marks found on British ceramics (see Lehner (1988) for an 'encyclopedia' of U.S. marks).

A second set of research projects is concerned with elucidating the life histories of product types. Most product types in industrial consumer societies pass through three stages: invention, commercialization, and adoption (Schiffer 1996: 656–8). We now briefly define each stage.

In the *invention* stage, people – working alone or in behavioral components such as corporations – devise models and prototypes of new artifacts that can be used to demonstrate the invention to potential entrepreneurs or financiers. In evolutionary terms, invention is a major source of new variants; most inventions, however, fail to reach the next stage.

During the *commercialization* stage, products enter production and are brought to market, sometimes after a lengthy and costly period of research and development. Commercialization is often undertaken by corporations, but individuals, government agencies, and so forth can also bring products to market. Once the commercialization process is characterized – perhaps by drawing upon data in antique collector catalogs or by reconstructing company histories through archival research, oral history, or both – a major goal is to identify the technological, social, cultural, and behavioral factors responsible for changes in the diversity of manufacturers and products. Another important focus in commercialization studies is to explain artifact designs. Specific designs represent compromises in performance characteristics responsive to varied technical, social, cultural, and behavioral factors (see Schiffer and Skibo 1997).

*Adoption* is the purchase of commercialized products; this stage ends when the purchase of a product type, as *new* goods, ceases. Reliable data on adoption are surprisingly difficult to obtain from documentary evidence. However, the archaeological record itself, especially secondary refuse, is an important – often unique – source of information on adoption.

Many questions about technological change can be fruitfully considered in the context of adoption processes, particularly when there is competition between different artifact types or technologies (see O'Brien *et al.* 1994; Schiffer 1996). In explaining adoption patterns, the archaeologist often takes various social groups as the unit of analysis, seeking to specify relationships between products and social groups defined, for example, on the basis of class, gender, ethnicity, and religion. Let us now look more closely at large-scale patterns of adoption, which furnish an important empirical basis for developing the archaeology of consumerism.

In his pioneering 1976 study, Stanley South identified artifact groupings associated with certain historical-period activity sets, such as food preparation in the household and military activities in frontier forts of the eastern United States. In subsequent studies, investigators have refined and extended South's patterns. All such studies, in effect, examine large-scale adoption/consumption processes and thus contribute directly to the archaeology of consumerism. As their units of analysis, these studies employ social groups or 'behavioral components' (*sensu* Rathje and Schiffer 1982; Schiffer 1992: 14–15).

Many archaeological studies of adoption have been carried out in relation to social class and ethnicity. The actual unit of analysis, however, is usually families and households whose socio-demographic characteristics are gleaned from documentary evidence. Consumption is inferred mainly from the contents of refuse associated with structures (LeeDecker 1994). On the basis of household refuse samples, one generalizes about consumption patterns of socio-demographic groups.

The adoption/consumption patterns of task units, communities, regional systems, and empires can also be characterized. Because these larger behavioral components consist of ever-greater aggregates of households, variability in large-scale artifact patterning is explained in part by the factors that influence household consumption. Other factors are at work in the larger behavioral components because they contain organized religions, polities, corporations, and so on, which engage in their own consumption processes.

We propose that the kinds of studies just enumerated, which many archaeologists are already undertaking and for which methods are well developed, provide a firm foundation for approaching higher-level questions about consumerism. Indeed, it is time to step boldly beyond the study of consumption, which archaeologists have always investigated, to the study of consumerism. According to Martin (1993: 143), consumption implies a process or means by which consumer goods and services move through the general economy; its study ranges widely to include the institutions that produce, market, and sell those goods and services. By contrast, the concept of consumerism extends well beyond acquisition; it subsumes the cultural relationship between humans and consumer goods and services, including behaviors, institutions, and ideas. It is potentially a unifying concept for many areas of scholarship (Martin 1993: 142–3).

## Mapping out the scope of a consumerist archaeology

Martin (1993: 142) outlines what she considers to be the most important thrusts of the study of consumerism: (1) the way material goods mark or confer position in a social hierarchy; (2) the role of fashion and demand in spurring economic growth and changing manufactures; and (3) the ways in which people can construct their own meanings for objects produced by themselves or others.

The themes identified by Martin are, of course, not new. Her point is that their contemporary study, within the context of consumerism, 'moves the scholarly eye from institutional forces to personal choices' (Martin 1993: 142) and places more emphasis on the role of bourgeois consumers of non-utilitarian goods and services, particularly women, as agents for change in the material culture repertoire of a society.

In this section, we present a series of broader themes and related questions that can help to build on Martin's points to map out an expanded scope for a consumerist archaeology. While we agree that inquiries into the role of the consumer are central to any reasoned study of modern material culture, it is also important to consider a variety of other issues to help us round out investigations of makers, buyers, and users.

### Structural and behavioral aspects of the emergence, growth, and maintenance of consumer societies

How do structural factors, such as capitalism, mercantilism, relatively 'free' markets (for goods, services, and labor), profit-making corporations not controlled by polities, lack of sumptuary rules, and social mobility, interact over time and contribute to the emergence of specific consumer societies? By what processes are a society's laws and regulations modified to provide favorable conditions for the growth of consumerism? By what general processes does any activity become 'consumerized?' That is, how does it come about that an activity's competent performance requires continual expansion and updating of the required material culture? What do long-term changes in toys, games, models, and books reveal about the role of children's material culture in reproducing the values, attitudes, skills, and activities of a consumer society (see Berger 1992; Formanek-Brunell 1993; Schiffer 1991)? How have huge corporations, only loosely under the control of nation-states, reconfigured people's lives during this century by internationalizing manufacturing, marketing, and consumption? Although consumer societies are resource- and energy-intensive, under what conditions do concerns over resource and energy exhaustion begin to affect policies, activities, and technologies? What role is the ideology of 'sustainability' coming to play in the maintenance of consumer societies?

### Effects of consumerism on the life histories of specific products

When and how does novelty in material culture become highly valued as 'progress?' How does the pursuit of novelty in products become actualized in the consumption patterns of middle- and working-class people? When, where, and for what products does the annual model change become an effective strategy for selling products to varying kinds of households and to other behavioral components? By what processes did the annual model change spread to an ever greater variety of consumer, commercial, and industrial products?

### Advertising and communication

How are the mass communication media – newspapers, magazines, radio, television, and now the Internet – involved in the maintenance and spread of the 'novelty orientation' and other values necessary for the functioning of consumer societies? Magazine ads by the Radio Corporation of America in the 1920s proclaimed, 'A Radiola for every purse.' By what processes did price-based differentiation spread to virtually every kind of product – from houses to neckties?

### Explaining apparent alternatives/reactions to consumerism

Are certain 'nonconformists' practicing strategies of resistance to consumerism, such as hermits, people of means who buy only used products or only 'organic' foods, families without televisions, and ethnic enclaves that reject most modern technologies? In what ways do these people employ artifacts to create meaning and define their own identities? What ideologies justify these lifestyle alternatives? Do institutions such as universities promote resistance to the vulgar ideologies of consumerism (that is, new = progress = good)? If so, are contrasting ideologies realized in different consumption patterns? How and why do handcrafted products of traditional societies become integrated into the consumption patterns of industrial consumer societies?

### Commercialization process of consumer services and societal practices

How do religious observances and objects become secularized, commercialized, and consumerized? By what processes have personal services, such as grooming and medical diagnosis and treatment, been consumerized?

### Ideological expressions of consumerist societies

When and how did the ideology of science and technology as founts of wondrous new products become entrenched? How is this ideology related to the artifacts purchased by middle- and working-class people over the last century? How is the erection of monumental architecture in cities since 1850 related to changes in the relative wealth and social power of churches, polities, various kinds of corporations, and sports franchises?

### Where to look for answers

Many of the questions above have been raised previously by students of consumerism in other disciplines. However, the answers tendered by these investigators tend to be just-so stories, foundering in abstract discourse divorced from the materiality of human life. In contrast, the archaeological perspective, which illuminates concrete consumption patterns by exploiting myriad lines of evidence in relation to artifact life histories, furnishes an empirical foundation for research on consumer societies that goes well beyond the study of consumption itself. Below we provide an example of how a particularly informative material class – historical ceramics – can be used to study some of the more salient questions related to consumerism.

Why ceramics? As a material class, ceramics have long been a favored focus of analysis for both prehistoric and historical archaeologists. In addition to being plentiful in archaeological deposits, they are the primary tools for establishing chronology and site function, and are also used to establish behavioral information about such topics as the social status, ethnicity, and foodways of a site's prior occupants. Being at the same time fragile and durable, ceramic objects tend to enter the archaeological record fairly frequently and survive to be recovered at a later date. Because there is such wide variability in ceramic composition and style, wares are readily identifiable with adequate study.

The example brings together pieces of information from archaeology, the decorative arts, history, and economics to illustrate that a consumerist approach is a viable means of integrating multiple disciplinary perspectives. To explore the feasibility of using this approach, we first outline the state of 'foundational' knowledge about the topic and provide contextual background. We then briefly consider the life history of ceramics made in a particular late-nineteenth-century 'style' – the Japanese-influenced Aesthetic movement – before moving on to an assessment of the potential value of the information for investigating some of the higher-level questions regarding consumerism posed earlier. Although the Aesthetic movement flourished on both sides of the Atlantic, our primary focus will be on its expression in America.

## Ceramics as a mirror of consumerism

As noted above, ceramics are perhaps the most ubiquitous material class found in archaeological sites dating to the historical period. Apparently, however, they represent a minor class of goods in terms of overall household expenditures (e.g., see Wettstaed's (1999) analysis of early nineteenth-century day books from a store in the Missouri Ozarks). Nonetheless, they are powerful tools for the archaeologist, and provide a range of information critical to site interpretation. Blaszczyk (1994: 126) notes that 'Expenditures on ceramics constituted a small portion of consumers' annual budgets, but the act of possession mattered more than the money spent. Ceramics were signs whose cultural value was derived from their inherent qualities and, to a lesser extent, from their prices.' In this section of the chapter, we consider a small subset of historical ceramics – those decorated in Aesthetic-movement style, and even more specifically those influenced by Japanese arts and crafts. Given a working knowledge of the technology of ceramic production and stylistic trends, we can use ceramics to study and illuminate many of the themes outlined above.

As background to the example, we offer a brief introduction to nineteenth-century trends in the decorative arts. The reader should keep in mind that two basic decorative styles (in all areas of design) will prevail at any one time: the style(s) of the moment ('high style,' or 'popular style') and traditional styles (Majewski 1996). A ceramic example close in time to our own experience would be wares influenced by the tenets of modernism (stark design, minimal or stylized decoration, form incorporated into style) produced during the 1950s compared with contemporary traditional wares, such as those decorated with floral decal sprays. The focus here will be on 'high style,' keeping in mind that these coexisted with traditional styles in the material culture repertoire.

### Nineteenth-century styles and ceramic expression

Prior to the beginning of Aesthetic influences in design, two high styles – Neoclassical and Gothic revival (Samford 1997) – followed one upon the other in popularity. The Neoclassical style was at its peak from the late eighteenth century to *circa* 1830, with an emphasis on classic revivals in architecture, ceramics, and other media. Some of Wedgwood's most famous products were made in imitation of Etruscan and classical Greek forms. Neoclassical ceramics were characterized by clean lines, symmetrical proportions, and restrained decoration. Transfer-printed motifs used at the time included urns, acanthus leaves, columned temples, and figures in classical garb. The Gothic-revival style was in vogue from the 1830s through the 1860s, and heavily influenced architecture, particularly public forms, but made an impact on the decorative and useful arts as well. Gothic-revival-style ceramics often exhibited angular, panelled shapes, which were frequently decorated with transfer-printed scenes of architectural ruins or buildings with turrets, arches, towers, or battlements.

These styles or movements were parts of the lengthy Victorian era (1837–1901), a critical time for the Western world in general, but in particular for America. Howe (1976: 3) sees this era as one of crucial transformation for the United States, in terms of industrialization, rapid developments in knowledge and communication, immigration and significant population growth, urbanization, geographical expansion, and changing race relations. These transformations accelerated after the American Civil War. Literacy increased, and communication networks expanded. Industrialization and urbanization went hand in hand with modernization, which Howe (1976: 7) identifies as the central process characterizing the era. In addition to social and economic effects, the modernization process also had cultural impacts (also see Stein 1986). As a value system, Victorianism represented a combination of premodern modes of thought (patriarchalism, English common law) with ideals specifically linked to the modernization process (work ethic, delayed gratification, discipline, sexual repression, rational order, the cult of domesticity) (Howe 1976: 17–18, 25).

Cohen (1982: 292) writes that the American home 'from the 1840s to the 1880s mirrored the nation's transformation from an agricultural to an industrial society.' More importantly for the purposes of our discussion, she notes that:

> The home served as an accurate indicator of one's relationship to the industrial economy, not by accident, but as a result of the Victorians' contradictory attitude toward economic and technological change. Enthusiasm for, as well as anxiety toward, industrialization provoked both an appetite for new products and a need to incorporate them carefully into private life ... The home embodied a contradiction as both the arena for and the refuge from technological penetration. Insofar as people could tolerate this contradictory domestic environment, the home provided a setting for gradual adaptation to a technological and commercial world ... The parlor best represented this accommodation to industrial life.
> (Cohen 1982: 292–3)

Victorian parlors, whether located in Great Britain or in the as-yet-untamed American West, were crammed with carefully arranged, store-bought, mass-produced objects (Figure 3.1).

During the decade beginning *circa* 1870, the ceramic 'market basket' (described by Miller 1990, 1993; also see Majewski 1996; Majewski and O'Brien

*Figure 3.1*  The interior of an officer's home at either Fort Huachuca or Fort Bowie,
Arizona, in the late nineteenth century. (Courtesy: Fort Huachuca Museum.)

1987) available to American consumers primarily consisted of heavy,
semivitreous white-bodied wares, either left plain or with molded body
decoration (properly called 'white granite,' but also known as 'ironstone' by
antique collectors and some archaeologists). White granite and nonvitreous
white-bodied earthenwares ('c.c.,' or cream-colored) remained popular in some
regions until well into the early twentieth century. Transfer-printed wares are
relatively uncommon in collections from sites dating to the early 1870s, though
some traditional styles continue, such as the willow pattern, which has been in
continuous production since it was first introduced onto the market in the late
eighteenth century (Copeland 1980). Occasional traditional-style floral transfer-
printed patterns were introduced to consumers during this period.

'Aesthetic' influences, however, dramatically changed Victorian design
concepts, including those expressed on ceramics. The Aesthetic movement –
the prelude to Art Nouveau – was one of the most original art movements in
British history. It began in England in the 1860s as a reaction by a 'few architects
and designers' (e.g., Christopher Dresser) against Victorian excesses and
eclecticism in decoration (Aslin 1969: 13; also see Kurland *et al.* 1993). The
term itself refers to the introduction of principles that emphasized art in the
production of furniture, metalwork, ceramics, glass, textiles, wallpapers, and
books. During its height, from the mid-1870s through the 1880s, the movement
affected all levels of society in both England and America (Aslin 1969: 13; Burke
*et al.* 1986: 19). The Arts and Crafts movement was also influential in Aesthetic

design. In America, these two 'styles,' together with the Colonial Revival style, contributed to the formulation of an aesthetic that would replace European-inspired and technologically sophisticated styles (Cohen 1982: 293). William Morris's Gothic Medievalism and the work of the Pre-Raphaelite Brotherhood also had an important impact on the Aesthetic movement, but probably the strongest contributions to the style were made by things Japanese.

Impetus for the movement came with the 'opening up' of Japan in the 1850s (thanks to the American Admiral Perry) – an event that revitalized taste in Europe. Japanese or 'Japonesque' motifs were applied everywhere – sprays of cherry blossoms and clumps of bamboo, birds, diaper patterns, fan shapes and cartouches with scenes within a scene, and stylized clouds to name but a sampling, were placed with casual asymmetry on everything from pots to postcards (Figure 3.2). The Japanese decorative arts and architecture displayed at the 1876 Centennial Exposition in Philadelphia (and at expositions later in the century) began a widespread interest in Japanese art in America. This phenomenon is variously referred to as the 'Japan Idea,' Japonism, Japonisme, and the 'Japan Craze' (see Cameron 1986; Hosley 1990; Rydell 1984; Spencer 1973).

Partly as a vehicle for expressing aesthetic motifs on ceramic tablewares, teawares, toilet sets, tiles, and decorative wares, the use of transfer printing as a

*Figure 3.2* Earthenware platter showing typical elements of Japanese-influenced Aesthetic decoration; 'Sitka' pattern; manufactured by Thomas Hughes, Burslem, England. (Hughes Collection; photo: Gerhardt Alt.)

decorative method was 'revived' and surged in popularity beginning in the late 1870s through the end of the century. The underglaze transfer-printing process began with engraved copper plates into which ceramic color mixtures have been worked. Special papers were then laid over the plate to make an impression of the motif. The paper was then laid on an unfired ceramic body, smoothed on, and removed. The design was then dried on prior to glazing and firing (Drakard and Holdway 1983; Majewski 1996; Majewski and O'Brien 1987). Colors used for late nineteenth-century transfer prints differed in tone from those used earlier. Especially popular for 'revival' transfers were subdued or even dull colors, particularly a range of dull greens and browns. The use of secondary or tertiary colors was the aesthetic reaction to the bright, harsh colors favored in the mid-1800s (Aslin 1969: 63).

An interesting variation includes non-Japanese motifs displayed in Japanese style or together with Japanese motifs (Figure 3.3). This strategy was likely an attempt on the part of the creators of pottery designs to reach an even greater portion of the market, i.e., those who preferred more traditional motifs on their

*Figure 3.3* Earthenware plate with European-style arch within a 'reserve,' combined with Japanese motifs (asymmetrically arranged foliage and insects) arranged in Aesthetic style. Rectangular arch-within-a-block arch element is an imitation of a Japanese woodblock print. Printed diamond-shaped registry mark on reverse for May 6, 1882; 'London' pattern mark; and mark indicating manufacture by Powell, Bishop & Stonier, Hanley, England. (Hughes Collection; photo: Gerhardt Alt.)

ceramics, such as English country scenes or architectural or nautical elements. Other colors were used in various anglicized adaptations of the style, e.g., turquoise and various other bright overglaze colors on bone china; pastels on majolica; and red, black, blue, and blue-black on transfer-printed earthenwares. One pattern might be transformed into many through the use of handpainted accents, gilding, or luster decoration. While underglaze transfer printing was the primary method of decoration for Japanese-style earthenwares, some earthenware and bone china forms were handpainted (painted under the glaze) or enameled (painted over the glaze).

Other wares were concurrently produced and marketed alongside Japanese-style earthenwares and bone china. The 1880s *Silber & Fleming Glass and China Book* (Silber & Fleming 1990) includes examples of traditional wares with handpainted rim banding and others with floral borders. The catalog also includes undecorated white earthenware (c.c. ware), much of which is shown in utilitarian forms such as foot baths, bed pans, chamber pots, and slop pails – a perfect illustration of Miller's (1993) concept of 'demand entropy' in operation. As applied to ceramics, demand entropy results in a situation where, through time, originally popular wares cycle down in price and form or drop out altogether.

Although monochrome outline decals, or lithotransfers, were used as the basis for handpainted fill-in by 1885 (U.S. Department of Commerce 1915: 156; Wood 1953: 77, 487), and thus would have been available to potters decorating in the popular Aesthetic style, it did not appear to be the decorative method of choice. Polychrome decaling, however, essentially replaced transfer printing by around 1900 (Fryman and Majewski 1995), and in the 1950s was still 'the most common decorative technique used for dinnerware' (Taylor 1950: 33).

By the 1890s, the Japanese style was no longer popular in ceramics, but asymmetrical placement of transfer-printed motifs (e.g., floral sprays) continued as did use of more muted hues and restrained handpainted color accents and gilding. A resurgence in popularity of flow-blue transfer-printed floral patterns occurred (on British and non-British wares), often on thinly potted bodies with some relief molding (Gaston 1983). Also occurring late in the century were bold floral handpainted motifs combined with cut-sponge stamping, and vessels with transfer-printed stylized Chinese motifs, often with luster accents and other light color washes (exported to America from Great Britain and Holland). Both of these types can be considered traditional in the sense that they were reincarnations of styles popular in early centuries.

'China painting' on porcelain blanks (frequently Bavarian or French) was a favorite avocation for women during the last part of the nineteenth century and into the early twentieth century. Many pattern books with instructions were available and frequently featured Aesthetic designs, particularly those in the Japanese taste (Blaszczyk 1994; Hosley 1990; Wood 1953). From the late 1890s until *circa* 1910, Art Nouveau-style motifs were popular with amateur china painters.

## Aesthetic-movement ceramics as case study

An investigation of the Aesthetic movement – as expressed in the Japanese-style decoration used on ceramic goods – can provide useful insights into the development of consumerism in the second half of the nineteenth century. Although the movement was infrequently mentioned in publications on the decorative arts sources written prior to the 1980s, a considerable amount of research on its context and influence on various kinds of media has been accomplished since that time. From a decorative-arts perspective, much of the foundational work has been done. We essentially know when, where, and by whom Aesthetic-influenced artifacts were manufactured (see Blaszczyk 1994; Hosley 1990).

Much of the supporting data for answering these questions comes from backmarks containing manufacturer and temporal information found on Japanese-style pieces in private collections and museums, published sources, and archaeological specimens. While some Aesthetic-influenced wares were produced in America (see Blaszczyk 1994), most were potted in Great Britain. Hosley (1990: 154–60) lists some of the most well-known British manufacturers: Gildea & Walker; Brownhills Pottery Co.; Wedgwood; Henry Alcock & Co.; Edge, Malkin & Co.; Minton and Company; Royal Worcester; and Belleek. From 1842 to 1883, Victorian ceramics bore a diamond-shaped mark to indicate that the design or shape had been registered at the Patent Office in London (see Godden 1964: 526–9 for information on how to 'read' these marks). Registration provided protection from 'design piracy' for an initial period of three years, and apparently could be renewed. Beginning in January 1884 (and continuing into the twentieth century), registered designs no longer appeared as diamond-shaped marks, but were numbered consecutively following the prefix 'Rd.' or 'Rd. No.' These trends in ceramic registration and marking illustrate that proprietary design was becoming an increasingly important concept by the mid-nineteenth century.

Still lacking, however, is a complete understanding of the behavioral processes associated with the life histories of these artifacts. As noted above, home interiors were the vehicle for displaying the occupants' level of articulation with the popular trends of the times. Hosley (1990: 16) notes that 'Where Victorian Americans at mid-century [1850] knew little more about Japan than its place on the map, a generation later Americans of all classes and backgrounds exhibited a cultlike fascination with the distant island nation.' If we are to equate a person's intellectual acceptance of the 'Japan Idea' with ownership of the material trappings of the movement, we are required to learn how effectively goods in Aesthetic style reached American homes of all social classes. This will allow us to begin to evaluate the movement's impact on American culture. A combination of historical and archaeological research can begin to fill in the gaps.

Historical sources are particularly useful for answering behavioral-process questions. Photographs, stereographs, and illustrations from contemporary printed materials of late nineteenth-century home interiors may be used to document the use of Aesthetic ceramics and other items of material culture in decorative and useful contexts (e.g., Blaszczyk 1994; Formanek-Brunell 1993; Frelinghuysen 1986; Hosley 1990). Illustrated period catalogs, such as those from Silber & Fleming (1990) and A. A. Vantine & Company (see Hosley 1990: 44), illustrate the range of items available in popular versus traditional styles at a particular time. A casual perusal of the Silber & Fleming catalog, originally published *circa* the 1880s, indicates that at least 50 per cent of the ceramic items illustrated were decorated with Aesthetic-influenced Japanese-style motifs. Other useful printed materials include art books, periodicals, and variety and women's magazines, as well as domestic-advice books and women's 'do-it-yourself' art manuals for decorating ceramic blanks.

Japanese-style ceramics may have been widely available to most consumers, but investigating issues related to consumer choice is more difficult. The archaeological record may provide some answers (see Majewski and O'Brien 1987 and Spencer-Wood 1987b for discussions of this topic). Archaeological evidence for the distribution and pervasiveness of Japanese-influenced Aesthetic-style ceramics must necessarily be cumulative and focused on household contexts. Descriptive and quantitative information on materials found in both urban and rural sites from throughout the United States is necessary to understand how extensively the 'Japan Idea' penetrated all aspects of American life. Consistency in identification and recording of ceramics decorated in this style is an essential first step (see Hosley 1990; Samford 1997).

As noted earlier, excavation must be accompanied by archival research designed to uncover the identity, social class, family composition, and ethnicity of a site's occupants if we are to understand the behavioral implications of the materials recovered. Optimal contexts for analysis are those features that can be linked to known households. Recent work on late nineteenth-century deposits at the Superblock site in downtown San Bernardino, California, has yielded promising results in this vein (Doolittle and Majewski 1997). One of the 50 features excavated at the site, a privy, was associated through archival research with the dwelling of a particular middle-class family – the Whaleys – who apparently lived at that location from *circa* 1860. Almost 800 ceramic sherds representing 150 vessels were recovered from the privy, and most dated to the 1870s and 1880s. Figure 3.4 illustrates two examples of transfer-printed vessels from this feature that were decorated in Japanese-influenced Aesthetic-movement style. The next step would be to begin constructing profiles of ceramic use by this household and other contemporary households in the area and elsewhere (e.g., percentage of popular versus traditional wares, range of forms used, etc.). Comparisons of ceramic use profiles and use profiles for other archaeologically recovered Aesthetic-influenced materials with those from contemporary sites in California and elsewhere could be used to build a broader understanding of the impact of the Aesthetic movement on the material culture of the times.

*Figure 3.4*  Transfer-printed Aesthetic-movement ceramics from a privy feature
associated with the Whaley household at the Superblock site, San Bernardino,
California: left, reconstructed, partial earthenware toothbrush holder
decorated with an unknown pattern (unmarked, but may have been potted
by William Brownfield & Sons, Cobridge, as early as 1880); right,
reconstructed, partial earthenware saucer with a printed diamond-shaped
registry mark for January 6, 1881, and pattern name 'Paiva' on the base
(probably manufactured by Benjamin & Sampson Hancock, Bridge Works,
Stoke, England). (Statistical Research, Inc., archives; photo: Cynthia Elsner
Hayward.)

In situations where households can be linked to archaeological deposits, what
can be learned about the 'lady of the house'? Women were likely the primary
purchasers of Aesthetic-style goods that were used and displayed in the home.
Formanek-Brunell (1993: 15–17 and caption to her Figure 4) notes that
shopping had become a central activity for middle-class women after the
American Civil War. At this time, Americans were becoming increasingly
affluent. Personal incomes were rising, and new outlets were available to
consumers – retail stores for those who lived in urban settings and mail-order
catalogs for those who did not. Middle-class Americans were now able to
purchase items formerly available only to the wealthy. First published in England
in 1868, Charles Locke Eastlake's *Hints on Household Taste in Furniture,
Upholstery, and Other Details* was published in America in 1872 (Voorsanger
1986: 423). Lynes (1949: 100) notes that households were completely
refurbished to follow the book's teachings.

In summary, studies of Aesthetic-influenced Japanese-style ceramics, whether
based on documentary or archaeological evidence (or both), can provide specific
information on the life histories of products associated with this apparently

pervasive, but short-lived movement. Understanding the role of international expositions in promoting material culture associated with the Japan Idea is pertinent to the invention stage (Blaszczyk 1994; Hosley 1990), and an intensive examination of available documentary and published materials of the period would illuminate the commercialization stage. Study of the latter would also benefit from an analysis of the source materials for the engraved copper plates used in transferring Aesthetic designs to ceramic bodies. For example, one might investigate why some of the designs were more Europeanized. The adoption stage can be elucidated through analysis and interpretation of the archaeological record. Particularly interesting will be archaeological data relating to 'competing' artifact types (popular versus traditional) being produced at the same time.

## Moving beyond foundational studies

In the previous section we introduced the reader to some of the foundational information necessary to understand Japanese-influenced Aesthetic-movement ceramics from the late nineteenth century within a consumerist perspective. Emphasis was placed on defining the basic parameters of the artifact type and making specific inferences about behavioral processes in its life history. Here we would like briefly to relate this information to some of the broader themes raised earlier.

Perhaps most obvious is the potential of the example to contribute to our understanding of the structural and behavioral aspects of the emergence, growth, and maintenance of consumer societies. We have outlined some of the processes that led to consumerization of Aesthetic-movement ideals. During its 10-year heyday, the movement made an enormous impact on the material culture of the late nineteenth century. Traditional nineteenth-century British design, and most early American design, was based on the symmetrical arrangements of elements in decorative arts, architecture, etc. Aesthetic designers introduced an entirely new grammar and syntax of ornament. Some design innovations introduced during this period, particularly the asymmetrical arrangement of motifs, carried over into the subsequent Art Nouveau and Art Deco popular style movements. Thus, consumers were in a sense 'preconditioned' to accept the later styles that were completely alien to their way of thinking. Nonetheless, while the Aesthetic movement may have emerged as a 'contradiction' or 'opposition' to contemporary Victorian norms, it coexisted with traditional Victorian material culture and in some instances even merged with it.

Written sources emphasize the pervasiveness of Aesthetic-movement goods in American culture. This is difficult to quantify, however. We have suggested that data from the archaeological record, while challenging to collect, may provide some of the best information on the actual use of these materials by members of different social classes. In addition, the ideological impacts of the movement (see Stein 1986) have yet to be fully investigated from an archaeological perspective.

The Aesthetic movement might accurately be termed a 'late nineteenth-century fad.' As such, looking at how it played out can help us to understand the role of fashion and demand in spurring economic growth and changing manufactures, one of Martin's (1993) most important thrusts for the study of consumerism. The roots of the movement are traceable to the opening of Japan in the 1850s, and its success in America was fueled by a combination of factors: the consumer's desire for something new (a reaction against Victorian excess); increased prosperity following the Civil War; expanded opportunities for consumption through catalogs and retail stores; and expanded communication, transportation, and advertising networks. By the late nineteenth century, women were the primary purchasers of household goods, a fact that has not received the attention it deserves in research on consumer behavior and the consumerization process.

This example also contributes to our understanding of how and when novelty in material culture becomes valued as progress. Products and artifacts have always gone through cycles of popularity, and demand entropy (Miller 1993) is one way of characterizing what happens when an item is on the downward spiral. Take the example of Josiah Wedgwood's creamware, developed in 1743 but not perfected until the 1760s (Young 1995: 9). During the 1770s, the ware graced the tables of European royalty; by late in the century the elite were losing interest, and use of the ware was more widespread among the middle and lower classes. By the early 1800s, creamware had been replaced in popularity by other wares, but as a ceramic body it persisted until well into the twentieth century. In the late nineteenth century, it was known as 'c.c. ware,' and was one of the materials of choice for manufacturing chamber pots, urinals, invalid feeders, and foot baths!

Something different began happening in the late nineteenth century, however. It is interesting that at the height of the 'Japan Craze,' Japanese-influenced Aesthetic-movement motifs appeared on ceramics of all levels of quality and cost, from bone china down to the cheapest earthenwares. This may be one of the earliest examples of price-based differentiation (though we suspect it was also occurring with goods other than ceramics). We suggest that by compiling quantitative and distributional information on popular- versus traditional-style tablewares, teawares, and toilet sets, it may be possible to gain insight into how 'novelty' products become actualized in the consumption patterns of middle- and working-class people.

Studying 'high style' material culture invites a consideration of alternatives to consumerism. In the example we presented, we noted that many consumers continued to choose traditional forms. Manufacturers of Aesthetic-style goods even catered to potential consumers by producing 'toned-down' expressions of the style using non-Japanese motifs (see Figure 3.3). The coexistence of traditional and popular styles is an important research theme in the study of consumerism, and is one that can benefit from information provided by the archaeological record.

Aesthetic-movement design elements even made their way into the late nineteenth-century bathroom. In keeping with the Victorian obsession with cleanliness and sanitation, a profusion of hygiene-related products were available. In the ceramic medium, 'toilet sets' contained numerous pieces, including basins, ewers, slop pails, and a variety of soap dishes and toothbrush holders (see Figure 3.4). Well over 50 per cent of the examples illustrated in the Silber & Fleming 1880s catalog (Silber & Fleming 1990) are decorated in Japanese-influenced Aesthetic style, which illustrates that the influence of the movement had spread into even the most personal areas of life.

An equally fascinating topic for further study relates to how children's material culture serves to reproduce the values, attitudes, skills, and activities of a consumer society. In an important study of the relationship of dolls to the commercialization of American girlhood during the period 1830–1930, Formanek-Brunell (1993: 20) points out that in the decades following the American Civil War:

> Adults expected girls to imitate the new rituals of high society with their largely imported dolls in their nurseries. Elaborately dressed dolls were thought useful in the instruction of social conventions such as housewarmings. Far more common, however, were dolls' tea parties, frequently depicted in stereographs, tradecards, and books like *The Dolls' Tea Party*. Adults proudly noted that 'The children's doll parties of to-day are counterparts of grown-up people's receptions.'

There are numerous extant complete or partial examples of children's tea sets decorated with Japanese-influenced Aesthetic-movement motifs in museums and private collections, which apparently indicates that the 'Japan Idea' had been deliberately introduced to society's youngest members in a way that would be used to prepare them for their roles as adults in a consumer society.

The themes touched upon here are only a few of those that can be used to investigate the development of consumerism. To build upon the work presented here, comparative studies would be productive, focusing on ceramics decorated in later styles, such as Art Nouveau and Art Deco, or on earlier styles (e.g., Rococo, Neoclassical, or Gothic revival). This would not only allow for the development of a temporal perspective on the themes discussed here, but could suggest other equally productive avenues of research.

## Conclusions

In this chapter we have outlined a strategy for investigating the development of consumerism that is grounded in compilation of foundational and life-history information about material culture and artifacts. This essential basic information is then used to investigate broader themes. Our approach is multidisciplinary, cumulative, comparative, and inclusive, but emphasizes the unique contributions that can be made using archaeological data.

Archaeologists, especially historical archaeologists, are in a position to use their intimate familiarity with archaeological and historical evidence pertaining to particular classes of goods to answer higher-level questions about consumerism. The information presented in this chapter is only the beginning, but we can already envision linking what we have learned about the consumerization of household ceramic goods with information about other classes of material culture. It is our earnest hope that the ideas presented here will foment synergies among practitioners of ethnoarchaeology, historical archaeology, and modern material culture studies to develop an explicit archaeology of consumerism, an enterprise that will contribute importantly to discussions of consumerist societies taking place across the academy and in other contexts.

## Acknowledgments

The authors would like to thank the many colleagues who commented on various drafts of this paper, particularly Patrick McCray, who suggested several useful references. Figures 3.2 and 3.3 appear courtesy of Mr Vernon Hughes, of Clarksville, Missouri, and TM would like gratefully to acknowledge the insights he has shared with her over the years regarding Aesthetic-movement ceramics.

## References

Adams, William H. (1973) 'An Ethnoarchaeological Study of a Rural American Community: Silcott, Washington, 1900–1930' Ethnohistory 20: 335–46.

Aslin, Elizabeth (1969) The Aesthetic Movement: Prelude to Art Nouveau. New York: Excalibur Books.

Berger, Arthur A. (1992) Reading Matter: Multidisciplinary Perspectives on Material Culture. New Brunswick: Transaction Publishers.

Binford, Lewis (1976) 'Forty-Seven Trips: A Case Study in the Character of Some Formation Processes of the Archaeological Record' in The Interior Peoples of Northern Alaska, edited by E. S. Hall, Jr., pp. 299–381. National Museum of Man Mercury Series No. 49. National Museums of Canada, Ottawa.

Blaszczyk, Regina Lee (1994) 'The Aesthetic Moment: China Decorators, Consumer Demand, and Technological Change in the American Pottery Industry 1865–1900', Winterthur Portfolio 29: 121–53.

Burke, Doreen Bolder, Jonathan Freedman, Alice Cooney Frelinghuysen, David A. Hanks, Marilynn Johnson, James D. Kornwolf, Catherine Lynn, Roger B. Stein, Jennifer Toher, and Catherine Hoover Voorsanger, with the assistance of Carrie Rebora (1986) 'Preface' in In Pursuit of Beauty: Americans and the Aesthetic Movement, pp. 19–21. New York: The Metropolitan Museum of Art/Rizzoli.

Cameron, Elisabeth (1986) Encyclopedia of Pottery and Porcelain 1800–1960. New York: Facts on File Publications.

Carlson, Shawn Bonath (1990) 'The Persistence of Traditional Lifeways in Central Texas', Historical Archaeology 24(4): 50–9.

Claassen, Cheryl (1994) 'Washboards, Pigtoes, and Muckets: Historic Musseling in the Mississippi Watershed', *Historical Archaeology* 28(2): 1–142.

Cohen, Lizabeth A. (1982) 'Embellishing a Life of Labor: An Interpretation of the Material Culture of American Working-Class Homes, 1885–1915' in *Material Culture Studies in America*, compiled and edited by Thomas J. Schlereth, pp. 289–305. Nashville: AASLH Press.

Copeland, Robert (1980) *Spode's Willow Pattern & Other Designs after the Chinese*. London: Studio Vista/Christie's.

Delgado, James P. (1992) 'Recovering the Past of USS Arizona: Symbolism, Myth, and Reality', *Historical Archaeology* 26(4): 69–80.

Doolittle, Christopher J., and Teresita Majewski (eds) (1997) *Archaeological Investigations at the Superblock Site (CA-SBR-7975H), San Bernardino, California*. Technical Series 62. Tucson: Statistical Research, Inc.

Drakard, David, and Paul Holdway (1983) *Spode Printed Ware*. London: Longman.

Eastlake, Charles Locke (1868) *Hints on Household Taste in Furniture, Upholstery, and Other Details*. London.

Ferguson, Leland (1977) 'Historical Archaeology and the Importance of Material Things' in *Historical Archaeology and the Importance of Material Things*, edited by Leland Ferguson, pp. 5–8. Special Publication Series No. 2. Society for Historical Archaeology, California, PA.

Flannery, Kent V. (1982) 'The Golden Marshalltown: A Parable for the Archeology of the 1980s', *American Anthropologist* 84: 265–78.

Formanek-Brunell, Miriam (1993) *Made to Play House: Dolls and the Commercialization of American Girlhood, 1830–1930*. New Haven: Yale University Press.

Frelinghuysen, Alice Cooney (1986) 'Aesthetic Forms in Ceramics and Glass' in *In Pursuit of Beauty: Americans and the Aesthetic Movement*, by Doreen Bolder Burke, Jonathan Freedman, Alice Cooney Frelinghuysen, David A. Hanks, Marilynn Johnson, James D. Kornwolf, Catherine Lynn, Roger B. Stein, Jennifer Toher, and Catherine Hoover Voorsanger, with the assistance of Carrie Rebora, pp. 198–251. New York: The Metropolitan Museum of Art/Rizzoli.

Fryman, Robert J., and Teresita Majewski (1995) 'The Great Decal Debate: New Perspectives on a Polychrome Problem'. Paper presented at the 1995 Conference on Historical and Underwater Archaeology, Washington, DC.

Gaston, Mary Frank (1983) *The Collector's Encyclopedia of Flow Blue China*. Paducah: Collector Books.

Godden, Geoffrey A. (1964) *Encyclopaedia of British Pottery and Porcelain Marks*. London: Barrie & Jenkins.

Goldthwaite, Richard A. (1993) *Wealth and the Demand for Art in Italy, 1300–1600*. Baltimore: Johns Hopkins University Press.

Gould, Richard A. (1990) *Recovering the Past*. Albuquerque: University of New Mexico Press.

Gould, Richard A., and Michael B. Schiffer (1981) *Modern Material Culture Studies: The Archaeology of Us*. New York: Academic Press.

Hayden, Brian (ed.) (1987) *Lithic Studies among the Contemporary Highland Maya*. Tucson: University of Arizona Press.

Hayden, Brian, and Aubrey Cannon (1984) *The Structure of Material Systems: Ethnoarchaeology in the Maya Highlands*. Papers No. 3. Society for American Archaeology, Washington, DC.

Hosley, William (1990) *The Japan Idea*. Hartford: Wadsworth Atheneum.

Howe, Daniel Walker (1976) *Victorian America*. Philadelphia: University of Pennsylvania Press.

Ingersoll, Daniel W., Jr., and Gordon Bronitsky (eds) (1987) *Mirror and Metaphor: Material and Social Constructions of Reality*. Lanham: University Press of America.

Kent, Susan (1984) *Analyzing Activity Areas*. Albuquerque: University of New Mexico Press.

Kingery, David W. (1993) 'Painterly Maiolica of the Italian Renaissance'. *Technology and Culture* 34: 43–57.

Kingery, D. W. (1996a) 'Materials Science and Material Culture' in *Learning from Things: Method and Theory of Material Culture Studies*, edited by David W. Kingery, pp. 181–203. Washington DC: Smithsonian Institution Press.

Kingery, David W. (ed.) (1996b) *Learning from Things: Method and Theory of Material Culture Studies*. Washington DC: Smithsonian Institution Press.

Kurland, Catherine, Lori Zabar, and Shawn P. Brennan (1993) *Christopher Dresser: The Power of Design*. New York: Kurland Zabar.

LeeDecker, Charles H. (1994) 'Discard Behavior on Domestic Historic Sites: Evaluation of Contexts for the Interpretation of Household Consumption Patterns', *Journal of Archaeological Method and Theory* 1: 345–75.

Lehner, Lois (1988) *Lehner's Encyclopedia of U.S. Marks on Pottery, Porcelain, & Clay*. Paducah: Collector Books.

Lubar, Steven, and W. David Kingery (eds) (1993) *History from Things: Essays on Material Culture*. Washington DC: Smithsonian Institution Press.

Lynes, Russell (1949) *The Taste-Makers*. New York: Harper & Brothers.

McCray, W. Patrick (1996) 'The Culture and Technology of Glass in Renaissance Venice'. Unpublished Ph.D. dissertation, Department of Materials Science and Engineering, University of Arizona, Tucson.

Majewski, Teresita (1996) 'Historical Ceramics' in *Three Farewells to Manzanar: The Archeology of Manzanar National Historic Site, California*, by Jeffrey F. Burton, Part 3: Appendices and References, pp. 793–862 (Appendix D). Publications in Anthropology No. 67. USDI National Park Service, Western Archeological and Conservation Center, Tucson, Arizona.

Majewski, Teresita, and Michael J. O'Brien (1987) 'The Use and Misuse of Nineteenth-Century English and American Ceramics in Archaeological Analysis' in *Advances in Archaeological Method and Theory*, vol. 11, edited by Michael B. Schiffer, pp. 92–209. San Diego: Academic Press.

Martin, Ann Smart (1993) 'Makers, Buyers, and Users: Consumerism as a Material Culture Framework', *Winterthur Portfolio* 28: 141–57.

Miller, Daniel (1987) *Material Culture and Mass Consumption*. Oxford: Basil Blackwell.

Miller, D. (1994) *Modernity, an Ethnographic Approach: Dualism and Mass Consumption in Trinidad*. Providence: Berg.

Miller, D. (1995) 'Consumption as the Vanguard of History: A Polemic by Way of an Introduction' in *Acknowledging Consumption: A Review of New Studies*, edited by Daniel Miller, pp. 1–57. London: Routledge.

Miller, George L. (1990) 'The "Market Basket" of Ceramics Available in Country Stores from 1790 to 1860'. Paper presented at the 23rd Conference on Historical and Underwater Archaeology, Tucson, Arizona.

Miller, G. L. (1993) 'Demand Entropy as a Byproduct of Price Competition: A Case Study from Staffordshire'. Paper presented at the School of American Research Seminar 'The Historical Archaeology of Capitalism,' Santa Fe, New Mexico.

Noël Hume, Ivor (1970) A Guide to Artifacts of Colonial America. New York: Knopf.

O'Brien, Michael J., Thomas D. Holland, R. J. Hoard, and G. L. Fox (1994) 'Evolutionary Implications of Design and Performance Characteristics of Prehistoric Pottery'. Journal of Archaeological Method and Theory 1: 259–304.

Orser, Charles W., Jr., and David W. Babson (1990) 'Tabasco Brand Pepper Sauce Bottles from Avery Island, Louisiana', Historical Archaeology 24(3): 107–14.

Poicus, Gerald L. (ed.) (1991) Living in a Material World: Canadian and American Approaches to Material Culture. Social and Economic Papers No. 19. Institute of Social and Economic Research, Memorial University of Newfoundland, St. Johns.

Rathje, William L. (1979) 'Modern Material Culture Studies' in Advances in Archaeological Method and Theory, vol. 2, edited by Michael B. Schiffer, pp. 1–37. New York: Academic Press.

Rathje, William L., and Michael B. Schiffer (1982) Archaeology. New York: Harcourt Brace Jovanovich.

Rydell, Robert W. (1984) All the World's a Fair. Chicago: University of Chicago Press.

Samford, Patricia M. (1997) 'Response to a Market: Dating English Underglaze Transfer-Printed Wares', Historical Archaeology 31(2): 1–30.

Schiffer, Michael B. (1991) The Portable Radio in American Life. Tucson: University of Arizona Press.

Schiffer, M. B. (1992) Technological Perspectives on Behavioral Change. Tucson: University of Arizona Press.

Schiffer, M. B. (1996) 'Some Relationships between Behavioral and Evolutionary Archaeologies', American Antiquity 61: 643–62.

Schiffer, Michael Brian, and Andrea R. Miller (1999) The Material Life of Human Beings: Artifacts, Behavior, and Communication. London: Routledge.

Schiffer, Michael Brian, and James M. Skibo (1997) 'The Explanation of Artifact Variability', American Antiquity 62: 27–50.

Silber & Fleming (1990) The Silber & Fleming Glass and China Book. Wordsworth Editions, Ware, England. Facsimile of a circa 1880s edition.

Skibo, James (1994) 'The Kalinga Cooking Pot: An Ethnoarchaeological and Experimental Study of Technological Change' in Kalinga Ethnoarchaeology: Expanding Archaeological Method and Theory, edited by William A. Longacre and James M. Skibo, pp. 113–26. Washington DC: Smithsonian Institution Press.

South, Stanley (1976) Method and Theory in Historical Archaeology. New York: Academic Press.

Spencer, Charles (ed.) (1973) The Aesthetic Movement 1869–1890. London: Academy Editions.

Spencer-Wood, Suzanne M. (1987a) 'Introduction' in Consumer Choice in Historical Archaeology, edited by Suzanne M. Spencer-Wood, pp. 1–24. New York: Plenum.

Spencer-Wood, Suzanne (ed.) (1987b) Consumer Choice in Historical Archaeology. New York: Plenum.

Stein, Roger B. (1986) 'Artifact as Ideology: The Aesthetic Movement in its American Cultural Context', in In Pursuit of Beauty: Americans and the Aesthetic Movement, by Doreen Bolder Burke, Jonathan Freedman, Alice Cooney Frelinghuysen, David A.

Hanks, Marilynn Johnson, James D. Kornwolf, Catherine Lynn, Roger B. Stein, Jennifer Toher, and Catherine Hoover Voorsanger, with the assistance of Carrie Rebora, pp. 22–51. New York: The Metropolitan Museum of Art/Rizzoli.

Taylor, S. (1950) *China and Other Dinnerware*. New York: Fairchild.

Toulouse, Julian Harrison (1971) *Bottle Makers and Their Marks*. Camden: Thomas Nelson.

U.S. Department of Commerce (1915) *The Pottery Industry*. Miscellaneous Series No. 21. U.S. Department of Commerce, Washington, DC.

Voorsanger, Catherine Hoover (1986) 'Dictionary of Architects, Artisans, Artists, and Manufacturers' in *In Pursuit of Beauty: Americans and the Aesthetic Movement*, by Doreen Bolder Burke, Jonathan Freedman, Alice Cooney Frelinghuysen, David A. Hanks, Marilynn Johnson, James D. Kornwolf, Catherine Lynn, Roger B. Stein, Jennifer Toher, and Catherine Hoover Voorsanger, with the assistance of Carrie Rebora, pp. 401–87. New York: The Metropolitan Museum of Art/Rizzoli.

Wettstaed, James R. (1999) 'Purchasing Frequency Versus Archaeological Visibility: Comparing Store Records and Early 19th Century Archaeological Sites in Southeast Missouri'. Paper presented at the 64th Annual Meeting of the Society for American Archaeology, Seattle, Washington State.

Wood, Serry (1953) *Hand-painted China*. Watkins Glen, NY: Century House.

Wood, W. Raymond (ed.) (1991) *Archaeology and World War II*. Monographs in Anthropology No. 10. University of Missouri, Columbia.

Young, Hilary (ed.) (1995) *The Genius of Wedgwood*. Victoria & Albert Museum, London.

# Chapter 4

# Archaeology as the design history of the everyday

*Greg Stevenson*

> Now people no longer have any opinions; they have refrigerators. The only way to catch the spirit of the times is to write a handbook on home appliances.
> (A German critic of creeping American consumerism at the Brussels World Fair of 1958, quoted in Wittner 1974: 120)

## Our fixation with things

The turn of the millennium has coincided with an intensification of public interest in design, and the stories and people behind the objects we use in the home. The coffee tables of the middle classes are laden with publications on the design 'classics' of the twentieth century, and museums are busy building collections of what they see as the icons of the modern movement. Through this process the status of the individual designer has risen, and today more people are familiar with names like Louis Comfort Tiffany, Charles Rennie Mackintosh or René Lalique than they ever were when the designers were alive. The popular consumption of terminologies once restricted to the world of design history has led to a diversification of their meaning. Terms such as 'Art Deco' or 'Art Nouveau' which once determined specific characteristics are now used as catch-all phrases to encompass what is envisioned as the spirit of an era.

Design studies as a discipline has grown alongside public consciousness about design and the designers of our homes and furnishings. Interior décor publications have expanded from the realm of the housewife into a wider readership. These transitions impact on our work as archaeologists as the received meaning of designs are changing with secondary consumption. Goods that once spoke of specific contexts are now received as iconic signifiers of imagined halcyon days. The material culture of the recent past is no longer culturally inanimate, in the right hands it becomes representative of a time, a person, or a place; it evokes the story of something.

As the cultural significance of the items of the contemporary past change with every example put behind the glass of the museum case, the goods themselves are once again commodified. Commercial markets have developed in supplying reproduction goods that play on the signifiers of the real thing (see Stevenson 1997). Artificially distressed rustic pine furniture dressers evoke rural Tuscany, swags of rose-print chintz arouse an image of the English country house, and spelter figures of 1920s dancers epitomise what it is imagined was the excitement of the 'jazz age'. Historical concepts have become embodied in icons and signifiers.

Inter-disciplinary interest in material culture is reflected in the publishing shift from sporadic articles to specialist volumes. Publishers Routledge and Berg have introduced book ranges dealing with material culture and consumption, and new journals such as *things*, 'the forum for the free discussion of objects, their histories and meanings', and *The Journal of Material Culture* have found a solid following. Things are, it seems, the fashionable thing. As more people become fixated with objects, the role of the archaeologist as one of the arbiters of the relationships between people and things must come to the fore. Now is the time to embrace the world of design studies and add our voices to the many telling the stories of the contemporary past. The very least that we can contribute is a balance to the misrepresentation of the past propounded by some of the more vulgar commercial re-interpretations of recent design historical styles.

## Problems of traditional design analysis

The case for the archaeologies of the contemporary past is easily made when you look at the pitfalls of traditional design analysis. In concentrating on the broader picture rather than everyday consumables, traditional design history has neglected the complexity of people/material culture relationships. Complicated issues have been compartmentalised into simplistic and neat categories that make consumption of the story of design easier. The heterogeneous nature of design has become constricted by frameworks that oversimplify reality.

Archaeologists are similarly guilty of adopting universalising narratives in much of their work, but the wealth of contextual evidence in the contemporary past means that the cracks simply cannot be plastered over with generalised assumptions. The distillation of design history into the big names and the 'classic' designs makes for palatable stories, but usually says little about the day-to-day life of the people that lived through those times. One role that the archaeology of the contemporary past could take would be in writing the design history of the everyday.

The process through which the aesthetics of the contemporary past have been compartmentalised into design historical terms such as 'Art Nouveau', 'Art Deco', and 'Pop Art' is not entirely the fault of design historians. The wider media are equally responsible for the creation of such terms. Films, television dramas and commercial companies all have an interest in identifying niche interest markets, and catering for them. Who can say just how significant the televised images of Agatha Christie's crime novels have been in painting the popular images of 1920s England? Publishing divisions have also played their part in the creation of the perceived 'evolution' of design. Books on ceramics, glass and furniture have traditionally been seen as for the collector/antiques market, whereas 'bigger' issues such as architecture and fine art have been seen as being more academic. This has left the material culture of the everyday to be serviced by a publishing industry led by the antiques trade. Popular distortions of the contemporary past need to be addressed by the archaeologist in writing our archaeologies of modernity. The 'twenties weren't 'roaring' for everyone and the 'sixties didn't 'swing' for all that lived through them.

Traditional design histories have tended to reflect the collecting tastes of the author, been biased by unrepresentative survival rates, retrospective evaluation or the collecting policies of the major museums, and generally tended to ignore the work of women. Many have assumed that material goods are socially inert artefacts that simply *reflect* human taste or fashion. Bruno Latour (1988a,b) illustrated how supposedly inanimate material culture is *active* in human social process, and that people and things are connected through 'actor networks' in which people and things are on an equal footing and with an equal contribution. The archaeology of the contemporary past has a role to play in bringing social sciences theory to the world of art history.

## The archaeology of the contemporary past

It is now widely understood that the consumption of material culture can be significant in the social construction and negotiation of our identities. Therefore in-depth deconstruction and analysis of the network of design metaphors in material culture can lead us to a broader understanding of human relationships. Political messages, group and individual aspirations and romantic fantasies are just some of the histories reflected in industrial goods used on a daily basis. An examination of the process through which these social ideals become part of an artefact's design, and the process through which the ideals are subsequently consumed, can lead us to a deeper understanding of our relationships between ourselves and the goods we use.

Anthropologically informed archaeology that specifically examines relationships between the social and the material has great potential in interpreting the recent past. Unlike archaeologies of pasts more distant and where we may never recover context-specific meanings, no great leap of imagination is required to make at least reasonable assertions of intended signifiers and consumed ideologies in material from the twentieth century. Original designers, original advertisements and original consumers are often available, though it should be remembered that this does not mean the interpreter is any less likely inadvertently to introduce bias into his or her interpretations.

By approaching the past through the objects of the everyday the archaeologist is acting to redress the imbalance created by design histories which have over-concentrated on the work of the great and the good. Twentieth-century design history is so mangled in the metanarrative of omnipotent designers and linear design evolution that simply by looking at real homes and real people outside of the buying circle of the avant-garde we can make a valuable contribution to our understanding of this century. By looking first to what was actually being bought, we can then trace back through design translations to the design sources of the 'great and the good', if indeed they are even there. The archaeology of the recent past may not only enhance our understanding of recent periods but may also challenge our perception of the relationships between people and things.

As archaeologists we have a duty to look beyond the aesthetic to the social. It is this emphasis that will ultimately separate our work from that being done on modern design in other disciplines. We can draw on the work done in design history, the sociology of technology, and art history to take a holistic, contextualised view and investigate *inter-active* relationships between objects and people. We do not have to start with the grand metanarratives of classic design history (modernism comes home), we can start with the products of daily life. For example, Pablo Picasso, Marcel Breuer and Terence Conran have all had very little direct effect on the domestic lives of the average person. Yet they have had an effect on the industrial designers who produce the products of everyday life. It is in deconstructing the design translations from these trend-setters to the industrial producers, and again to the individual consumer and how they use and consume design, that we can see the real picture of how design works in the lives of the individual and the group. It is cups on the breakfast table, not the chairs in the design showroom of capital cities, that form the design facts of design history.

## Case study: Clarice Cliff and the deco-ration of the inter-war home

Clarice Cliff (1899–1972) was an industrial designer, a woman who modelled the pots seen on the breakfast tables of Britain in the 1930s and sold them by the million. Her work is neither rare nor unique, yet its use of brilliant enamel colours on geometric shaped pots has attracted a significant following amongst modern-day collectors. Popular texts written for the antiques market dub her the 'Doyenne' of British Art Deco. These approaches to the ceramics of inter-war Britain have at best considered pots as inactive artefacts reflecting contemporary fashions, and at worst been shallow reviews of the output of the factories whose goods are now collectable in the international antiques trade. Such work has failed to grasp the social significance of inter-war ceramics.

Clarice Cliff's work fits into the revival of flatbrush on-glaze decoration made popular after the 1925 Paris exhibition. Many manufacturers were selling lines with speedily painted representations of flowers in bright oranges and greens, Cliff went a stage further by introducing elements of modern and cubist art into her work. Competition was fierce between the four hundred or so ceramic manufacturers in Stoke-on-Trent between the wars. A depressed market and increases in imports from Germany, Czechoslovakia and Japan meant that manufacturers had to consolidate an individual identity to survive. Commercial pressures amongst smaller and medium-sized manufacturers to produce eye-catching tableware designs at affordable prices meant it was they who largely brought Art Deco influenced and modern inspired designs to the British public.

New designs appeared by the late 1920s echoing exotic continental shapes and patterns. Streamlined modernistic shapes influenced by architectural and engineering developments appeared in decorative vases. Some manufacturers copied directly from continental designs and others copied each other. Popular tea-ware gained angular outlines and bright floral decoration. These modern lines would typically be placed prominently in displays to add prestige to cheaper, traditional lines that sold in greater numbers.

From 1927 to 1937 Cliff produced some of the most daring designs and patterns ever seen on commercially produced ceramics in Britain. She dazzled consumers with bright colours and fashionable, continental looking shapes, and brought great commercial success to her employers Wilkinsons. Cliff was the first woman to design both shapes and decoration of commercial tableware, and she produced hundreds of new shapes for manufacture. Nobody rivalled the volume or breadth of her design output in the inter-war years, and eight million pieces of her Bizarre Ware sold altogether in the 1930s.

Cliff is of interest to the archaeologist because she was a commercially driven designer who was responsive to the changing tastes of Britain in the 1930s. It is, after all, the minor industrial designers who produced the products that made inter-war Britain. Analysis of Cliff's work shows that she adopted and translated modern and *art décoratifs* styles seen on the continent for the British palate. The way that she took the images of artists such as Mondrian, Modigliani and Edouard Benedictus and translated them onto earthenware gives us a real story of the influence of modernism on people's lives. A look at the broader ceramics industry of the period (Stevenson 1998) shows us that it was the failure of most of Britain's successful designers to adopt modernism, or to grasp even the true meaning of the French *art décoratifs* style that make for the archaeology of the period.

Britain as a whole was not ready for truly modern ceramics in 1927 when Cliff started to produce pots for her employers A.J. Wilkinsons – a medium-sized earthenware manufacturer in Burslem, Stoke-on-Trent. The buying public was, however, ready for pots which they felt embodied the 'new look' popular on the continent. Designers such as Cliff saw an opening in the market and started to produce watered-down half-interpretations and translations of continental design aesthetics. She often copied 'the look' popular in Paris without adopting the philosophy of modernism. Angular pots were produced that spoke of clean lines and functionalism, but which were not in fact the product of a modern production process. Cliff proceeded to decorate these modernistic shapes with landscape, floral and geometric images in brilliant contrasting colours.

Cliff was guilty of copying shapes and patterns from French, German and Dutch artists and designers. There was however nothing unusual about this at the time, and to Cliff's credit she succeeded in creating something new in her misappropriation of modernist styles. Clarice's pots were original in the way they blended a host of design signifiers. Few others would have dared paint rustic cottage scenes onto decoration-eschewing modernist shaped teapots, but in doing so Cliff captured the spirit of the 1930s buying public. Her work makes an excellent case study of the way that the modern aesthetic entered the British home in the 1930s.

Clarice Cliff's success is linked to the changing face of Britain in the 1930s, and it is through investigating the relationship between the pots and how they were consumed that we undertake our archaeological 'excavation'. Cliff's relationship with the changing Britain is clear. She deliberately marketed herself as a 'modern' designer in home décor publications, she deliberately targeted developing niche markets with her 'bachelor' tea-sets and small place-setting dinner services, and she adapted continental patterns and shapes in designs that would be compatible with the new suburban domestic style.

Cliff recognised the active role that her pots played in the home. She sometimes designed her ceramics within holistic interior design concepts. Magazines such as *Modern Home* supplied cross-stitch patterns so that women could copy Clarice Cliff patterns onto their cushion covers or paint them onto lampshades. Cliff even went to the effort of dressing shop-window displays herself. Brilliant shop-front displays of top-of-the range cubist inspired pots were used to draw people in to shops where most left with cheaper, restrained floral pieces. The name Clarice Cliff became a fashionable one to display in a culture where more and more people were checking underneath to see who made the pots on their tables and the tables of their friends.

Whereas times were very hard for some in inter-war Britain, the living standards of many were rising, and the middle classes benefited from improvements in housing. If the 'consumer society' had been born before WWI, then it was certainly in the inter-war years that it was consolidated. In the late 1920s many people found that they could move into accommodation that they owned themselves (the majority had rented before WWI) and there was a house-building boom on the outskirts of many large towns. The suburbs swelled with estates of semi-detached 'Tudorbethan' homes, a pastiche of Tudor, Elizabethan or Jacobean styles. They shared common architectural styles and were designed to provide domestic arenas for new consumer practices.

> The sort of house which the great majority of inter-war suburbans wanted, escaping as most were from the monotony of terraces in central or inner-urban areas, was something like a country cottage of some historical style, preferably individually sited and individual in character. Ideally, it might be a Tudor cottage in a country lane, but equipped with modern conveniences and supplied with nearby shops, schools and transport.
>
> (Burnett 1978: 263)

Despite being slated by contemporary design critics for their lack of imagination (see for example Bertram 1938: 58) and famously by author D.H. Lawrence for being 'horrid little red mantraps', the romantically clad 'semi' remained popular. As home-ownership expanded and family size diminished, the importance attached to the home constantly increased, and in this respect the inter-war generation can be seen as a home-centred one. As far back as 1914 Elsie de Wolfe introduced her *House of Good Taste* by claiming,

> I know of nothing more significant than the awakening of men and women throughout the country to the desire to improve their houses ... It is no longer possible, even to people of faintly æsthetic tastes, to buy chairs merely to sit on or a clock merely that it should tell the time.
>
> (de Wolfe 1914: 3)

The cult of home décor was aided by magazines such as *Good Housekeeping* which sold around 100,000 copies a month in the early 1930s. Image was now emerging at the root of consumer practice (Benson 1984). For the first time in the history of the British home we see a degree of deliberate aesthetic uniformity and attention to compliance with the latest fashion. Knowledge about these fashions was fuelled by the communications revolution taking place at the time (see Thorpe 1992). By 1934 around 20 million people listened to the radio, read a national rather than regional newspaper and visited the cinema at least once a week. It was now quite possible for people of modest incomes to have an understanding of what the latest fashions were in London or Paris.

The homes of inter-war suburbia bizarrely blended nostalgic romanticism and 'scientific' futurist design, bridging the dichotomy between old and new, romance and convenience, fantasy and practicality. And at the same time there is a recurrent theme of the dawning of a bright new age, about the wonders of science, and of wildly optimistic futurism. Romanticism is inherent in the modern condition, as it has been throughout modern consumer practice (Campbell 1987). Inter-war suburbia was not about the consumption of avant-garde design, but the consumption of popular dreams. The inter-war home was in many ways a new way of seeing and understanding the world. For those occupying newly built suburban houses it was a new environment inhabited largely by a young, new generation experiencing new technologies and the changes that came with them.

If the advertisements and features in the popular housekeeping magazines of the time are to be taken as indicative, people were buying Clarice Cliff's pots to decorate these new suburban settings. With her plates garishly mimicking the styles of cubist paintings Cliff brought modern art to suburbia (Figure 4.1). Conical bowls in patterns inspired by Picasso sat comfortably on grotesque oak veneer copies of Jacobean sideboards. The British public opted for both historical romanticism and modernistic design in their new homes, and Cliff catered for every taste. She designed modernistic angular pots for the kitchen (where clean

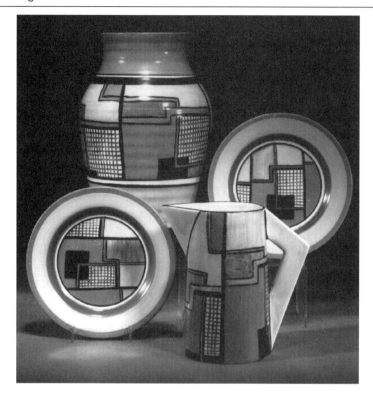

*Figure 4.1* Ceramics by Clarice Cliff for Wilkinsons, 1929/30 in the 'Football' pattern. Cliff brought modern art to suburbia with her earthenware interpretations of Cubist and De Stijl art. (Courtesy: Christie's SK.)

lines projected an image of hygiene and futuristic aesthetics) and floral wares for the bedroom (in her specially produced 'Early Morning Tea sets to be taken in bed') (Figure 4.2). In a combination of seemingly antagonistic philosophies, *streamline moderne* styling took hold in the kitchen and bathroom whilst the front room remained romantically *Jacobethan*.

Suburbia was the meeting place of nostalgia and futurism, and the new suburbians happily blended a pastiche of historical styles with the very latest in technical innovation. Consumers did not define between the apparently opposing interests of functionalism and romanticism in the way that art historians have since. Looking to the broader picture we see similar contradictions between design metaphors in other material cultures of Britain. The archaeology of the contemporary past reveals the complexities of the relationships between design ideas and practical realities.

It is often assumed, for example, that the term Art Deco can be adopted when discussing British design 1925–1939. The term Art Deco, coined in the 1960s and largely used in the antiques/collector trade, refers to the fashions made popular by the 1925 Paris 'Exposition Internationale des Arts Décoratifs et

TEA FOR THE INVALID – The first essential is to make the tray dainty and gay. When milk is not allowed, tea can be served with lemon.

*Figure 4.2* Tea for one by Clarice Cliff. Cliff copied the shape of this 1930 'Stamford' tea-set from a white metal original by French designer Jean Tétard. She then had it decorated with the floral 'Soloman's Seal' design and sold it in tea-sets which catered for the changing domestic arrangements of Britain. Sets could be purchased as here with just one cup as a 'Bachelor Set', with two cups as an 'Early Morning Set' or with more cups as desired. (Photograph by Greg Stevenson.)

Industriels Modernes'. The typical work on display at the exhibition rejected the twisting naturalistic forms popular in Art Nouveau in favour of symmetrical shapes and a pursuit of refinement in material, form and decoration. However, a thorough investigation of the actual material culture and architecture of Britain at the time suggests that the style was so transformed by British designers that we cannot really talk about Art Deco Britain at all.

The continental style of leading figures such as Ruhlmann, Lalique and Cartier had indeed influenced a generation of British designers, but the Deco philosophy of refined luxury became crystallised into the adoption and repetition of popular symbols. Images of the sun rising and Egyptian and ziggurat motifs abound in British design of the period. Such icons became signifiers of the new style and were often employed independently of the wider design philosophy in an attempt to make 'non-Deco' items appear 'Deco'. For example, furniture often retained Edwardian styling yet gained walnut veneer and Egyptian-style marquetry. This superficial adoption of Art Deco is widely seen in British ceramics of the period, and in the work of the 'Doyenne' of Deco, Clarice Cliff.

Cliff's work is significant to the archaeologist as she was conscious of the need to please both conservative and modern tastes. Even whilst bringing avant-garde 'modern art' to the British breakfast table she still produced more reserved lines such as her signature pattern *Crocus* and fantasy romantic landscapes with thatched farmhouses in brilliant colourways. The ceramics market catered for many tastes, and Cliff pitched her designs at as many sectors of the market as she could. Rather than following the philosophy of modernism, or attempting to produce the finest *arts décoratifs* goods, she drew on the aesthetics of the major design movements of the time and adapted them to make them more commercial.

Cliff's story is important precisely because she never was part of the design establishment. Unlike contemporary Susie Cooper she had no interest in carrying the mantle of modernism, and neither was her aim to produce the highest quality earthenware on the market. Cliff was not trying to distil the British Art Deco style any more than she was trying deliberately to change the fashions of the breakfast table. She produced what would sell, and sell it did. So when we look at her work we may stand in awe at her audacious re-interpretation of De Stijl and cubist patterns, and simultaneously cringe at her homely floral moulded pieces of the later 1930s.

To describe her place in the history of British ceramic design, Cliff was an unusually innovative designer of a middle-of-the-range earthenware manufacturer who had an uncanny ability to produce the 'right' goods at the right times. She was there in 1927 selling Egyptian styled 'Original Bizarre' when Egyptomania was going strong. In 1929 she was one of the first to produce the angular geometric pots that echoed the European avant-garde. By 1933 she was producing fantasy landscapes which catered for the British taste for something modern looking, yet not too outrageous. It is precisely her responsiveness to the market that means she is important when we look back at the history of ceramic design. Her successful designs really do provide litmus to the domestic tastes of Britain 1927–1937.

Her pots are important because of the way they were active in 1930s society. Having Cliff's pots in your front room in the 1930s was playing a small part in the modern dream. Whereas Britain failed to embrace the philosophy of modernism, many consumed what they considered to be the look of modernism, and Clarice Cliff was one way into that world. Britain was not ready for truly modern design, and people wanted pots that took a fresh approach to rural nostalgia and traditional patterns. This is exactly what Cliff gave to Britain – modern 'looking' pots decorated in what most people thought was the fashionable continental look. Her work is neither modern, nor truly Art Deco. But it does say more about Britain at the time than any number of designs from the big names of the Modern movement or the Art Deco style. Investigations of Cliff's work reveals the subtleties involved in the deco-ration and modern-isation of the British home.

## Conclusions

The modern period with its rich contextual sources is ideal ground on which to write archaeologies of the everyday. Terms such as 'Georgian' and

'Victorian' are words that the public can relate to as the recent past. When we research the archaeologies of houses that people still live in, when we write about the relatives in the photographs on our walls, then we add relevance to our discipline. When archaeology deals with the life of the man-next-door, or even readers themselves, then it becomes even more engaging. Up until now however, our attempts at dealing with the material from this century have been few and far between. The turn of the millennium is an appropriate time for archaeologists to take a look at the twentieth century, and illustrate how, more than any other century, it was created by people and their relationships with material culture and material environments. People constructed their identities through material consumption in the twentieth century as in no other time. The scope for the archaeologist in telling these stories is substantial.

Our interpretations will be aided by the wealth of contextual material associated with the contemporary past. In looking at the relationships between designer, item and consumer we may glean a good deal about the process by which we employ material culture as social actors. It is through the deconstruction of design and consumer metaphors that archaeology can be a useful socio-historical tool in telling the stories of the twentieth century.

In writing design-based archaeologies of the contemporary past we need to take objects as linked to a wealth of contextual design metaphors. Material culture is actively participating in social life. Objects may contribute to, but not necessarily sit comfortably within design 'movement' boundaries. It is in the minutiae of everyday items that 'thought styles' and fashions (and thus social history) are created and maintained. It is not the case that industrial design is always a reflector of the work of the 'leaders' of design fashion. We should be aware of the fact that material culture can embody many identities, which can change according to individual and general contexts, and over time.

Finally, it must not be forgotten that the role of the archaeologist is that of the designer, in that we 'design' social relationships, stories and narratives of how things might have been. Without deeper investigation of the relationships between the designed and the consumed, and the everyday realities of design history, there cannot be a comprehensive and balanced understanding of the contemporary past as a whole.

## References

Benson J. (1984) *The Rise of Consumer Society in Britain 1880–1980* London: Longman.
Bertram A. (1938) *Design* Harmondsworth: Pelican.
Burnett J. (1978) *Social History of Housing 1815–1970* London: David & Charles.
Campbell C. (1987) *The Romantic Ethic and the Spirit of Modern Consumerism* Oxford: Blackwell.
Latour B. (1988a) 'The Prince for machines as well as machinations' in *Technology and Social Process* ed. B. Elliott, Edinburgh: Edinburgh University Press.

Latour, B. (1988b) 'Mixing humans and nonhumans together: the sociology of a door-closer' in *Social Problems* Vol. 35 No. 3 June.

Stevenson G. (1997) 'Better than Bizarre' *things* Vol. 7 pp. 110–13.

Stevenson G. (1998) *Art Deco Ceramics* Princes Risborough: Shire.

Thorpe A. (1992) *Britain in the 1930s* Oxford: Blackwell.

Wittner L.S. (1974) *Cold War America: From Hiroshima to Watergate* NY: Praeger.

de Wolfe E. (1914) *The House in Good Taste* London: Sir Isaac Pitman & Sons.

# Chapter 5

# Integrated archaeology
## A garbage paradigm

*William Rathje*

As founder and director of the Garbage Project, most of my career has been spent cheek-to-jowl with modern refuse. From the outset, the primary goal of Garbage Project research was to demonstrate the utility of archaeological methods and theories for achieving a better understanding of issues of current public concern – including assessments of resource waste and proposed methods of waste minimization, measures of diet and nutrition, evaluations of household participation in recycling programs, identification of household-level sources of hazardous wastes, cross-validation of census counts of minority populations, and providing base data for the design of new 'environmentally friendly' packages (for first-decade and second-decade summaries see Rathje 1984a and Rathje 1996a). As a result, I have rarely discussed what the Project's understanding of the relation between contemporary garbage and the society that generates it means to archaeology. After twenty-five years of *garbology*, it is time to make those observations in an archaeological forum (one rationale for archaeological studies of contemporary industrial societies is presented in Rathje 1979a; see also Rathje *et al.* in press).

Over the past five decades there have been several archaeologists concerned with identifying the most productive type of archaeology – *new, behavioral, postprocessual, consumption-based*, and more. This paper suggests that none of these approaches alone can provide a comprehensive perspective of the present – or of the past. Only by combining them all into an *Integrated* archaeology can the most complete understanding of human behavior over the centuries, and including today, be acquired (see Rathje 1979b).

The key reference for the foundation of an *Integrated* archaeology is *Unobtrusive Measures: Nonreactive Research in the Social Sciences*, written in 1966 by Eugene Webb, an economist and jack-of-all-disciplines, and a few colleagues. The premise of the book is quite simple: neither interview-surveys of participants nor observations of participants are sufficient, either by themselves or in combination, to adequately describe, analyze, and understand the ways social systems both behave and evolve. The book argues for adding the analysis of material trace measures – archaeologists' expertise – to the mix. And, because none of the data acquisition perspectives are sufficient in themselves, the book further argues for 'triangulating' mental, behavioral, and material records into a richer multi-dimensional perspective of the social systems under study. It took only a few years of archaeological garbage research for me to arrive at the same conclusion.

When the Garbage Project began in 1973, I believed – as most social scientists have come to understand, whether they admit it or not – that what people report they do and/or what they themselves believe they do is often very different from their actual behavior. Twenty-five years of Garbage Project studies strongly suggest that this belief is correct. For example, Garbage Project comparisons of interview-survey reports and alcohol containers in respondents refuse (sorting done with discarders' permission) quickly determined that respondents underreport the amount of alcohol they drink by 40 to 60 percent (see Rathje and McCarthy 1977, Rathje 1978, Dobyns and Rathje 1987, Rathje and Murphy 1992).

Such misreports of alcohol consumption, of course, came as no surprise. Nor was it a surprise that market researchers hired by alcohol purveyors and academic and rehabilitation alcohol researchers were already familiar with this pattern (see Rabow and Watts 1982, Rabow and Neuman 1984) – they did not know the exact underreports for specific population segments, but they did know that reports were almost always substantially lower than actual consumption. There was, however, one surprise for the Garbage Project – that, for a variety of reasons, these researchers focusing on alcohol use did not care to identify actual levels of consumption – alcohol researchers, because an alcohol problem is an alcohol problem whether a subject consumes one beer too many per day or fifteen, and market researchers, because, if the actual quantity of over-consumption of a market segment of drinkers were accurately reported, beer companies would be under immense pressure to curb ads and financially support alcohol treatment programs.

The point is that what people said they drank and observations of drinking behavior in controlled settings were not valid representations of actual drinking, and no one seemed to care about what the artifacts of drinking indicated. In effect, what they knew was enough for their own purposes, but not enough to comprehensively and accurately assess patterns of alcohol consumption. The same disinterest in the material realities of behavior is pervasive throughout our society. The keepers of U.S. Department of Agriculture's (USDA) national records as well as medical researchers did not want to know that their reports were not accurate representations of food use behavior. That would call into question decades of USDA records and medical research conclusions. As this reality became clear to the Garbage Project, it also became obvious that the only reason garbage archaeologists were asked to conduct studies of fresh refuse was because some major gaffe showed up in traditional interview-survey or observational methods.

As one example, the USDA sent out an RFP (request for proposals) in the late 1970s to verify its 'Nationwide Food Consumption Survey' (NFCS) interview-protocols, which were to measure in-home food use in 30,000 households in 1980. Amazingly, the traditional way to 'verify' interview data is to give the interview again – no matter that the same biases would be in place. In spite of this easily applied traditional method of verification, all of the research groups responding to the RFP asked the Garbage Project to examine refuse to further cross-verify respondent reports. To our surprise, the company that won the grant received it on the condition that the garbage aspect of the study be removed! I was told that was because the USDA could not afford to study garbage from even a subsample of 30,000 study households. As you might suspect, I was slightly disappointed.

My funk lifted considerably when the two components of the completed NFCS – (1) interviews of someone reporting for the whole household and (2) interviews of individuals within the household – were compared. The comparison showed that the final USDA survey results were out of kilter with each other by 40 percent – the households as a whole were reported to use 40 percent more food than the individuals within the households admitted to using. In 1982, the Garbage Project was contracted by USDA to find out what was wrong. That year, we duplicated the NFCS interview-survey in a sample of homes in Tucson (see Harrison *et al.* 1983, Ritenbaugh and Harrison 1984). It was reassuring that the Tucson results documented virtually the very same whole household/individual residents gap as the national results. Thanks to the permission of respondent households for the Garbage Project to sort their refuse, it was possible to compare food use recorded from package labels and from food preparation debris to interview reports (for more on the Garbage Project's methodology, see Hughes 1984, Dobyns and Rathje 1987).

Garbage/interview comparisons documented that the 'use' (this is the term of choice for nutritionists) of virtually every food was misreported, both in whole household and in individual responses, by 10 percent or substantially more – and all for what seemed to be interesting reasons (see Rathje 1984b, Dobyns and Rathje 1987). For example, we discovered the 'Good Provider Syndrome' – that the woman of the household usually overreported virtually everything the family ate as a whole; the 'Lean Cuisine Syndrome' – that individuals almost always dramatically underreport what they themselves eat as individuals; and the 'Surrogate Syndrome' – if you want to know how much alcohol the residents in a household consume, do not ask the drinkers, rather ask a non-drinker (Rathje and Dobyns 1987). Was the result of the Garbage Project study the addition of a garbage component to the NFCS? No, the result was the end of the NFCS and a whole new in-home/out-of-home 24-hour recall interview methodology that the Garbage Project could not possibly cross-verify on a large scale.

Medical researchers paid little attention to our similar cross-verification of the NCI's (National Cancer Institute's) Food Frequency Questionnaire (FFQ) which produced similar garbage/interview results (see Johnstone and Rathje 1986, Johnstone 1986). There was no attention, that is, until the recent report of a study in the *New England Journal of Medicine* that concluded that a high-fiber diet was not protective against colon cancer (Fuchs *et al.* 1999). This report was based on the occurrence of colon cancer in a sample of 88,000 nurses who had been given the FFQ every couple of years over the past 16 years. The study found that nurses who reported diets high in fiber were just as likely to contract the disease as those who reported that they ate relatively little fiber.

Suddenly, when the results did not meet researchers' expectations, medical and nutrition specialists were willing to concede that diet reports may be flawed. In fact, a Garbage Project cross-verification of the NCI's FFQ found that misreports of many high-fiber items and other foods ranged between 10 and 65 percent (Johnstone and Rathje 1986, Johnstone 1986). That Garbage Project study was completed 12 years ago!

Other areas of garbage research have led to results that have similarly been ignored. Take HHW (Household Hazardous Waste) (see Rathje et al. 1987a,b). At first, the Garbage Project found that HHW 'collection days' did not significantly diminish HHW in household refuse in three study communities (see Rathje and Wilson 1987, Wilson et al. 1994). In fact, in communities that did not publicize continued disposal opportunities for HHW, the quantities of HHW actually increased after one highly publicized community-wide event. This is probably because people were informed through media ads and community-flyers that they had HHW in their homes. When householders missed the pickup, they most likely felt that discarding HHW in their refuse was the only legal disposal opportunity they had available (Rathje and Wilson 1987, Rathje et al. 1987a). How happy do you think the cities that contracted the Garbage Project were to have these results published?

Today, relative to HHW there is another problem. For some reason, people tend to drastically misreport the quantities of specific forms of HHW they discard in one year (a typical interview-survey question) (see Rathje et al. in press). I personally don't know how much paint or how many batteries I throw out in a year – do you? As an example of the report problem, consider the responses to a telephone survey covering Marin county compared to hands-on sorts of the refuse from some 2000 households refuse pickups sampled in the phone-survey neighborhoods (see Rathje and Wilson 1987, Rathje et al. 1987a).

Two divergences in the survey versus garbage data jumped out immediately. Marin householders, especially if they were male, were likely to report changing their motor oil themselves and then discarding the old oil improperly. Motor oil was not common in sorted refuse. In fact, while motor oil represented 46 per cent of reported HHW discards, in actual garbage it was recorded as exactly half that figure – 23 per cent. In contrast, yard-related HHW was recorded as 16.6 per cent of total HHW in garbage sorts, but scored less than 2 per cent on phone survey records. An explanation? I believe the motor oil reports are Marin male macho – men want to believe that they change their own motor oil even when they don't. As for the yard wastes, most Marin residents hire landscaping services to care for their yards and don't pay attention to what their employees discard. End result: How can community services target those products that most need to be properly discarded if they receive information for interview-surveys that are nearly the opposite of what is recorded in the garbage by hand sorts?

I thought at the outset of the Project that people might be intentionally misreporting. I no longer believe that. I believe that either they do not have any concrete idea of what they consume and discard – likely, since we are not trained to remember such things as 'how many ounces of green beans did you eat yesterday' – or, people are fooling themselves. In some ways, it really does not matter which explanation is correct – deceit, ignorance, or not wanting to know. The end result is that what people say and/or believe they do is often strikingly different from their actual behavior. And, all too often, the response of companies, government agencies, and even academic researchers, is 'so long as our society keeps working, so what?'

Archaeology has traditionally been about what happens after the dust settles – literally. That settlement is, of course, thousands, hundreds, or dozens of years after the fact. But why wait until all or most of the subjects in a study are dead to truly understand the way their behavioral system worked? To understand what has transpired – or, perhaps more relevant to the current members of our society, what is transpiring – do we not need to understand all of the aspects of society? Do we not need to know the mental, behavioral, and material elements of our actions and how they all fit together in ways that keep society functioning no matter how incongruent its various components may seem to each other? In fact, I believe that no one can fully interpret one component of a social system without all the others!

One final, but critical, example of our lack of knowledge about ourselves in today's hyper-studied society: because of its mutagenic nature, fat from red meat was a big concern to nutritionists and medical researchers. In 1978 the USDA called the Garbage Project and asked how much of the 'separable' fat on steaks, roasts, and chops people cut off and discarded. The Garbage Project replied that we did not know much about the discard of meat fat. We considered meat fat to be inedible and did not record it as a distinct waste. The USDA representatives responded that the fat had calories and asked us to start recording it. We did, and we were greatly surprised by a summary of our data records a few years later (Rathje and Ho 1987).

We were able to record the amount of 'separable fat' on cuts of meat because the USDA constantly analyzes numerous pieces of meat to identify the quantity of separable fat that can be expected on various cuts, say a Porterhouse steak or a T-bone steak. Since we usually found meat packages labeled by both cut and weight, we could estimate the quantity of separable fat that would have entered the household. On the other hand, dogs and cats eat our data, or it may be ground down in garbage disposals. Nevertheless, there were no major changes in the frequency of dogs, cats, or garbage disposals in Tucson over the study years. As a result, we could look at trend data.

We found that the percentage of meat fat cut from fresh red meat that we were actually able to weigh and record remained constant between 1979 and 1982. But that percentage doubled in 1983 and has remained at that higher level since! In addition, we found that households began purchasing fewer steaks, roasts, and chops in 1983. There was no reason for this we could think of, except that the National Academy of Science had published a highly publicized report in early 1983 that fat from red meat was a risk factor for breast and colon cancer (Committee on Diet, Nutrition, and Cancer 1983). Garbage Project results, at first, made the USDA and the NAS quite happy.

The problem was that in place of fresh red meat, people were not buying chicken or fish. They were buying salami, bologna, hot dogs, and other processed red meats in higher quantities. These processed red meats, of course, have higher fat content than most cuts of fresh red meat. The end result, which no one expected, was that the fat content in the diet from red meat remained the same or actually increased (Rathje and Ho 1987)!

Was the cause lack of understanding of medical jargon? In fact, most residents of sample households we asked about these behaviors thought that 'fat from red meat' – the medical jargon reported in the media – meant steaks, roasts, and chops; and that if the doctors had meant salami, bologna, and hot dogs, they would have 'said so.' Or was it the desire for convenience? We do not know. What we do know is that the picture of the American diet and people's understanding of what the medical community was saying was 'good' for them to eat were not in sync. To me, this says that, if they can, behavioral scientists should know all of the variables – mental, behavioral, and material – before they draw conclusions. Otherwise, historians might draw one conclusion from media reports – that people were concerned about disease prevention and cutting down on fat in their diet, while archaeologists might draw another – that in order to increase their energy intake, people were switching to higher fat sources! Only when all the data are available does the puzzle of inconsistencies become somewhat clearer.

I believe that this study clarified my thinking. As I have mentioned, I used to believe that people intentionally 'lie' in interviews today – in the past in texts and on monuments. Now, I wonder if the differences between mental and material realities are not mainly simple cases of people not mentally recognizing material realities and fooling themselves. This is a question for future archaeologists and other behavioral scientist to answer in tandem. For now, however, I believe that this is one of the most important questions related to human behavior for all behavioral scientists to answer. Only when all of these realities are in sync with each other can people plan rational public policies and make rational personal decisions that lead to expected results. And the only way to begin to provide quantitative information to bring the realities of behavioral systems into sync is to compare the separate realities all humans share – mental, behavioral, material – over time in an *integrated* archaeology! An *integrated* archaeology means reconstructing at least six very distinct and separate 'realities' that are components of behaviors. Such an integrated approach is important because the various behavioral measurement perspectives in use today are not mirrors of each other. They each have different biases. They each record different data. Thus, each adds a new and important dimension to the study of our behavioral system.

To an archaeologist, material artifacts are the starting point. Based on the significant role of material culture in our lives today, the role of these *material traces* (Rathje 1979b) in the methodology of behavioral science needs to be revised – and greatly heightened in prominence. The reason is that in both archaeology and the other social sciences, material traces have usually been measured as 'reflections of behavior' to document change. But material traces are not a simple mirror; they are a critical component that plays a leading role in the direction of behavioral change. Are McDonald's and other fast-food restaurants only a reflection of changing family eating habits and values, or were McDonald's *et al.* a part of the cause? To sort out roles in behavioral change, the recording and analysis of material culture must be a significant perspective in any behavioral science methodology designed to understand change – new patterns in artifacts, behaviors, and perceptions. I believe an *integrated* perspective should begin with actions. Actions are composed of a complicated integration of perception, behavior, and artifacts. To be complete, even a simplified model of actions must include all three of these domains along with specific perspectives within each domain (see Figure 5.1).

*Perception elements* are (1) general cultural rules and values that can be elicited from informants and (2) informant perceptions of what behavior, their own and the behavior of others, actually occurs as a result of these rules.

*Behavioral elements* are (3) records or direct observations of behavior and (4) common behavioral shorthand concepts (income level, ethnicity, demography, education level) used to classify people in ways assumed to have significance in terms of some degree of shared behaviors. One of the primary opportunities presented by an *integrated* research approach is to test such assumptions.

*Material traces elements* are quantitative data in the form of standardized measures of (5) material culture and its traces in specific environments and (6) the general natural, social, and economic environments in which human actions occur.

No one of these dimensions and perspectives provides a more correct or accurate view of reality than the others. They are, in fact, each equally real. The challenge comes from attempting to fit these separate realities into a coherent description and understanding of a behavioral phenomenon. The value of a holistic perspective that combines traces with other measures can be illustrated through an idealized analysis of food loss behaviors based on a series of actual Garbage Project studies. The central focus is the amount of food discarded, but a variety of perspectives define the elements of food loss actions and their synergistic effects. This is currently an active area of Garbage Project research.

1   *General cognitive rules and values.* Informants would be interviewed to determine the rules they use to make decisions about when to throw out food. For example, questions would be asked to determine an informant's general understanding of food knowledge, such as when food is safe to eat and when it is not.

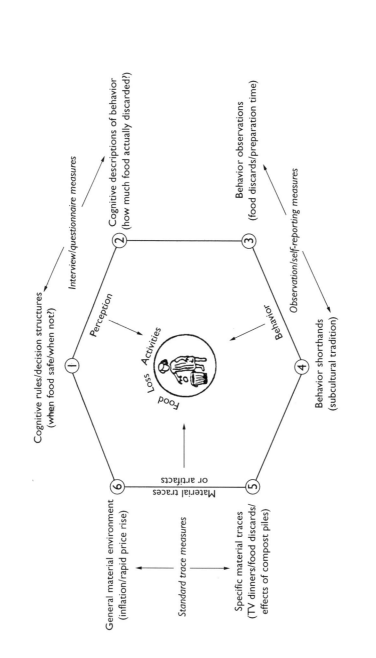

*Figure 5.1* An integrative model of behavioral science research.

2   *Self-perceptions of behaviors.* To quantify the results of applying the cognitive rules described under perspective 1, informants would be asked to describe their own behavior. How much beef, for example, is actually discarded and how often in, say, a six-month time-frame?

3   *Behavior observations and records.* For this perspective, behavior would be directly observed; if it were not possible to make such observations, informants would be asked to self-report and keep records of their actions. These data would include information on actual discards that resulted from applying cognitive rules during an 'observation' period, say one week.

4   *Behavioral shorthands.* This perspective would be derived from census and other public data that record those variables considered significant in our society as ways of categorizing people – age, sex, education, income, and ethnicity.

5   *Material traces (material culture).* Household procurement and utilization would be derived from household refuse by recording packaging (such as microwave dinner trays and boxes, cereal boxes and bags, etc.), preparation debris (such as avocado pits), and food discards (actual weights of discarded once-edible food). Interview/garbage studies would be used to identify potential material trace biases, such as compost piles or garbage disposals.

6   *General material environments.* This viewpoint would record general natural, economic, social, political, and other environmental variables, including inflation rates and the general availability of food and other resources.

Although each of these separate realities may give an impression of internal coherence, the most useful coherence comes from comparing and integrating these independent perspectives. A few examples from Garbage Project studies will illustrate this point. Because archaeologists start from a materialist perspective, I will relate the other perspectives to item number 5 above, specific material traces.

5-1   *General cognitive rules – material traces.* Economists have argued that household food loss is a conscious choice that is made as a trade-off for more free time. As a result, they argue that studying specific food loss patterns would be pointless. In contrast to this argument, one survey/refuse comparison study indicates that a major correlate of food discard is the level of informant knowledge of food safety – the less knowledge, the more waste (Harrison 1976). As a result, education to a few simple rules of food safety might be useful in decreasing food waste.

5-2   *Self-perceptions of behavior – material traces.* Garbage Project studies indicate that it seems likely that the more people admit to waste, the less they actually waste. In other words, people sensitive to food loss may admit more waste, but actually waste less than those who are largely unaware of their waste patterns. Consider what the Garbage Project calls the 'Fast Lane Syndrome.' Those households that buy more pre-prepared foods and less fresh food, waste the highest percentage of fresh food. The result is that the households that buy less fresh food waste more of it than households that buy much more fresh produce (Rathje and Hughes 1977, Rathje 1996b). Ironically, householders who buy very little fresh food believe that they waste very little, when they actually waste quite a lot.

5-3 *Behavior observations and records – material traces.* It is also likely that preparation time relates to waste: the less time invested in preparing food, the more food is discarded. Back to the 'Fast Lane Syndrome.'

5-4 *Behavior shorthands – material traces.* There are lower food loss rates in Mexican-American neighborhoods than in White neighborhoods (Harrison *et al.* 1975, Harrison *et al.* 1983, Dobyns and Rathje 1987). This is likely attributable to the Mexican-American cultural background, both in terms of attitudes and values and in terms of types of foods used, preparation techniques, and ease of incorporating leftovers into other meals.

5-5 *Material traces – material traces.* Various attributes of packaging may affect loss and cross-cut population segment distinctions. Rates of food loss can be compared to types of package configurations and be recorded across neighborhoods to identify general loss/package patterns. For example, preliminary results show that canned vegetables are discarded at a lower rate than frozen vegetables. More important, food that is used regularly and comes in standard-sized packages is discarded at a much lower rate than specialty foods in specialty packages. The best example is bread. There is very little waste associated with standard 16 oz and 24 oz 'sliced bread' loaves. In most households, the slices are used regularly – toast at breakfast, sandwiches for lunch, and plain bread on the table at dinner. On the other hand, most wasted bread is specialty items, such as hamburger and hotdog buns, muffins, biscuits, etc. These breads are used irregularly for cookouts, for other special meals, and the like. Such specialty breads are wasted at a rate of 40 to 60 percent (Rathje 1986, 1996b, Rathje and Murphy 1992, Wilson *et al.* 1991).

5-6 *General material environments – material traces.* One early surprise in the Garbage Project's refuse studies was that during the well-publicized 'beef shortage' of 1973, the waste of edible beef was three times higher than it has been since. The increased loss of sugar products during the 1975 'sugar shortage' fit the crisis buying model worked out to explain the consumer reaction to the beef shortage (Rathje 1977).

While each of the six perspectives presented here is incomplete alone, together they form a comprehensive and integrated approach to any behavioral problem.

Environmental psychology is one of the forms of behavioral science closest to this total perspective. It concentrates on the relation between people's perceptions and behaviors and their physical environments, often national parks or buildings (Heimstra and McFarling 1978, Proshansky 1970). Nevertheless, usually only one perspective, either perception or behavior, is used to collect study data. One example is Yancey's (1970) discussion of the behavioral consequences of the architectural design of Pruitt-Igoe, a low-income housing project in St Louis which won design awards but soon turned into a complete failure – in fact, it was blown up on national television in 1973. Yancey meticulously quantified and analyzed resident's perceptions. In contrast, few behavior observations were reported and no specific distributions of trash or trash collection facilities, unfinished construction, broken windows or graffiti were reported. Needless to say, actual behaviors and traces might have added depth and patterning in new dimensions unrecognized by either residents or researchers.

Two examples will suffice. First, researchers noted a urine smell on the elevators, but they did not mention that there were no ground-floor facilities for the legions of little children who played around the building. How many kids plan ahead for a slow or broken elevator when they are playing and nature calls? Second, there were no shutes on the building's floors for garbage; for proper disposal, residents had to carry their trash down an elevator or stairs and to the back of the building. While researchers did not comment on this physical reality, they did mention that it was obvious that some residents threw their refuse out their upper-story windows. How much will architects learn from one or two analysis perspectives on Pruitt-Igoe versus a wide range?

The value of an *integrated* multi-perspective analysis is also illustrated by Schensul, Paredes, and Pelto's study (1968) of rural northern Minnesota. The authors interviewed informants in rural areas and in Minneapolis-St Paul about their perceived quality of life and quantified their material possessions. The resulting total system was characterized as a 'twilight zone of poverty,' where poverty was experienced in rural households primarily in terms of self-perceived deprivations relative to the affluent sectors of society presented on TV, rather than as a quantifiable deprivation of specific material goods. Schensul and his colleagues concluded that investigation of poverty 'should include both the specific objective descriptions of the researcher and the perceptions of the members of the group under study.'

The approach of treating traces as independent variables does not alter the basic assumption of trace studies – that traces are related in a systematic manner to behavior/perceptions. This assertion has been demonstrated by the Garbage Project's research that identified the *First Principle of Waste*, derived by combining a series of Garbage Project studies (see 5-4, 5-5, 5-6 above). This principle originated with an explanation for the high rate of beef waste recorded during the nation-wide 'beef shortage' in 1973.

The Garbage Project's interpretation of high waste during the beef shortage was that consumers responded to the hype surrounding the shortage by purchasing meat when they found it in unfamiliar cuts (usually cheaper) and unfamiliar quantities (usually larger). Improper preparation and improper storage of these abnormal cuts and quantities resulted in waste. One year later, a 'sugar shortage' produced a strikingly similar pattern in residential refuse – the waste of sugar and sweets doubled while both were expensive and in short supply.

Recording these patterns led to the proposal of the *First Principle of Food Waste*: the less food use behavior varies over time, the less food is wasted. This principle explained why common sliced bread is wasted at a rate of less than 10 percent of purchase, while specialty breads are wasted at a rate of more than 35 percent. It also explains why Hispanics waste less food than Anglos: while prepared Hispanic foods are diverse, their basic ingredients are relatively few compared to the larger variety of foods in common Anglo diets. These and other patterns which can be deduced from the *First Principle of Food Waste* have implications for shopping and meal planning as well as for the design of pre-prepared foods and food packaging.

A form of corroboration for the *First Principle of Food Waste* came from an unexpected source. In 1986, the Garbage Project conducted the EPA's first study of household hazardous wastes in New Orleans and Marin County. One clear pattern in both communities was that potentially hazardous household commodities involved in regular maintenance tasks were wasted at much lower rates than those, such as paints and stains, which are used sporadically and were often wasted in bulk (Rathje *et al.* 1987a and 1987b, Wilson *et al.* 1991 and 1994). This last discovery, confirmed in every subsequent Garbage Project household hazardous waste study, led to the realization that the *First Principle of Food Waste* also covered hazardous discards and was more properly the *First Principle of Waste* (Wilson *et al.* 1991).

While the *integrative model* does not propose that archaeologists change their recording methodologies, it does propose that traces are not merely remains or reflections of behaviors; they are important components of behavior. This perspective is particularly useful today, when we face environmental, energy, and other crises that focus on mental–behavioral–material interactions. In fact, the role of traces in our behavioral systems has never been more relevant ... and the archaeologists needed to document that role have never been more in demand!

## References

Committee on Diet, Nutrition, and Cancer, Assembly of Life Sciences, National Research Council (1983) *Diet, Nutrition, and Cancer*, Washington, D.C.: National Academy Press.

Dobyns, S. and W.L. Rathje, eds (1987) *The NFCS Report/Refuse Study: A Handbook of Potential Distortions in Respondent Diet Reports*, 4 Volumes, Report to the Consumer Nutrition Division, U.S. Department of Agriculture, Washington, D.C.

Fuchs, C.S., M.D. Edward, L. Giovannucci, G.A. Colditz, D.J. Hunter, M.J. Stamper, B. Rosner, R.E. Speizer and W.C. Willett (1999) 'Dietary fiber and the risk of colorectal cancer and adenoma in women', *The New England Journal of Medicine* 340(3): 169–76.

Harrison, G.G. (1976) 'Socio-cultural correlates of food utilitzation and waste in a sample of urban households', unpublished doctoral dissertation, University of Arizona, Tucson.

Harrison, G.G., W.L. Rathje and W.W. Hughes (1975) 'Food waste behavior in an urban population', *Journal of Nutrition Education* 7(1): 13–16.

Harrison, G.G., W.L. Rathje, C.K. Ritenbaugh, W.W. Hughes and E.E. Ho (1983) *The Food Loss Project: Methodologies for Estimating Household Food Losses.* Report to the Consumer Nutrition Division, U.S. Department of Agriculture, Washington, D.C.

Heimstra, N.W. and L.H. McFarling (eds) (1978) *Environmental Psychology,* Monterey: Brooks/Cole.

Hughes, W.W. (1984) 'The method to our madness', *American Behavioral Scientist* 28(1): 41–50.

Johnstone, B.M. (1986) 'Alternative approaches to nutritional assessment for studies of diet and disease: an anthropology perspective', Ph.D dissertation, Department of Anthropology, University of Arizona, Tucson.

Johnstone, B.M. and W.L. Rathje (1986) 'Building a theory of the differences between respondent reports and material realities', paper presented in the Symposium on Different Approaches to Using Food Consumption Data Bases for Evaluating Dietary Intakes, Institute of Food Technologies AM, Dallas.

Proshansky, H.M. (1970) 'Environmental psychology: a methodological orientation' in H.M. Proshansky, W.H. Ittelson and R.G. Rivlin (eds) *Environmental Psychology,* New York: Holt, Rinehart and Winston.

Rabow, J. and C.A. Neuman (1984) 'Garbaeology as a method of cross-validating interview data on sensitive topics', *Sociology and Social Research* 68(4): 480–97.

Rabow, J. and R.K. Watts (1982) 'The role of alcohol availability in alcohol consumption and alcohol problems' in M. Galanter (ed.) *Recent Developments in Alcoholism,* New York: Plenum Publishing.

Rathje, W.L. (1977) 'In praise of archeology: Le Projet du Garbàge' in L.G. Ferguson, (ed.) *Historic Archaeology and the Importance of Material Things,* Society for Historical Archaeology.

—— (1978) 'Archaeological ethnography' in R.A. Gould (ed.) *Explorations in Ethnoarchaeology,* Albuquerque: University of New Mexico Press.

—— (1979a) 'Modern material culture studies' in M.B. Schiffer (ed.) *Advances in Archaeological Method and Theory 2,* pp. 1–37. New York: Academic Press.

—— (1979b) 'Trace measures' in L. Sechrest (ed.) *Unobtrusive Measures Today: New Directions for Methodology of Behavioral Science,* San Francisco: Jossey-Bass, Inc.

—— (1984a) 'The garbage decade', *American Behavioral Scientist* 28(4): 9–29.

—— (1984b) 'Where's the beef?', *American Behavioral Scientist* 28(4): 71–91.

—— (1986) 'Why we throw food away' *The Atlantic Monthly* 257(4): 14–16.

—— (1996a) 'The archaeology of us' in C. Ciegelski (ed.) *Encyclopædia Britannica's Yearbook of Science and the Future – 1997,* pp. 158–77, New York: Encyclopædia Britannica Inc.

—— (1996b) 'The mother lode for source reduction', *MSW-Management* 6(4): 13.

Rathje, W.L. and S. Dobyns (1987) 'Handbook of potential distortions in respondent diet reports' in S. Dobyns and W.L. Rathje (eds) *The NFCS Report/Refuse Study, Vol. 1,* Report to the Consumer Nutrition Division, U.S. Department of Agriculture, Washington, D.C.

Rathje, W.L. and E.E. Ho (1987) 'Meat fat madness: conflicting patterns of meat fat consumption and their public health implications', *Journal of the American Dietetic Association* 87(10): 1357–62.

Rathje, W.L. and W.W. Hughes (1977) 'Food loss at the household level: a perspective from household residuals analysis' *Proceedings, RANN 2, the Second Symposium on*

*Research Applied to National Needs*, Vol. 3: 32–5. National Science Foundation, Washington, D.C.

Rathje, W.L. and M. McCarthy (1977) 'Regularity and variability in contemporary garbage' in S. South (ed.) *Research Strategies in Historical Archaeology*, New York: Academic Press.

Rathje, W.L. and C. Murphy (1992) *Rubbish! The Archaeology of Garbage*, New York: Harper Collins.

Rathje, W.L. and D.C. Wilson (1987) 'Archaeological techniques applied to characterization of household discards and their potential contamination of groundwater', paper presented at the Conference on Solid Waste Management and Materials Policy, New York City.

Rathje, W.L., D.C. Wilson, W.W. Hughes and R. Herndon (1987a) *Characterization of Household Hazardous Wastes fron Marin County, California, and New Orleans, Louisiana*. U.S. EPA Environmental Monitoring Systems Laboratory, Report No. EPA/600/x-87/129, Las Vegas.

Rathje, W.L., D.C. Wilson and W.W. Hughes (1987b) *A Characterization of Hazardous Household Wastes in Marin County, California*, Association of Bay Area Governments, Report No. P87004HAZ, Oakland.

Rathje, W.L., D.C. Wilson, W.W. Hughes and T. Jones (1988) *The Phoenix Report: Characterization of Recyclable Materials in Residential Solid Wastes in Phoenix and Tucson, Arizona*. A report prepared for the Department of Public Works, the City of Phoenix.

Rathje, W.L., V.M. LaMotta and W.A. Longacre (in press) 'Black hole archaeology' in B. Cunliffe *et al.* (eds) *Archaeology: the widening debate*, London: The British Academy.

Ritenbaugh, C.K. and G.G. Harrison (1984) 'Reactivity of garbage analysis', *American Behavioral Scientist* 28(4): 51–70.

Schensul, S., A. Paredes and P. Pelto (1968) 'The twilight zone of poverty: a new perspective on an economically depressed area' *Human Organization* 27(1): 30–40.

Webb, E.J., D.J. Campbell, R.D. Schwarts and L. Sechrest (1966) *Unobtrusive Measures: Nonreactive Research in the Social Sciences*. Chicago: Rand McNally.

Wilson, D.C., W.L. Rathje and W.W. Hughes (1991) 'Household discards and modern refuse: a principle of household resource use and waste' in E. Staski and R. Wilk (eds) *The Ethnoarchaeology of Refuse Disposal*, Arizona State University Anthropological Research Papers No. 42: 41–51.

Wilson, D.C., W.L. Rathje and M.K. Tani (1994) *Characterization and Assessment of Household Hazardous Wastes in Municipal Solid Wastes*. Final Report to the Water Quality Engineering Program, National Science Foundation, Washington, D.C.

Yancey, W.L. (1970) 'Architecture, interaction, and social control: the case of a large-scale public housing project' in H.M. Proshansky, W.H. Ittelson and R.G. Rivlin (eds) *Environmental Psychology*, New York: Holt, Rinehart and Winston.

# Part II

# Remembering and forgetting

# Chapter 6

# Between remembering and forgetting

*Victor Buchli and Gavin Lucas*

Between landfills and monuments there may seem a vast difference, but there is a structural similarity between the two. The issue of excess dominates many aspects of archaeological investigations of the recent past – late captialist societies are almost hyperactively proficient in their sacrificial consumptive economies (Miller 1998 and Bataille 1991). The result is that many aspects of twentieth-century experience disappear, buried within this prodigious accumulation of excessive discourse and material goods, not just our own consumption practices, but a whole range of experiences, many of them painful. The contributions of the previous sections negotiate this superfluity, either through the identification of general processes (Rathje and also Majewski and Schiffer) or obscured narratives and experiences as suggested by Stevenson. They all sort through the obscuring superfluities characterising the material culture of modern experience. Indeed, as we become increasingly mired and unavoidably 'dirty', environmentally unsustainable, increasingly less sanitised, more excessive, profligate, blaspheming and dissolute, the 'dirt' of the 'dirt archaeologist' has changed qualitatively and quantitatively. Thus archaeologists working on the contemporary past tend to direct themselves to that which is forgotten, to attempt literally and metaphorically to find what has been 'buried' and obscured, sorting through the hyperactive creation and dissipation of resources, information and material goods.

In the Freudian model of the mind, all memories are potentially intact; it is his stratified model of the mind (unconscious/preconscious/conscious) which enables this, while at the same time making it susceptible to those pathologies he wrote so much about. For Freud, forgetting was therefore never really about loss but merely distortion. Forgetfulness becomes, essentially, a *failure* of remembering and is subject to a subtle classification (i.e. repression, distortion, condensation). Remembrance therefore becomes something that is normal, and forgetting, by contrast, pathological (Lucas 1997). Underlying this is the concept of the *copy* or reproduction with remembrance as the reproduction of an original experience, forgetting as its non-reproduction through the aberrant copy.

From this derives the predominant conception of the relationship between material culture and the processes of remembrance or forgetfulness – that of the *supplement* or *substitute*, letting objects carry the *excess* of ideas and images which our limited minds cannot contain (Forty 1999: 2). If memory is a mere copy, mementoes are copies of copies. From books to computers, from mementoes to war memorials, material culture shoulders the larger responsibility of our personal and collective memory. The corollary of this, of course, is that the decay or destruction of these objects brings forgetfulness. It is precisely this character that made de Certeau write that objects are the enemies of memory (de Certeau 1984: 87). Not that such a model implies material culture as passive – the explicit materialisation or de-materialisation of events can act to forge memories or facilitate forgetting, they produce memories, not simply recall them. Yet it is precisely the weight of this excess that should perhaps make us stop and rethink the role of material culture as supplement. Can we in fact envisage memory without these so-called substitutes – indeed, could it possibly be that memories are not frequently created from the material strategies we use? In an interesting study on the souvenir, Susan Steward turns this whole formula on its head – she argues that souvenirs are needed for events whose materiality escapes us; rather than acting as a supplement to our memory, they fulfil a basic lack, and establish contexts of perpetual consumption for an experience that is otherwise fleeting – but not necessarily trivial (Steward 1984: 135). She argues that while the souvenir initially acts as a metonym or trace of an original experience, it ultimately displaces this experience as a point of origin as subsequent narratives focus around the souvenir – the narrative in fact becomes the supplement to the object which now becomes the authentic point of reference. Her argument equally applies to all mementoes, whether souvenirs or monuments.

What then are the material strategies we use in the processes of remembering and forgetting? At one level, they follow the same continuum or cycle of objects we discussed in the last part, the cycle between production or construction and decay or destruction – although given a more specific twist by Lowenthal's apt terms, to memorialise or anathematise (Lowenthal 1999: xi; 1993). Through the construction of memorials in almost every village across Britain after the world wars, communities and the nation sustained the recollection of the events and sacrifices made; through the demolition of statues of Lenin and Marx throughout soviet eastern Europe after 1989, and the fall of the Berlin wall, the past started to be forgotten. And yet, it is not that simple. It is not just that memorials commemorate and iconoclasm causes forgetfulness; the relation between remembrance and forgetfulness is not a linear process but a struggle, a tension – in every memorial, something has been left out or forgotten, in every removal, something is left behind, remembered. In both cases, it is what is *not there*, what is *absent* that causes this tension. The empty space left behind in the wake of the collapse of the Berlin wall, the omission or exclusion of the pain and horror of war on those memorials – these gaps, these absences attest to a greater complexity. It is the more active nature of forgetfulness that adds a more complex dimension, indeed we agree with Forty when he says that '... forgetting has, in a manner of speaking, been *the* problem of the twentieth century' (Forty

1999: 7) just as the related problem of waste. Forgetting forges a common social project, a project to forget that which has been painful and contradictory (see Forty and Küchler 1999).

By focusing on the material processes of remembering and forgetting, we argue for an image of the processes of memorialisation and anathemisation being traversed by those of the constituted and unconstituted. These axes inscribe a space that enables the tension between remembering and forgetting to be kept open, rather than reduced to one or the other term (Figure 6.1). The spaces where these axes cross demarcate specific fields of materiality: the two obvious cases are construction and destruction which involve constituted strategies of materialising or dematerialising monuments, objects or sites to remember or forget. The two less obvious cases are the excess or residues, left behind in the wake of destruction, which are all that remain of an event, while the deficit or gap refers to those things that are excluded in the construction of monuments or souvenirs. Both of these are unconstituted materialities, one through a process of fragmentation, the other through omission. Moreover these two lines implicate quite different practices of re-constitution: in the one, an archaeology or forensics is involved in the reconstruction of memory from those residual fragments, while in the other a material culture study or reading is involved in the deconstruction of memory to uncover the gaps.

The three chapters that follow all explore different facets of this grid, in particular Hart and Winter focus on the problems and politics of memorialisation in the context of South Africa and heritage management, while both Wilkie and the Ludlow Collective deal with the issue of anathemisation, or forgetfulness, in particular how to sustain and reconstruct memories through archaeological work. Hart and Winter show how since apartheid, the question of memorialising the past requires rethinking, not only *what* gets designated a national monument, but *how* the whole process with its fixation on architecture and other structures is itself a product of the old order. On the one hand, in such monuments, there are silences and gaps, what is missing – either through being 'whitewashed', both literally and figuratively, or

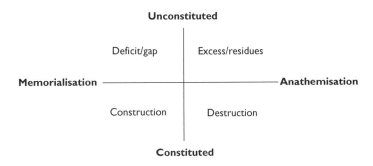

*Figure 6.1* Remembering and forgetting.

simply excluded; on the other, there is the deeper issue of how to memorialise the immaterial, the ephemeral. In either case, the unconstituted is what is ultimately at issue – whether what is missing in existing memorials or what is unmemorialised because it is immaterial – both literally and metaphorically.

With the Ludlow Collective and their work on the miners' massacre, they attempt through archaeology to make news again; memory of the massacre and its role in labour and working class history has all but been forgotten outside the mining community and yet its significance was and should remain much wider. Through excavation, the lives of the mine workers and their families are reconstituted, materially, and made to matter again. Similarly, Wilkie's work on black sharecroppers and white fraternities uses archaeology to engage with community memories, to help sustain and enrich them. In excavating sites, the memories of racial tension on the one hand and fraternity life on the other are drawn into a new and renewed discourse which extends beyond the boundaries of the local communities involved. In both these papers, archaeology, through the reconstitution of residues left behind of the past, plays a role in sustaining and potentially developing local and national memories of institutions and events.

The common theme to all these chapters is the question for whom does memory and forgetting serve. Conflicting interests mediate the processes of remembering and forgetting, articulated through the personal vs. the collective (social upheaval), the private versus the public (fraternities) or simply us and them (racism or class war). Two examples show how these processes can be explored further. Memorials of the Holocaust constantly face the problem of how to sustain memories of the atrocities lest it happen again yet at the same time not lose sight of the horror of it, sanitising it. For such a painful event, people want to forget, yet the need to remember means they need to face the horror. The problem is, how to produce a memorial that can sustain this tension. Consider here Daniel Liebeskind's recent Jewish Museum in Berlin which materialises the immaterial as a poignant monument to a disappeared community. The other example comes from South Africa and the Truth and Reconciliation Commission (TRC) – the evil of apartheid is dissected, events resurfaced and yet while reconciliation is the ultimate aim, it is the collectivity who benefits from this, not the individuals who have to re-live their experiences (de Kok 1998). Justice in this instance is at odds with humanitarianism. In many ways, the same tension, between personal memory and collective memorial, is expressed in the holocaust monuments and, as Forty remarks, once the personal memories go, the horror will be forgotten (Forty 1999: 6). The same tension can be seen across a range of monuments, and some meet with greater success, such as the famous Vietnam Memorial in Washington, where personal and collective grief can meet without one cancelling the other (Rowlands 1999), or the District Six Museum in Capetown, South Africa which mediates between the personal histories of those who were caught up in a mass forced removal during apartheid. Indeed, this tension between personal and collective memory/forgetfulness becomes a useful way to express the basic themes of this section as the contributions demonstrate. The examples just given of the Holocaust, apartheid or war memorials are all faced with the danger of subsuming the personal to the collective, where the personal becomes marginalised and unconstituted.

## References

Bataille, Georges (1991) *Accursed Share vol. 1*, New York: Zone Books.

de Certeau, M. (1984) *The Practice of Everyday Life*, Berkeley: University of California Press.

de Kok, I. (1998) 'Cracked heirlooms: memory on exhibition' in S. Nuttall and C. Coetzee (eds), *Negotiating the Past: The Making of Memory in South Africa*, Oxford: Oxford University Press.

Forty, Adrian (1999) Introduction, in A. Forty and S. Küchler (eds), *The Art of Forgetting*, Oxford: Berg.

Forty, Adrian and Susanne Küchler (eds) (1999) *The Art of Forgetting*, Oxford: Berg.

Lowenthal, David (1993) *Museum Management and Curatorship* 12: 171–82.

Lowenthal, D. (1999) Preface in A. Forty and S. Küchler (eds), *The Art of Forgetting*, Oxford: Berg.

Lucas, Gavin (1997) 'Forgetting the past', *Anthropology Today* 13: 18–14.

Miller, Daniel (1998) *A Theory of Shopping*, Cambridge: Polity.

Rowlands, Michael (1999) 'Remembering to forget: sublimation as sacrifice in war memorials' in Adrian Forty and Susanne Küchler (eds), *The Art of Forgetting*, Oxford: Berg.

Steward, Susan (1984) *On Longing: Narratives of the Miniature, the Gigantic, the Souvenir, the Collection*, Baltimore: Johns Hopkins University Press.

Chapter 7

# The politics of remembrance in the new South Africa

*David Hart and Sarah Winter*

## Introduction

Since the advent of a democratically elected government in South Africa in 1994, the state agency for heritage management, the National Monuments Council (NMC), has been required to redress the imbalance in the list of officially recognised heritage sites, namely those heritage sites declared as National Monuments in terms of the National Monuments Act (Act No. 28 of 1969, as amended in 1989.) This list has been heavily criticised as being largely composed of white colonial buildings or structures, generally neglecting those heritage sites of relevance to the majority of South Africans (Frescura 1992). In redressing this imbalance, there is a tendency towards the identification, interpretation and commemoration of heritage sites that are symbols and expressions of the recent political change and which promote the concept of a new South African identity and nation.

This chapter discusses the many conceptual challenges facing the NMC in a new political context. It discusses the new role of our National Monuments (both old and new) and explores the need for the NMC not only to revise its traditional architectural approach to heritage management but also to deal with the contested, ephemeral nature of our contemporary past and identity and recognise events and sites in a meaningful and creative manner. In doing so, the record of national monuments becomes a twentieth-century artefact reflecting the dominant ideologies of the time.

## The role of our old National Monuments in the new South Africa

The NMC has inherited a list of National Monuments that is comprised mostly of historical buildings declared as a result of their age and architectural interest. The list is heavily biased towards buildings of the Dutch and British colonial period and largely reflects Western aesthetics and cultural values. The NMC is now faced with the challenge of how best to proceed in its responsibility to protect and promote the cultural heritage of all South Africans. It is faced with the decision of what to do with a list of National Monuments belonging to the material legacy of the colonial and apartheid eras.

In 1999 new heritage legislation was implemented to enable the democratisation of heritage management in South Africa and to address the need for the list of heritage sites of national significance to contain sites that are significant to the nation as a whole. In terms of the new heritage legislation all existing National Monuments declared in terms of the existing legislation, will be reclassified as Provincial Heritage Sites. National Heritage Sites will have to be motivated afresh. (A small number of existing National Monuments will, by means of a schedule gazetted at the time of the passing of the new legislation, be automatically proclaimed National Heritage Sites. Robben Island, Table Mountain, the Castle of the Cape of Good Hope and Sterkfontein Caves amongst others are likely to be placed on that schedule.)

In reviewing the existing list of National Monuments, it is clear that the practice of heritage management has left us with a valuable archaeological record reflecting the changing political ideology of this century. This is reflected both in terms of those sites selected for conservation and the manner in which they have been conserved. As such, the entries in the list are twentieth-century artefacts informing future generations of the politics and values of society at the time of declaration. For example, the numerous eighteenth-century 'Cape Dutch' and nineteenth-century 'Victorian' buildings on the existing National Monuments list provide a valuable record of how European material culture was used to create, justify and reinforce the notion of dominant superior 'white culture'. Furthermore, the numerous eighteenth-century Cape Dutch buildings provide a valuable record of the political tensions existing between the English and Afrikaans speaking South Africans during this century. They also illustrate how Afrikaner nationalism during the 1950s and 1960s sought to claim and manipulate these eighteenth-century artefacts as symbolic of Afrikaner supremacy. The restoration of National Monuments of the Dutch East India Company (VOC) period (c. 1652–1795) until fairly recently generally presupposed the removal of all later layering from the buildings. Buildings were returned to their original appearance before the later addition of British period accessories, such as Victorian verandas and filigree detail. (Today, these additions are likely to be considered important elements of the historical layering of the building and warranting conservation.) To illustrate this point further, in the historical Western Cape town of Stellenbosch, an interpretative plaque placed on a Dutch period National Monument during the 1980s refers to the removal of Victorian additions which 'spoilt' its original Dutch appearance (Figure 7.1).

Out of the propensity to restore many historical buildings to their original appearance, a newly constructed Dutch culture of clean whitewashed historical thatched buildings emerged. The interiors of Dutch period buildings were painted white and joinery was painted green, purifying and brightening the impression. (Today, however, the original dark decorative interiors of these

*Figure 7.1* Cape Dutch house. (Photograph by David Hart and Sarah Winter.)

buildings are recognised, as well as the wide variety of colours used on their exteriors.)

In recognising the valuable contribution of South Africa's old National Monuments towards an understanding of the complex nature of our history and its society, the task of transforming heritage management is not simply one of replacing the existing list of National Monuments with a list of new Heritage Sites. The appropriate place within the new South Africa lies not in their removal from the record, but their reinterpretation within the current context. In this regard, the designation of existing National Monuments as Provincial Heritage Sites rather than their removal will serve to give recognition to their value as artefacts of the previous political and social system. This recognition will be emphasised by the fact that the bronze National Monument badges will not be withdrawn from the site, but will remain, reflecting their iconic status in the old order.

The NMC was recently involved in the erection of a new commemorative memorial and interpretative plaque at the site of the 'Battle of Blood River'. This is the place where the Afrikaners defeated the Zulus in 1838. It was a historic battle in which thousands of lives were lost. The new memorial and plaque is somewhat different from that previously erected within the old system. The original memorial, however, still remains. The old memorial emphasises Afrikaner victory and the fact that this victory was God's will. In contrast the new memorial emphasises reconciliation.

Possibly one of the most contentious old National Monuments is Dr Verwoerd's holiday house at Betty's Bay in the Western Cape. Dr Verwoerd is regarded as the architect of apartheid. The cottage, which was built by Dr Verwoerd himself, was declared a National Monument in 1973 during the height of apartheid. Clearly, re-interpretation of this site presents an interesting challenge.

## The new nature of our National Monuments and their role in the current political context

Many of the recently declared National Monuments have a markedly different character from those declared during the colonial and apartheid eras. Sites have become more contemporary in nature and symbolic of or associated with the recent political transformation. There is a shift away from the basic assumptions of age and aesthetics as being fundamental criteria for conservation and a move towards the recognition of sites associated with events or people, but which as physical objects are of little interest. Given the architecturally biased conceptual framework, which has dominated conventional conservation practice, the identification, interpretation and commemoration of Heritage Sites which is less bound to bricks and mortar is indeed a challenge for the NMC.

The following examples illustrate this shift in emphasis. After Mr Nelson Mandela's release, the NMC considered declaring as a National Monument the section of pavement on which he was arrested for the second time before his long imprisonment. The site of the aeroplane crash of Samora Machel, the late president of Mozambique, was recently declared a National Monument. In both these cases, these events were brief and the physical attributes of the site are largely inconsequential.

Houses where significant struggle leaders have lived or were born have also been declared or are recommended for declaration as National Monuments. For example, Mandela's house in Qunu, the house at Victor Vester Prison where he lived before his release and where the new constitution of South Africa is said to have been begun, Steve Biko's house in King Williamstown in the Eastern Cape and John Dube's house in Umlazi in Kwa Zulu Natal. These houses form the closest material link to our leaders in the recent political struggle and are recognised as national symbols of freedom.

Robben Island is an example of a Heritage Site whose recognised cultural value has shifted in the new political context. The original motivation for the declaration of the island (drawn up in the 1980s) focused on its rich natural and historical significance (from the period of the first European settlers in the Cape to the period of apartheid when the island was used as a political prison). In comparison the motivation for the declaration of the island as a World Heritage Site (drawn up in 1998) focuses largely on the island's more recent political apartheid history and its significance as an international symbol of hope, and triumph over adversity.

## Conceptual issues relating to our new National Monuments and their role in the current political context

There are number of conceptual challenges relating to our new National Monuments and their role in the current political context. These challenges are centred on the contested and ephemeral nature of a new South African identity and its contemporary past. The concept of a South African identity and nation cannot be viewed simplistically. In view of South Africa's history of cultural oppression and the complex nature of its society there is a lack of consensus as to what constitutes a South African identity or nation (Tomaselli and Mpofu 1997). Therefore, as expressions of a new South African identity, the challenge lies in the ability of our new National Monuments to express what Tomaselli and Mpofu (1997) term 'South Africa's creative tensions'. These tensions refer to the 'fine dialectic' between individual and collective, conflicting and common identities (Tomaselli and Mpofu 1997).

A further conceptual issue regarding the nature of our new National Monuments concerns the difficulty in conserving a heritage of our recent political past. The difficulty lies in the fact that there is much contemporary relevance in historical political issues in South Africa, many of which remain unresolved. Weyeneth (1996) makes a similar argument in his article on the conservation of Heritage Sites linked to the Civil Rights Movement in the United States during the 1950s and 1960s. He outlines the difficulty in conserving a Civil Rights Movement of the contemporary past, particularly after 1965. He explains that this is when 'the story becomes more complicated: when the heroes, victims, and villains become harder to define, when the violence seems to take on some utility; when society loses consensus about the meaning of the movement and what the future should hold' (1996: 28).

In the search for national symbols of the political struggle against apartheid, there is a current tendency to focus on the contribution of the leaders in the struggle. The declaration of the houses where these leaders were born or lived serves to immortalise their role in the struggle. One hopes, however, that this recognition will not be at the expense of the key role of many ordinary people in the struggle, of whom many were women and children. It is important to mention that while the physical fabric of these houses as political symbols are considered to be of little consequence in the motivation for their declaration – simple dwellings similar to thousands of others in South African's townships – they form part of the apartheid material legacy. It can be argued that the relevance of these houses lies most strongly in their materiality, which in its ordinariness is common to the experience of the multitude of oppressed people, and thereby demonstrates hope for triumph over adversity (Figure 7.2).

With the difficulty often in establishing a relevant material link to many events or people associated with our recent political past, the NMC has also been faced with the responsibility of constructing memorials such as that at Blood River, which is dedicated to events or people considered to be of national significance.

*Figure 7.2* Cape township. (Photograph by David Hart and Sarah Winter.)

The Department of Arts Culture Science and Technology, under which the NMC falls, recently constructed a concrete and steel memorial to Samora Machel at the site of the air crash in which he was killed. Samora Machel was the president of Mozambique who played an important role in the fight against colonial oppression. (At the unveiling ceremony, the then Minister of Transport was to announce a £2.6 million project to build a road to the memorial.)

One such case of a memorial building in which the NMC is involved is the site at the Union Buildings in Pretoria where in 1956, 20,000 African women demonstrated as part of the defiance campaign against introduction of the pass laws. The event is one that is vivid in the memories of many living today. In a space that has always been the political domain of the state, the conceptual challenge has been to claim the space from the oppressor for the people. Many of the women who participated in the march have been interviewed in order to collect information on the event. The proposed memorial is being put out to competitive tender.

Where there is no artefactual or material symbol representing the event, one is being created in order to express the need to recognise and honour the event. It should be noted that the Union Buildings are already a National Monument, so that declaration of the site for the specific commemoration of the march is not possible. From monument identification, the NMC is moving into the realm of monument building.

In the case of Enoch Satonga, who was responsible for composing the new South African national anthem, Nkosi Sikelela, the NMC went to some lengths to locate his unmarked grave, the most obvious existing tangible artefact relating to this person. The choice to erect a memorial on the grave and to declare the grave a National Monument came at the time where the anthem symbolised most strongly the rebirth of South Africa.

It is interesting to note that previously it was stated policy of the National Monuments Council not to declare physical monuments or memorials as National Monuments, and generally to remove itself from sites that were 'directly' political in nature. There are of course some obvious exceptions, such as the declaration of Dr Verwoerd's holiday cottage, and the underlying cultural bias of the so-called 'non-political' declarations is unarguable. Today, however, the policy not to declare memorials as National Monuments appears to have been cast aside, and the National Monuments Council is not only involved with the construction of memorials, but with declaring the sites on which to construct the memorials. Heritage conservation is clearly moving from the recognition and conservation of artefacts of the past, towards the construction of artefacts in order for the future to remember the present and contemporary past.

The need to create a material link to an event or person, or an appropriate and meaningful manner in which to celebrate and recognise an event or person, offers an exciting challenge. Although in certain cases the construction of a memorial might be considered appropriate, the opportunity of recognising events, or indeed celebrating heroes, in a more tangibly meaningful manner, which could have a direct positive impact on the lives of the community may be considered.

When we look at the total budget of the NMC (little over £500,000 per year nationally), it is questionable whether it should involve itself in the erection of costly monuments. Large impenetrable blocks of black marble, or massive concrete and steel structures erected at vast expense may often be inappropriate to the nature of the event or the person being commemorated. It might well be contested that monument building of the same scale and form and expense to the state as that of the past, should surely remain a material legacy of British imperialism and Afrikaner nationalism. We need to look for more resourceful ways of materialising the past. Nevertheless, the NMC has been placed in the position where it must redirect its scant budget to the construction of high-profile monuments such as those at the battle-site at Blood River, the memorial on the grave of Enoch Satonga and the women's march on the Union Buildings.

While the need to create a material link to an event is accepted, and the case for the construction of a monument or memorial may well be appropriate, the opportunity for a far more creative and imaginative approach to materialising the cultural significance of an ephemeral site must be sought. From the colonial period to the rise of Afrikaner nationalism, monument building has been a powerful tool to inscribe racial exclusivity and white supremacy (Thornton 1991 cited in Tomaselli and Mpofu 1997, Bunn 1998). David Bunn (1998), in his insightful deconstruction of the nineteenth-century colonial monuments and early twentieth-century Afrikaner memorials, shows how these monuments serve to keep selected memory alive. However, he also argues that in time the meaning of these monuments tends to become 'disjointed, partial and dismembered' (1998: 108).

'Monuments would like us to believe that they are haunted by the spirit of the past, that they are chambers echoing with the voices of the heroic dead. In time, however, most South African monuments have come to be haunted by what was repressed to achieve their exclusiveness and then their meaning has appeared to desert them' (1998: 108).

The conceptual challenge for monuments in a new South Africa is to ensure that their meaning, not only their structural form is durable. To do this there is a need to construct and identify monuments that represent our collective or public memories. A more accessible and positive manner of materialising the ephemeral events of the past would be to look towards a material improvement of the general quality of life and environment of the people who were marginalised by our oppressive past, and who continue to live in sterile and hostile environments, a legacy of apartheid ideology and planning.

Dolores Hayden argues that public spaces can help to nurture the profound, subtle and inclusive sense of what it means to be a citizen, where identity is intimately tied to memory: both our personal memories and collective or social memories are interconnected with the histories of our families, neighbours, fellow workers, and ethnic communities (Hayden 1995). Urban landscapes, she argues, are storehouses of these social memories, because the elements or features frame the lives of many people and often outlast many lifetimes – there is a need to restore some shared experience or public meaning – a recognition of a common and meaningful experience. Without lavish expenditures in poor living environments, it is possible to enhance the social meaning of public places that are sensitive to all citizens and their diverse heritage and developed with public process that recognises both the cultural and political importance of place.

Rather than creating expensive, monumental and dour memorials, the powerful but ephemeral events that have shaped our recent past might be better celebrated by an accessible and meaningful transformation of our public spaces. The argument for this is strengthened when one looks at the quality of our living environments – sterile, monotonous, uncontestable and dominated by apartheid ideology. With a recent past in which the voices of many ordinary people were heard only through protest in our public spaces and our streets, it would seem, once again, that these public spaces form the strongest and most accessible link to the collective memory of our contemporary past.

Catherine Howett's (1994) commentary on the new design for rehabilitating the 'white only' Kelly Ingram Park in downtown Birmingham in the United States is useful to the South Africa context, where one can draw similar parallels. The historical park was a venue for rallies and marches to protest against racial segregation during the 1960s, a time still vivid in the memory of those living today. It represents painful memories to the residents of Birmingham city. These protest marches and the police brutality against the protestors brought home to many Americans for the first time the reality of racism against black citizens, and eventually led to landmark civil rights legislation in 1965.

> Here is an example of an important place made new, its meaning enlarged not only by the events that took place within and around it, but by the interpretation of those events that the City of Birmingham has chosen to inscribe in the fabric of the park.
>
> (Howett 1994: 39)

There are many opportunities in South Africa, from Freedom Square to the dusty, grassless spaces in the numerous faceless townships that have been sites of unity of spirit and of social protest. Here, the memories of the past may be celebrated and the real quality of life of the residents greatly improved by the upgrading of their public living environment, and the interpretation of the events that occurred there.

The interpretations of the past can no longer be done, as they were in the past, by architects, planners and historians involved with traditional conservation practice. While we see a change in the list of our Heritage Sites from buildings being declared purely on their physical attributes towards the commemoration of events, people and movements, the conceptual challenge comes more from the interpretation than from the physical form. This will require the development of new skills and sensitivities in order to be able to access, understand and interpret the new demands placed on our heritage managers.

Our traditional heritage practices had been imbibed from the well-established mother countries whose comparative homogeneity, identity and value systems had evolved over many generations, leaving us with an archaeological record of heritage sites which until recently, in terms of criteria, may differ little from those accepted in Europe. Today South Africa appears to be rejecting the dominance of the previously accepted traditional system of heritage values, and as a new country with an extraordinary diversity of cultures – whose indigenous value systems have been damaged through years of cultural suppression – is still trying to establish its own rules. It is clear, though, that there is a strong need for the bodies responsible for heritage management to respond to the needs and opportunities being offered in this new awakening, and to facilitate the celebration of the country's heritages, past and present, in an imaginative, positive and durable way.

Whatever the case, the Heritage List of South Africa, when viewed as an archaeological record, proves a revealing reflection of the social and political order of the time, and indicates clearly the current changes in heritage needs with which the authorities responsible are trying to grapple.

Information for this paper was also obtained from various National Monuments Council records, including various NMC files on specific heritage sites.

# References

Bunn, D. (1998) 'Whited sepulchres: on the reluctance of monuments' in Hilton Judin and Ivan Vladislavic (eds), *Architecture, Apartheid and After*, Netherlands Architecture Institute Publishers, Rotterdam, pp. 93–115.

Frescura, F. (1992) 'Monuments and the monumentalisation of myths', paper presented at the Myth – Monument – Museums conference, University of Witwaterstrand.

Hayden, D. (1995) *The Power of Place: Urban Landscapes as Public History*, Massachusetts: MIT Press.

Howett, C. (1994) 'Interpreting a painful past: Birmingham's Kelly Ingram Park', *Cultural Resource Management* 17(7), pp. 38–40.

*National Heritage Resources Act* (Act No. 25 of 1999), Pretoria: Government Printers.

*National Monuments Act* (Act No. 28 of 1969, as amended in 1989), Pretoria: Government Printers.

Thornton, R. (1991) 'The Monument to Paul Kruger, Pretoria South Africa: genealogy of violence and autochony', mimeo.

Tomaselli, K.G. and Mpofu, A. (1997) 'The rearticulation of meaning of National Monuments: beyond apartheid culture and policy', *A Journal of the Australian Key Centre for Cultural and Media Policy* 8(3), pp. 57–75.

Weyeneth, R.R. (1996) 'Historic preservation and the Civil Rights Movement', *Cultural Resource Management* 2, pp. 26–8.

# Chapter 8

# Archaeology of the Colorado Coal Field War 1913–1914

*The Ludlow Collective*

On the morning of April 20, 1914, Colorado National Guard troops opened fire on a tent colony of 1,200 striking coal miners at Ludlow, Colorado. They continued shooting until late afternoon, and then swept through the camp looting it and setting it aflame. When the smoke cleared twenty of the camps inhabitants were dead including two women, and twelve children. The Ludlow massacre is the most violent and the best-known event of the 1913–1914 Colorado Coal Field War, but its significance goes far beyond this struggle. The killing of women and children at Ludlow outraged the American public and helped to turn popular opinion against violent confrontations with strikers. It marks a pivotal point in U.S. history when labor relations began to move from class warfare to corporate and government policies of negotiation, co-option, and regulated strikes. Today, however, popular memory of the massacre has been largely lost outside of union circles, and the realities of class struggle in the United States buried.

The State University of New York at Binghamton, the University of Denver, and Fort Lewis College sponsor the Archaeology of the Colorado Coal Field War project. The Ludlow Collective includes faculty and students from these and other institutions. We are working to recover the memory of Ludlow and to exhume the class struggle of 1913 to 1914 in the coalfields of southern Colorado. To do this we are building an archaeology of the American working class that speaks to a working-class audience about working-class history and experience.

## Class

Archaeology as a discipline serves class interests and those interests are frequently contrary to the interest of the working class in the United States. In the United States both scholars and the general public frequently confuse class with economic status and they define class in terms of income levels. This focus on income obscures the structural realities of class in the United States (Wurst 1999). The class structure of the twentieth-century United States minimally includes three positions: (1) a bourgeoisie that owns or controls the means of production, (2) a working class that labors for wages, and (3) a middle class of administrators, professionals and small business owners who mediate between these two classes. These classes do not form uniform masses and we can define class fractions rooted in regional, racial, and cultural differences (Patterson 1995).

Archaeology has typically served middle-class interests. It is part of the intellectual apparatus (things such as schools, books, magazines, organizations, and arts) that produces the symbolic capital (things such as esoteric knowledge, shared experience, certification, and social skills) that individuals need to be part of the middle class. This apparatus, including archaeology, developed as part of the historical struggles that created the capitalist middle class (Trigger 1989; Patterson 1995). Because it is set in the middle class, archaeology attracts primarily a middle-class following, and often does not appeal to working-class audiences (Sennett and Cobb 1972; Frykman 1990; Potter 1994: 148–9; McGuire and Walker 1999).

We feel that archaeology can be mobilized to address the interests of more than just the middle class. We seek to fuse our scholarly labor with working-class interests. We have entered into the developing dialogue between organized labor and scholars in the United States. The election of John Sweeny as president of the AFL-CIO in 1995 has led to a revitalization of the organization as a broad-based social interest movement. As part of this movement a joint labor/academic teach-in was held at Columbia University on October 3–4, 1996 with over 2,500 people in attendance (Tomasky 1997).

We are contributing to these efforts by studying a history that has meaning for working people and addressing their interests in this history. The Colorado Coal Field War of 1913–1914 is not exotic or ancient history. It is familiar, close to home, relevant, and concerns issues that still confront workers today.

## Goals of the project

Our project incorporates theoretical, scholarly, and political goals. We strive to address multiple audiences including scholars, people outside the academy, and most importantly working-class people. On a theoretical level we wish to build a praxis of archaeology that entails knowing the world, critiquing the world and changing the world.

As scholars we are integrating archaeological evidence with archival evidence to test propositions about how mundane experience shaped the strike. We are demonstrating that similarities in the day-to-day life of miners' families crosscut ethnic and cultural differences within the community of miners, and that these similarities helped to form a common class-consciousness necessary for group action. Strikes do not just involve male miners; women and children were major participants in the 1913–1914 strike. We are showing how their participation sprang from their lived experience, and how the struggle changed that experience. We are obtaining the data to test these propositions through excavations of domestic deposits dating from the period immediately before the strike, during the strike, and in the decade after the strike. Our results will have implications for understanding this important event in U.S. history, the process of labor struggle in the United States, and for current theoretical debates in archaeology over the forces of cultural change.

Our project is a form of memory. Our excavations at Ludlow draw attention to what happened there. Local people come out and they tell us the story of their grandmother or great uncle who lived in the camp. The excavations also attract the attention of the media, newspapers, television and radio. Our excavations make the events of 1914 news once again. We are also developing programs for students and teachers that tell the story of the strike. We do not have to recover this memory for a working-class audience, especially a union audience, but we can lend our expertise to assist them in maintaining this memory. The memory of Ludlow is strong in the United Mine Workers, the place is sacred to them. Memory is one way to address a working-class audience, to speak to their experience, in a language that they can understand, about events that interest them and about events to which they feel directly connected.

## The Colorado Coal Field War of 1913–1914

In 1913 Colorado was the eighth largest coal-producing state in the United States (McGovern and Guttridge 1972). Most of this production centered on the bituminous coal fields in Huerfano and Las Animas counties north of Trinidad, Colorado. These mines primarily produced coke for the steel mills at Pueblo, Colorado. The largest company mining coal in this region was the Rockefeller-controlled Colorado Fuel and Iron Company (CF&I). This company employed approximately 14,000 miners in 1913, 70% of whom were immigrants. The conditions of the mines, and of miners' lives, were appalling (Beshoar 1957; McGovern and Guttridge 1972; Papanikolas 1982). In 1912 the accident rate for Colorado mines was triple the national average (Whiteside 1990). The mines in southern Colorado operated in flagrant violation of several state laws that regulated safety and the fair compensation of miners. The miners lived in rude, isolated coal camps owned by the companies. Companies controlled the housing, the store, the medical facilities, the town saloon, and all recreational facilities. Company guards acted as police and regulated who could enter or leave the communities. The companies also dominated most of the local political structure and instructed their employees on how to vote. Contemporary accounts described the situation as feudal (Seligman 1914).

In 1913 the United Mine Workers (UMW) launched a massive organizing campaign in southern Colorado and launched a strike in the fall of that year (Beshoar 1957; McGovern and Guttridge 1972; Papanikolas 1982). The strikers demanded the right to unionize, higher pay, and that existing Colorado mining laws be enforced. Simultaneously the companies brought in the Baldwin Feltz detective agency to violently suppress the organizing efforts and later the strike. On September 23, 1913, over 90% of the miners left the shafts to begin the

*Figure 8.1* Ludlow tent camp a few days before the massacre. (Courtesy of the Denver Public Library.)

strike. The companies forced people out of their company-owned housing and several thousand people moved into tent camps set up by the UMW. Ludlow, with approximately 150 tents and about 1,200 residents, was the largest of these camps and the UMW strike headquarters for Las Animas county (Figure 8.1). Each of these camps contained a mix of nationalities including Italians, Greeks, Eastern Europeans, Mexicans, African Americans, and Welsh.

Violence characterized the strike from the very beginning, with both sides committing shootings and murders (Beshoar 1957; McGovern and Guttridge 1972; Papanikolas 1982). In October the governor of Colorado called out the National Guard. Over the winter of 1913–1914 relations between the strikers and the guard deteriorated, especially in April when the governor removed the regular troops and the mining companies replaced them with their own employees under the command of Colorado National Guard officers. In Ludlow the strikers dug cellars under their tents as refuges for women and children.

On April 20, 1914 the Guard attacked the tent camp at Ludlow. At about 9:00 that morning the Guard commander ordered Louis Tikas, the leader of the colony, to meet him at Ludlow Station. Fearing that this might be a pretext for an attack, armed strikers took up a position in a railroad cut overlooking the station. The National Guard had positioned a machine gun on a hill one mile to the south of the tent colony. Someone fired and the guardsmen began firing the machine gun into the tent camp. As the day progressed up to 200 guardsmen joined the fight and a second machine gun was added to the first. After a few hours of firing the tents were so full of holes that they looked like lace (Thomas 1971). The armed strikers engaged the Guard and tried to draw their fire away from the camp. In the camp there was pandemonium. Some people sought refuge in a large walk-in well, and many people huddled in the cellars under their tents. The camp's leaders worked all day trying to get people to a dry creek bed north of the camp. In the early afternoon a 12-year-old named William Snyder came up out of a cellar to get some food and was shot dead.

As dusk gathered a train stopped in front of the machine guns and blocked their line of fire. With a brief respite from the machine gun fire the majority of the people left in the camp and the armed strikers fled, while the guardsmen swept through the camp looting and burning the tents. Four women and eleven children in a cellar below tent 58 huddled in fear while the flames consumed the tent above them. The guardsmen seized Louis Tikas and two other camp leaders and summarily executed them. When the morning came the camp was a smoking ruin and in the dark hole below tent 58 two of the women and all eleven children were dead.

Following the attack the strikers throughout southern Colorado took up arms and took control of the mining district. The strikers destroyed several company towns and killed company employees. Finally, after ten days of war, President Wilson sent federal troops to Trinidad to restore order. The strike continued until December of 1914 when a broken UMW had to call it off.

The killing of women and children at Ludlow shocked the nation (Gitelman 1988). Prominent progressives such as Upton Sinclair and John Reed used the events to demonize John D. Rockefeller Jr. The United States Commission on Industrial Relations investigated the events of the strike, and issued a 1,200 page report. In response to this national attention Rockefeller hired the first corporate public relations firm and instituted a series of reforms in the mines of southern Colorado. It is not clear what practical impacts these reforms had on the lives of miners and their families but throughout the 1920s the district was embroiled in strikes. Union recognition in southern Colorado only came with the New Deal reforms of the 1930s (McGovern and Guttridge 1972).

## What can archaeology tell us about the Colorado Coal Field War?

Several major historical works on the strike have mined the rich archival record of documents and photos related to the Colorado Coal Field War (Beshoar 1957; McGovern and Guttridge 1972; Papanikolas 1982). These studies have focused on the events, the strike leaders, and the organizational work of the UMW. They have tended to emphasize the male miner and the commonalities of the work experience as the source of the social consciousness that united ethnically and racially diverse miners. The histories usually imply, and sometimes assert, that the miners shared a common lived experience at work but then returned to ethnically different home lives. In this way they accept a very traditional hypothesis of labor action that emphasizes the agency of men and downplays the role of women. This hypothesis tends to equate class and class struggle with active men in the workplace, and ethnicity and tradition with passive women in the home.

We, and many others, are skeptical of this traditional view (Long 1985, 1991; Beaudry and Mrozowski 1988; McGaw 1989; Cameron 1993; Shackel 1994, 1996; Mrozowski et al. 1996). We agree that ethnic identities cross-cut class in southern Colorado and that they hindered the formation of class consciousness but we question the equation of class = workplace= male, and ethnicity = home= female. Alternatively we would propose that class and ethnicity cross-cut both workplace and home, male and female. We would thus expect to find that working-class men in the mines and working-class women in the homes shared a common day-to-day lived experience that resulted from their class position and that ethnic differences divided them in both contexts.

We can demonstrate from existing analyses that ethnic divisions existed in the workplace. In southern Colorado the miners worked as independent contractors and formed their own work gangs. These work gangs were routinely ethnically based (Beshoar 1957; McGovern and Guttridge 1972; Papanikolas 1982; Long 1991). Historical and industrial archaeologists have also demonstrated in many other cases that nineteenth- and early twentieth-century workplaces were ethnically structured (Hardesty 1988; Bassett 1994; Wegars 1991). In the traditional hypothesis it is the commonality of the work experience that overcomes these ethnic divisions in the workplace and in an ethnically based home life to create a class consciousness. The idea that there existed a commonality of lived experience in the home that also aided in the formation of a common class consciousness is harder to demonstrate from existing analyses. The histories all agree that the day-to-day lives of miners' families were hard, but they provide little more than anecdotal evidence of the reality of these conditions. The historian Priscilla Long (1985), in an analysis that supports our alternative hypothesis, has demonstrated that women in the Colorado coal fields shared a common experience of sexual exploitation, but she also lacks detailed data on the realities of day-to-day lived experience in the home.

Our alternative hypothesis stresses the importance of the home in the creation of class consciousness. We seek to prove that the day-to-day material conditions of home life cross-cut ethnic divisions, before, during, and after the strike. If this is the case then we will argue that women and children were active agents, with male miners, in formulating a social consciousness to unify for the strike. Alternatively, if our analyses show that each ethnic group had distinctive day-to-day material conditions of home life then we will accept the traditional notion that families followed the lead of male miners who acquired a common class identity in the shafts.

Historical archaeology offers a very productive arena for archaeologists to examine the relationship between social consciousness, lived experience, and material conditions to cultural change (Orser 1996; Shackel 1996). In historic periods the archaeologist can integrate documents and material culture to capture both the consciousness and material conditions that form lived experience (Beaudry 1988; Leone and Potter 1988; Little 1992; Leone 1995; De Cunzo and Herman 1996). In the documents, people speak to us about their consciousness, their interests, and their struggles, but not all peoples speak in the documents with the same force or presence. Also, they rarely speak to us in detail about their day-to-day lives. People, however, create the archaeological record from the accumulation of the small actions that make up their lived experience. Thus the archaeological record consists primarily of the remains of people's mundane lives and all people leave traces in this material record.

Archaeological research provides one means to gain a richer, more detailed, and more systematic understanding of the everyday experience of Colorado mining families. These families unknowingly left a record of that experience in the ground. Archaeologists can recapture it in the burned remains of their tents, in the layout of camps, in the contents of their latrines, and by shifting through the garbage that they left behind. Linking this information with documentary and photographic sources gives us a useful way to reconstruct that experience. By applying these methods to company towns occupied before the strike, the strikers' tent camps, and to the company camps reopened after the strike we can test our propositions. The United Mine Workers maintain the site of Ludlow as a shrine to the workers who died there. There is presently a monument at the site but little or no interpretative information (Figure 8.2). In this context our archaeological work also becomes a powerful form of memory and action.

## Archaeological work to date

We have completed two years of excavations both at Ludlow and in the company town of Berwind. The massacre site itself represents a near perfect archaeological context. It is a short-term occupation that was destroyed by fire and subsequent use of the area has had little impact on the archaeological remains. In Berwind, the streets, foundations, latrines, and trash pits remain visible on the surface.

At Ludlow we have been able to find features associated with the strike camp and to define the distribution and types of artifacts at the site. The site is quite shallow with features appearing at depths of 10 to 20 cm. We have found and excavated tent platforms and privies. The distribution of artifacts matches the plan of the camp as shown in contemporary photographs.

From photos we know that the tents were constructed by first digging a shallow basin, then laying wooden joists directly on the ground to support a wooden platform and frame. Once covered with canvas the strikers piled a ridge

*Figure 8.2*  1997 archaeological field crew in front of the Ludlow monument.
(Photograph by Randy McGuire.)

of dirt around the base of the tent. In 1998 we excavated one platform and we were able to define it by stains in the earth, remains of the shallow excavation, and rows of nails that followed the joists (Figure 8.3). A wide range of small artifacts were associated with the tent including fragments of miners' lamps, buttons, ceramics, bottle glass, and fragments of shoes. A collection of religious medals suggests that the occupants of the tent were Italian Catholics.

Photographs have proven a great aid in our excavations and a rich source of information. Several hundred photographs exist of the strike including dozens of the Ludlow tent colony. One photo taken from nearby a railroad water tower shows the camp a few days before the massacre. We used a technique pioneered by Gene Prince (1988) and James Deetz (1993) to define the position of the tents and other features in the colony. We had a 35 mm negative made of the photo and then mounted it on the ground glass of an SLR camera with a removable viewfinder. With the negative in position we could look in the viewfinder and see through the negative. We know where the water tower was and we placed a lift jack on that spot and raised it. At that point we could view the site area with the tents in the negative superimposed on it. We were able to locate over a quarter of the tents in the colony using this technique.

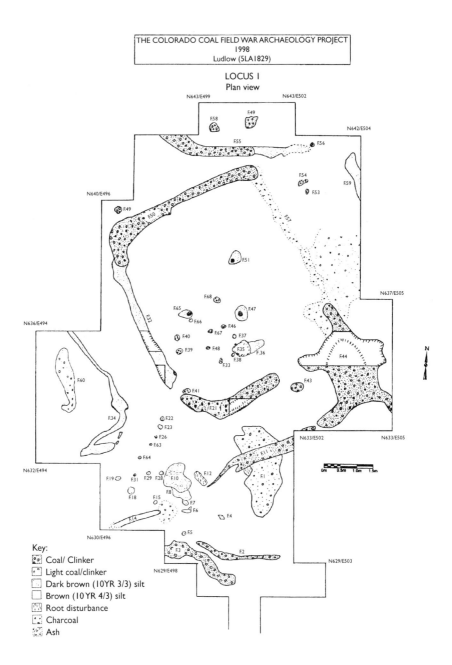

*Figure 8.3* Plan of a tent platform excavated in 1998.

Berwind was a CF&I town located in Berwind canyon near Ludlow, occupied before and after the strike. Many of the strikers at Ludlow originated from there. CF&I built the town in 1892 and abandoned it in 1931. In 1998 we made a detailed map of the community and we were able to define numerous discrete residential neighborhoods. Test excavations revealed stratified deposits of up to 50 cm deep in the yards associated with houses. We have been able to sort these deposits into ones dating before, during, and after the strike. Our preliminary examination of artifacts from the tests, of photos of the community at different points in time, and of company records indicates that some of the neighborhoods date to before the strike, while others were constructed as part of the program of town improvements that followed the strike. We also contacted and started doing oral history interviews with people who lived in Berwind during the 1920s and 1930s. Currently we are excavating in trash deposits and latrines dating to before and after the strike.

## Archaeology as memory

The story of the 1913–1914 Coal Field War and Ludlow is a history that has been hidden, lost, or at best selectively remembered outside of union circles. Within the union movement Ludlow is a shrine and a powerful symbol used to raise class consciousness and to mobilize union members. The new signs on the interstate identifying the exit to the 'Ludlow Massacre Memorial' draws a small but steady stream of summer tourists to the site. Most of the individuals arrive expecting to find a monument to an Indian massacre. In this context our excavations become a form of memory that recalls what happened at Ludlow, the sacrifices of the strikers, and that the rights of working people were won through terrible struggle. Memory leads to action as working people realize how their contemporary struggles are a continuation of the struggle at Ludlow.

The story of Ludlow has great popular appeal. The violence of the events and the death of women and children make the history a compelling story. It is also not a tale of distant or exotic past. Descendants of the strikers still regularly visit the site and the United Mine Workers hold an annual memorial service at the monument.

Our focus on everyday life humanizes the strikers because it talks about them in terms of relations and activities that our modern audiences also experience. For example, relations between husbands and wives, parents and children, and activities such as preparing food for a family, or how to get the laundry done. The parallel between the modern realities of these experiences and the miners' lives provides our modern audience with a comparison to understand the harshness of the strikers' experience.

In the United States archaeological excavations are considered newsworthy. Our first two seasons of excavation both resulted in articles in every major newspaper in the state of Colorado. Eric Zorn, a columnist with the *Chicago Tribune*, picked up on our excavations for his Labor Day column in 1997. He titled the column 'Workers' Rights Were Won With Blood'. Our excavations give the events of 1913–1914 a modern reality, they live again and become news again. We have also focused on developing interpretive programs at the massacre site. The United Mine Workers have made Ludlow and the massacre a symbol of their struggle today. But, the tourists off the highway need educating. During the summer of 1998 over 500 people visited our excavations and heard the story of what happened.

At the Ludlow memorial service in June of 1999 we unveiled an interpretive kiosk. The kiosk includes three panels, one on the history of the strike and massacre, a second on our archaeological research, and a third on the relationship of Ludlow to current labor struggles. Over 700 working people viewed the kiosk and our traveling exhibit of artifacts, and listened enthusiastically to a short presentation on our work.

Working people in southern Colorado still struggle for dignity and basic rights. Several hundred of the participants in the June 1999 Ludlow memorial service were striking steelworkers from Pueblo, Colorado. They had been on strike from CF&I for two years to stop forced overtime and thus regain one of the basic rights that the Ludlow strikers died for, the eight-hour day. They have used the Ludlow massacre as a powerful symbol in their struggle. It is so powerful that the parent company (Oregon Steel) changed the name of their Pueblo subsidiary from CF&I to Rocky Mountain Steel to distance themselves from the events of 1914. The company now seems determined to break the union and to deprive the steelworkers of another of the basic rights that the Ludlow strikers struggled for, the right to collective bargaining. In June of 1999 we twice addressed the Pueblo steelworkers and afterwards several individuals insisted that we accept small donations of money to further our research.

An important component of our education program is the preparation of school programs and educational packets for the public schools of Colorado. We are currently writing a curriculum for middle school students on the history of labor in Colorado with the 1913–1914 strike as its central focus. During the summer of 1999 we held a Colorado Endowment for the Humanities sponsored training institute for teachers. The purpose of this institute was to educate the teachers on labor history and to develop classroom materials to use in the teaching of Colorado labor history.

In the Colorado Coal Field War Project we have built an archaeology that working people can relate to both emotionally and intellectually. It is one of the few archaeological projects devised in the United States that speaks to working-class people. It speaks to their experience, in a language that they can understand, about events that interest them and about events that they feel directly connected to. By doing this it also becomes a form of praxis that seeks to know the world, critique the world, and most importantly take action in the world.

## Acknowledgements

We would like to thank many people who have contributed to the success of our project and to this chapter. The planning of the project was accomplished with a faculty development grant from the State University of New York at Binghamton in the summer of 1996. The Colorado Historical Society funded the project in 1997, 1998 and 1999. District 22 of the United Mine Workers of America (UMWA) granted us permission to do our research at Ludlow. The UMWA Women's Auxiliary local 9856 maintains the Ludlow monument and hosts the annual memorial. We would single out Yolanda Romero and Carol Blatnick-Barros for the assistance that they have given our research. Michael Romero, president of UMWA local 9856, has also aided us in many ways. We have received great help and support from numerous individuals with the Colorado Historical Society including Paula Manini and Susan Collins. Trinidad State Junior College has provided us with housing and other forms of assistance. Larry Conyers of the University of Denver has performed several ground penetrating radar surveys on portions of the Ludlow site for us.

The Ludlow Collective are: Donna L. Bryant, Phil Duke, Jason Lapham, Randall McGuire, Paul Reckner, Dean Saitta, Mark Walker, and Margaret Wood.

## References

Bassett, Everett (1994) 'We Took Care of Each Other Like Families Were Meant To': Gender, Social Organization, and Wage Labor Among the Apache at Roosevelt. In *Those of Little Note: Gender, Race, and Class in Historical Archaeology*, edited by Elizabeth Scott, pp. 55–79. University of Arizona Press, Tucson.

Beaudry, Mary (ed.) (1988) *Documentary Archaeology in the New World*. Cambridge University Press, Cambridge.

Beaudry, Mary C. and Stephen Mrozowski (1988) The Archaeology of Work and Home Life in Lowell, Massachusetts: An Interdisciplinary Study of the Boott Cotton Mills Corporation. *Industrial Archaeology* 19: 1–22.

Beshoar, Barron B. (1957) *Out of the Depths: The Story of John R. Lawson, A Labor Leader*. Colorado Historical Commission & Denver Trades & Labor Assembly, Denver.

Cameron, Ardis (1993) *Radicals of the Worst Sort: Laboring Women in Lawrence Massachusetts 1860–1912*. University of Illinois Press, Urbana.

De Cunzo, Lu Ann and Bernard L. Herman (eds) (1996) *Historical Archaeology and the Study of American Culture*. Henry Francis du Pont Winterthur Museum, Winterthur, Delaware.

Deetz, James (1993) *Flowerdew Hundred: The Archaeology of a Virginia Plantation, 1619–1864*. University of Virginia Press, Charlottesville.

Frykman, Jonas (1990) What People Do But Seldom Say. *Ethnologia Scandinavica* 20: 50–62.

Gitelman, Howard (1988) *Legacy of the Ludlow Massacre: A Chapter in American Industrial Relations*. University of Pennsylvania Press, Philadelphia.

Hardesty, Donald L. (1988) *The Archaeology of Mines and Mining: The View from the Silver State.* Society for Historical Archaeology, Pleasant Hill, CA.

Leone, Mark B. (1995) A Historical Archaeology of Capitalism. *American Anthropologist* 97: 251–68.

Leone, Mark B. and Parker B. Potter Jr. (1988) Introduction: Issues in Historical Archaeology. In *The Recovery of Meaning: Historical Archaeology in the Eastern United States,* edited by Mark P. Leone and Parker B. Potter, Jr., pp. 1–26. Smithsonian Institution Press, Washington.

Little, Barbara (ed.) (1992) *Text-Aided Archaeology.* CRC Press, Boca Raton.

Long, Priscilla (1985) The Women of the CF&I Strike, 1913–1914. In *Women, Work, and Protest: A Century of U.S. Women's Labor History,* ed. By R. Milkman, Routledge & Kegan Paul, London.

Long, P. (1991) *Where the Sun Never Shines: A History of America's Bloody Coal Industry.* Paragon Books, New York.

McGaw, J. A. (1989) No Passive Victims, No Separate Spheres: A Feminist Perspective on Technology's History. In *In Context: History and the History of Technology,* edited by S. H. Cutcliffe and R. Post, pp. 172–91. Lehigh University Press, Bethlehem.

McGovern, George S. and Leonard F. Guttridge (1972) *The Great Coalfield War.* Houghton Mifflin Company, Boston.

McGuire, Randall H. and Mark Walker (1999) Class Confrontations in Archaeology. *Historical Archaeology* 33(1): 159–83.

Mrozowski, Stephen, Grace H. Ziesing and Mary C. Beaudry (1996) *Living on the Boott: Historical Archaeology at the Boott Mills Boardinghouses, Lowell, Massachusetts.* University of Massachusetts Press, Amherst.

Orser, Charles (1996) *A Historical Archaeology of the Modern World.* Plenum Press, New York.

Papanikolas, Zeese (1982) *Buried Unsung: Louis Tikas and the Ludlow Massacre.* University of Utah Press, Salt Lake City.

Patterson, Thomas C. (1995) *Towards a Social History of Archaeology in the United States.* Harcourt and Brace Co., Fort Worth.

Potter, Parker B. Jr. (1994) *Public Archaeology in Annapolis: A Critical Approach to History in Maryland's Ancient City.* Smithsonian Institution Press, Washington D.C.

Prince, Gene (1988) Photography for Discovery and Scale by Superimposing Old Photographs on the Present-Day Scene. *Antiquity* 62: 12–116.

Sennett, Richard and Jonathan Cobb (1972) *The Hidden Injuries of Class.* Vintage Books, New York.

Shackel, Paul (1994) A Material Culture of Armory Workers. In *Domestic Responses to Nineteenth-Century Industrialization: An Archaeology of Park Building 48, Harper's Ferry National Historical Park,* edited by Paul Shackel, pp. 10.1–10.7. U.S. Department of the Interior, National Park Service, National Capital Region, Regional Archaeology Program, Washington, D.C.

Shackel, P. (1996) *Culture Change and the New Technology: An Archaeology of the Early American Industrial Era.* Plenum Press, New York.

Thomas, Mary (1971) *Those Damn Foreigners.* Hollywood.

Tomasky, Michael (1997) Waltzing With Sweeny: Is the Academic Left Ready to Join the AFL-CIO? *Lingua Franca* February: 40–7.

Trigger, Bruce (1989) *A History of Archaeological Thought.* University of Cambridge Press, Cambridge.

Wegars, Priscilla (1991) Who's Been Workin' on the Railroad: An Examination of the Construction, Distribution, and Ethnic Origins of Domed Rock Ovens on Railroad-related Sites. *Historical Archaeology* 25: 37–65.

Whiteside, James (1990) *Regulating Danger: The Struggle for Mine Safety in the Rocky Mountain Coal Industry*. University of Nebraska Press, Lincoln.

Wurst, Louann (1999) Internalizing Class in Historical Archaeology. *Historical Archaeology* 33(1): 7–21.

# Chapter 9

# Black sharecroppers and white frat boys

## Living communities and the appropriation of their archaeological pasts

*Laurie Wilkie*

## Introduction

The archaeology of the early twentieth century is truly the archaeology of 'us' and the social and economic conflicts that have shaped our recent history. Today's society is not divorced from the experiences of the early twentieth century; racism and economic and social inequality are all issues that continue to shape today's social discourse. While younger generations may draw upon the early twentieth century to provide fuel for today's social lessons and debates, the generations that experienced the recent past first-hand are still among us. The early twentieth century is a very recent past ... the past of our parents, grandparents and great-grandparents, many of whom are still alive.

As archaeologists working in this time period, we are confronted with multiple voices, representing multiple generational, gender, socio-economic and ethnic/racial experiences and agendas. These are the voices of the people who created the archaeological sites, and their descendant populations. When these voices are raised in discord, expressing different interpretations of the past, archaeologists can be caught in the middle. In this chapter, I will discuss two recent projects, both dealing with early twentieth-century sites, one in California, the other in Louisiana. The California site was associated with a wealthy college fraternity community at the University of California, the Louisiana site was associated with an African-American sharecropping community. In both projects, I worked closely with individuals who had created the archaeological sites, as well as their descendant communities. Each group contained individuals who hoped to influence and shape the way their past was constructed. While attempting to negotiate between different community groups can be frustrating, in both instances, working with the community informants allowed the archaeological interpretation to become contextualized within early *and* late twentieth-century social debates, allowing for the construction of a richer social dialogue.

## African-American sharecroppers

As part of my research into the African-American past, I have been fortunate enough to work with living members and descendants of the specific plantation communities I have studied. Such efforts at community partnering are increasingly common and the subject of reflective and critical debate within historical archaeology (e.g. Potter 1991, 1993; Farnsworth 1993; McKee 1994; McDavid and Babson 1997). In research I conducted in the early 1990s, I attempted to reach and consult with the African-American community through oral history interviews, lectures, public outreach events, and through university class and volunteer events. Through these efforts, I was able to reach a wide breadth of individuals, including multiple generations of individuals whose life experiences involved the specific sites being studied, as well as the broader community. These different interactions allowed me not only to explain why archaeologists were interested in studying the African-American past, but also to listen to the concerns and interests of the community, which were incorporated into the research scheme. I do want to indicate, at this juncture, that by the standards considered appropriate by some authors writing in the years since I conducted this research (e.g. LaRoche and Blakey 1997; Epperson 1998), my community partnering efforts have been considerably weakened by the fact that I was only in contact with a small portion of the community prior to excavation. In my defense, excavations at Riverlake were conducted as salvage excavations, and the discussion about ways of brokering community interaction were still very young when both of these sites were studied. I do not write this discussion with the intent of providing a formula for community partnering, but rather, to illuminate the tensions and dynamics that characterize the dialectical relationship between informant and anthropologist.

While a wide range of community partnering approaches have been developed and discussed elsewhere by historical archaeologists (e.g. Derry 1997; LaRoche and Blakey 1997; McDavid 1997), in this discussion, I want explicitly to address the relationship between an archaeologist and people I have come to think of as 'community informants'. Community informants are those individuals whose personal experiences and direct ancestral ties link them with the archaeological sites being studied both in the past and present. I am using this term to distinguish from informants who may be culturally or consanguinely descended from the plantation communities, but did not live on the specific plantation being studied.

I will briefly discuss my experiences with community informants from Riverlake Plantation, located in the sugar-producing parish of Pointe Coupee. The plantation was founded in the late 1700s, occupied through the antebellum and Civil War periods, and farmed by sharecroppers during the periods of Reconstruction and Jim Crow. Riverlake's African-American quarter was only fully abandoned in the early 1990s (Wilkie 1994). The focus of archaeological research was to illuminate how African-American families, from the period of enslavement onwards, constructed a sense of identity in a context of oppression and racism.

The descendant community of Riverlake was easy to locate, in part, due to fortuitous timing. Riverlake had been the childhood home of African-American author, Ernest Gaines. Gaines was a member of the Riverlake community during his childhood in the 1940s and 1950s, and at the time of our 1993 excavations, his life had just been the subject of a television documentary. The documentary led several individuals to visit their old home, and thus, enabled us to introduce ourselves and the project. In addition, the film-maker introduced us to her informants, who introduced us to other family and community members. Riverlake was also used by former occupants for hunting and fishing, providing yet another opportunity to meet community members. Informants from Riverlake ranged in age from their early 50s to their late 80s. Ten informants were extensively interviewed, and an additional eight were informally interviewed. While I had hoped that the outreach efforts would enrich and make more relevant the archaeological research, I had not expected how clearly the community informant interviews would illustrate the social, political and racial contexts in which my informants had lived. Most striking were the differences between how members of the different generations perceived the potential of archaeology and their potential relationship to the past.

Intrinsic to any interview situation is the dynamic between informant and interviewer. While I had anticipated some racial tension, as a white person interviewing black people about aspects of plantation life, including racism, I had not fully anticipated the generational and regional subtleties. As I began interviews, I first only saw the similarities between interview experiences. Unwittingly, I had several aspects of my own personality and background that facilitated my ability to develop rapport with informants. First, it was clear from my accent that I was not a Louisianian. With all informants, this was commented upon as an advantage. I was not perceived as having any family locally, and therefore, there was no chance that I was related to any of the planter families referred to during interviews. As a northerner, or 'Yankee', who had even lived in California, I was also perceived as essentially more liberal than a southerner would be. I was also told by one informant that my beat-up old car and 'Clinton for President' bumper sticker reassured him of my sincerity. As a woman, I was perceived by my informants as less threatening and was assumed to be a more sympathetic listener. My perceived youth also made older informants more likely to talk to me about the past in parable-like terms: my informants were educating me. Many of the informants saw me as a voice through which to reach their own children and grandchildren. Because I was a teacher, my informants would often preface their stories by saying, 'Now the younger generation doesn't understand what life was like back then ... you be sure to tell your students about this.'

As I continued with interviews, however, I began to distinguish other patterns. Informants aged 60 years and younger had very different agendas in speaking with me than older informants. Younger informants were very forthright about discussing both the positive and negative aspects of life on the plantation. Although raised in sharecropper's cabins as farm laborers, most of my informants had successfully completed high school and college degrees, had found employment off the plantations, were homeowners in Baton Rouge or the surrounding suburbs, and had raised children who had attended college. The experiences of my informants during childhood were very different from the experiences of their children. In many cases, informants commented upon how their children had no concept of the past, and did not appreciate how much life had changed since the Civil Rights movement. In telling me about the past, these younger informants told tales with a moral: racism had been an evil that could only be successfully battled when people stood together as a community. The text they wanted repeated was how when the African-American community stood together, they were able to defeat racism. The stories they told to illustrate this moral had been told to them by their older relatives, and had been passed down to inspire them. The stories had inspired them, and now my informants were passing these stories on so that I could retell them and inspire others. These informants saw the oral history interviews as an opportunity to shape the way that the past was reconstructed and presented. In addition, as excavations progressed, these informants told me what they thought materials meant and wove these materials into their constructions of the past. In a real way, these informants used the archaeology to reinforce the stories they wanted told.

While anecdotes of racism and survival were told to me by younger informants, it became apparent that older informants were not comfortable talking about these issues. This was most dramatically illustrated when one of my younger informants introduced me to his uncle. The younger man had enthusiastically told me about how his grandfather had been gifted in mathematics. Every year when the sugar crop was harvested and annual debts were to be settled with the overseer, the black sharecroppers would come to his grandfather and have him check their bills to ensure they were not being cheated. In most cases, the overseers were trying to cheat them, and armed with information from the grandfather, families were able to earn their fair wage. The overseers learned who was responsible for helping the sharecroppers. Shortly afterwards, the Ku Klux Klan rode into the quarter of Riverlake, dragged the grandfather out of the family cabin and beat him severely as a warning.

The uncle had told the younger man this story, telling him how he had hidden under his bed and listened to his father being beaten outside. The younger man wanted me to hear the story directly from his uncle. However, when the nephew asked the older man to tell me the story, he looked his nephew straight in the eye and told him that he did not remember any stories like that. The two argued for several minutes until I asked the man about the plantation during his childhood. At that point, he talked to me about various aspects of his childhood on the plantation, including information about the school that the community had built, first in an abandoned sharecropper's cabin, then in the community's church. While he did not state so himself, the school had been founded by the community because the parish would not properly fund black education. The context of racism in which he had lived as a young man made it inappropriate to tell of his experiences to a white researcher. Furthermore, he did not see me, as an educator, or archaeologist, as a means of promoting any particular agenda or vision of the past. Instead, he told me about a past with which he thought I would be comfortable: a past in which happy children fished and chased turtles in False River and attended small one-room schools.

While these generational differences between informants is intriguing from the perspective of how individuals construct and politicize the past, these differences can also be used to enlighten archaeological interpretations of the times in which these individuals lived. The hesitance of older informants to discuss issues of race and power illustrates the impact that living in such a context had upon them. The younger informants had come of age during the Civil Rights movement, and as a result, were more forthright in discussions of racism and inequality. It is important to recognize, however, that it was the older informants whose generation had sparked the Civil Rights movement: through the attitudes and beliefs that they instilled in their children and families; through the schools they instituted and the churches and social institutions they founded. Evidence of these activities is clearly seen in the archaeology of these sites. Comparisions of ceramic patterns found in different cabins demonstrates evidences of food-sharing and neighborly interdependence. Faunal remains illustrate the range of wild foodstuffs used to supplement the diet and to help families minimize the amount of debt they owed annually to the plantation manager. The archaeological record also bears testament to the importance of education within the community, with slate writing tablets, pens and pencils being recovered from all of the cabins. Education ultimately became the key to freedom from the plantation for the younger generations.

To understand and interpret more fully the archaeology of early twentieth-century African-American life, it is important to consider not only the racism that was encountered on a daily basis by black families; but also to recognize how individuals and families forged strong resourceful communities outside the influence of white oppression. Children raised within these communities were taught the lessons of racism and resistance, and provided with the education and self-confidence necessary for them to force broader social reforms and change. Documentary history would inform us that the Civil Rights movement was a phenomenon of the post World War II world. Oral history demonstrates otherwise. However, had I pursued interviews and outreach with only the oldest community members, the social context of community internal activism would have been lost due to the legacy of racism these individuals had endured. By creating a dialectical relationship between the past and present, through the integrated use of archaeological data and community informants, a richer construction of the past was achieved.

## European-American fraternity brothers

The second research project that I will discuss began as an archaeological exercise in the construction of identity: how did the early twentieth-century fraternity population of Zeta Psi create a sense of community and identity within their house? However, in researching the site, it became apparent that in constructing identities from archaeological materials, archaeologists are creating consumable commodities. People who consume our interpretations do not necessarily consider the shifting and changing dynamics of group identity through time, and interpret our findings through late twentieth-century lenses.

A fraternity is an all-male community, whose members identify one another as brothers, or fictive kin. Potential members are drawn from individuals who are perceived to be of the same background as existing members. The criteria used to define this likeness may be socioeconomic, racial, ethnic, regional, occupational, or genealogical. The perceived commonalities, however, do not alone create the sense of identity within a fraternity. The creation of a shared ideology, reinforced through shared ritual and ceremony, a shared history and through shared experiences between members of the house lead to the construction of a common identity (Wilkie 1998, forthcoming).

The archaeological materials for this analysis and discussion were recovered from behind 2251 College Ave., on the University of California Berkeley campus. The structure was built in 1911 with funds generated by the fraternity, and designed and built to suit their needs (*Oakland Tribune* 1910; Zeta Psi Archive 1909). The materials were most likely to have been deposited around 1923–1925. Archaeological and contemporary documentary materials were analyzed for evidence of arenas of social interaction that may have allowed fraternity members to develop a sense of communal identity.

Porcelain ceramics bearing the fraternity crest were among artifacts recovered. The crest is meaning-laden, representing the act of initiation and the fraternity's values and rituals. The meanings of the crest are only revealed to initiated members, and would serve as a visual reinforcement of the fraternity's codes during meals. While the meals were highly ritualized, the poor quality of the food, as evidenced both archaeologically and in documents, was another arena that served to promote a sense of community (Wilkie forthcoming).

Social drinking, limited to fraternity brothers only, also served as a means of fostering camaraderie. Since the materials date to the period of Prohibition, the activity of consuming alcoholic beverages was illegal. Brothers were not only drinking together, but also colluding to obtain and dispose of the incriminating material. The construction of a multiple gender–age system within the fraternity that relegated brothers into symbolic adults or children, based on their college class level, created an additional family-like structure within the fraternity house (Wilkie 1998). A sense of shared male identity was reinforced through activities such as cross-dressing for plays or skits, an activity documented historically and suggested archaeologically (Wilkie 1998).

As part of this project, Zeta Psi fraternity alumni were interviewed. The national organization of Zeta Psi provided the names of two alumni who had been brothers of Zeta Psi at Berkeley, graduating in the classes of 1930 and 1931. One of these alumni was still alive, and was in touch with other members of his fraternity. In this way, we were able to contact five Zeta Psi alumni from the classes of 1929–1933. Additional alumni contacted us after news stories about the project were released. Reactions to the project were primarily enthusiastic. Alumni were interested in the artifacts, pleased with the attention of students and media, and proud to discuss their time as college students, always emphasizing that Zeta Psi had been the best and most prestigious of the fraternities on campus. They sang the praises of other alumni, and their accomplishments since graduation. Zeta Psi alumni included Olympic Gold medalists, prominent lawyers, doctors, businessmen and politicians.

It is important to remember that fraternities are secret societies, with histories and mythologies not meant to be known outside of the fraternity. During the course of interviews, it became apparent that the alumni were not always sure what facets of fraternity life should be public versus private. The alumni would tell stories, then think better of it, consult other alumni, then sometimes retract or retell their stories. The oral history of the fraternity became a changing and dynamic history, as much a product of a group collaboration as a remembrance of individual experiences (Wilkie forthcoming).

This tendency became particularly visible as media exposure to the site increased. Alumni who provided a certain set of information in a research context were very likely to provide different information to the media. For instance, one alumni who visited the lab to view the archaeological materials, when asked to identify artifacts interpreted as typically related to women's attire, identified the materials, unprompted, in a similar way. The alumni saw the archival photographs of Zetes dressed in drag and agreed that they were men in drag, but did not volunteer an interpretation of why they were doing this. In front of television cameras, however, he stoutly denied that any women's artifacts were found, stated that artifacts such as the hat pin were a tie clip, and stated that no Zeta Psi brothers would be involved in such 'monkey business' (Wilkie 1998, forthcoming).

Interest in the site has also been expressed by the international fraternal organization. Dan King, the webmaster for the Zeta Psi site, informed me that the fraternity is interested in building an on-line archive, and that it sees the research as appropriate and of interest to members. In addition, yet another branch of the organization has asked to borrow artifacts for display at their annual meeting. Andrew M. Nunez, the Executive Director of the International Organization of Zeta Psi Fraternity, wrote in a correspondence: 'After reading a few of the articles, I realize that the cultural material in the site provide not only a keen insight to the turn-of-the-century life in California, but our organization as well.'

Another affiliate of the international fraternity, who is responsible for retraining fraternity chapters in the traditional structure and values of Zeta Psi, was also interested in the research. He saw the archaeological materials as providing a tangible tie between the values, practices and traditions of the past and the future. According to this informant, the fraternity is in the process of redefining itself, and trying to revive the spirit and tradition of the fraternity. The archaeological materials provide a vehicle through which to make those ties.

The construction of 1920s Zeta Psi identity, as told through its archaeological remains, is of great interest to living members of the fraternal institution. It is evident that the fraternity alumni, in appropriating this archaeological history and the constructions of identity it proffered, wanted a certain presentation of their history told to the public, reflecting the current needs and philosophies of their organization.

The vision of the fraternity promoted by the media, however, removed the archaeological materials from their social historical context and presented the evidence of social drinking as evidence of massive drunken parties (although this conflicts with the documentary data), equating the historical site directly with stereotypical late twentieth-century fraternity life and behavior. In particular, comparisons were made by the media between the movie 'Animal House' and the early twentieth-century Zeta Psi brothers.

The media's emphasis may reflect socioeconomic class tensions that are symbolized by fraternities. In 'Animal House', the fraternity that served as the focus of the movie was situated on the fringe of the university community, harassed by the administration, and seen as having the lowest status of the fraternities on the campus. The members of the fraternity are slovenly, drunk, stoned, stupid, sometimes ugly, and essentially the reverse of what fraternity members aspired to be. As such, the members of the 'Animal House' become the heroes of the movie and the characters from other fraternities, who in actuality were closer embodiments of fraternity reality, become their nemeses.

The 'Animal House' fraternity is an every person's fraternity. Members (with the exception of one legacy who is begrudgingly accepted) do not appear to be selected for membership based upon socioeconomic class, intelligence, ethnic background, family connections or occupation. Instead, the fraternity is portrayed as equally accessible to all, even to the extent that the house is open to all at parties. The secret and solemn nature of true fraternity initiation is mocked in the movie and contrasted to the activities of the Animal House. The brothers of the house are portrayed as having little ambition or thought about their futures, again, in contrast to 'real-world' fraternity members who use fraternity membership as a means of creating and maintaining professional contacts after school. 'Animal House', therefore, is not a representation of what fraternities are or necessarily were, but the public's perception of how fraternities should be (Wilkie forthcoming).

The media and the public, by focusing upon the 'Animal House' parallels from the archaeological interpretations and ignoring other aspects of fraternity identity, in essence, created a populist fraternity, void of class distinctions. In many respects, some contemporary fraternity chapters have also embraced the 'Animal House' view of fraternities in constructing their own identities, as graphically illustrated by fraternity pledges at Massachusetts Institute of Technology and Louisiana State University, who died of alcohol poisoning related to rushing activities. National organizations, such as Zeta Psi's, are concerned that their chapters are losing their desired sense of identity, and constructing undesirable identities, thus the need to re-indoctrinate chapters in their fraternity's heritage.

## Conclusions

In many archaeological instances, our only opportunity to explore identity is through material culture. When discussing identity, archaeologists are often dealing with groups or communities and the collective ways that individuals within those groups define themselves. When studying change, our efforts often focus upon longer-term culture change (e.g. Lightfoot *et al.* 1997; Lightfoot *et al.* 1998) rather than changes that can take place within an individual's life. Despite growing awareness among archaeologists that an individual's identity shifts and changes throughout a person's lifetime (Jones 1997; Moore and Scott 1997; Sofaer-Derevenski 1994; Upton 1996; Wilkie 1998; Wright 1996), the bulk of archaeological research still ignores the individual.

Research at Riverlake plantation demonstrated to me how the inclusion of community informants into archaeological investigations can enrich our understandings of the relationship between past and present contexts that shape individual and societal experiences. In the case of Riverlake, the collection of oral histories from multiple generations of community informants provided a keener insight into how the experiences of and responses to racist oppression shaped the African-American past. Ironically, it was the informants who had most resisted the confines placed upon them by segregation who were least comfortable speaking about their actions outside of their families and communities. As a white researcher, the discourse of the interviews forced me to acknowledge how structures of racial inequality, established in the early twenieth century, continue to shape and limit my effectiveness as a white researcher working with African-American populations today.

The research at Zeta Psi allowed for the exploration of fraternity identity at multiple scales: that of individual experiences, as constructed through individual oral histories; that of a discreet synchronic population, as explored through the archaeology; that of a diachronic community, as studied through the integration of the archaeological, historical and oral historical data. The Zeta Psi fraternity project revealed how archaeological constructions of identity are consumed, be it by cultural descendants, the regional community, or the national public. Again, an essential aspect of this research required an acknowledgment of the dialectic relationship between those who lived the past and those who study it.

In his essay, 'Archaeology's Relationship to the Present and to the Past' in *Modern Material Culture: The Archaeology of Us*, Mark Leone explored how social dynamics of the present shape our presentation of the past in such public arenas as Colonial Williamsburg. While the past of Colonial Williamsburg and Leone's present were separated by 200 years, as more archaeologists delve into the archaeology of the early twentieth century, we will find the past and present more difficult to extricate from one another. The issues of the early twentieth century are the issues of the late twentieth century, and will follow us to the next century. As archaeologists, the discourse of post-modern decon-structionism has led us to question what we are learning through our research and how we make our archaeological questions of meaning and relevance to the general public and to living descendants of a cultural group (e.g. McDavid and Babson 1997; Potter 1993; Leone *et al.* 1987; Leone 1995). These projects have been enlightening in that I have been able to watch how several descendant communities from very different socioeconomic, regional and racial backgrounds, have differentially related to, appropriated, consumed and sought to influence archaeological knowledge. While African-American archaeology has been recognized as a politicized archaeological realm (e.g. McDavid and Babson 1997), the presentation and use of the past, even a seemingly recent and non-controversial past, like the fraternity, is multi-faceted and nuanced. Both of the projects discussed here were enriched through the incorporation of informant interviews. Not only did the interviews underscore how the present tries to create its own past, but also how the informants themselves were shaped by their times. Ultimately, by maintaining a dialectic between the past and the present, we can only improve the nature of our archaeological research and interpretations.

## References

Derry, L. (1997) 'Pre-Emancipation Archaeology: Does it Play in Selma, Alabama?', *Historical Archaeology* 31, 3: 18–26.

Epperson, T. (1998) 'Critical Race Theory and the Archaeology of the African Diaspora', unpublished paper presented at the Conference for Historical and Underwater Archaeology, Atlanta, Georgia.

Farnsworth, P. (1993) 'What is the Use of Plantation Archaeology? No Use at All, if No One Else is Listening!', *Historical Archaeology* 27, 1: 114–16.

Jones, S. (1997) *The Archaeology of Ethnicity: Constructing Identities in the Past and Present*. London: Routledge

LaRoche, C. and Blakey, M. (1997) 'Seizing Intellectual Power: The Dialogue at the New York African Burial Ground', *Historical Archaeology* 31, 3: 84–106.

Leone, M. (1981) 'Archaeology's Relationship to the Present and to the Past', in R. Gould and M. Schiffer (eds) *Modern Material Culture: The Archaeology of Us*, New York: Academic Press.

—— (1995) 'A Historical Archaeology of Capitalism', *American Anthropologist* 97, 2: 251–68.

Leone, M., Potter, P. and Shackel, P. (1987) 'Toward a Critical Archaeology', *Current Anthropology* 28, 3: 283–302.

Lightfoot, K. G., Schiff, A. M. and Wake, T. A. (eds) (1997) *The Native Alaskan Neighborhood: A Multiethnic Community at Colony Ross*, Berkeley: Archaeological Research Facility of the University of California.

Lightfoot, K. G., Martinez, A. and Schiff, A. (1998) 'Daily Practice and Material Culture in Pluralistic Social Settings: An Archaeological Study of Culture Change and Persistence from Fort Ross, California', *American Antiquity* 63, 2: 199–222.

McDavid, C. (1997) 'Descendants, Decisions, and Power: The Public Interpretation of the Archaeology of the Levi Jordan Plantation', *Historical Archaeology* 31, 3: 114–31.

McDavid, C. and Babson, D. (eds) (1997) 'In the Realm of Politics: Prospects for Public Participation in African-American and Plantation Archaeology', *Historical Archaeology* 31, 3.

McKee, L. (1994) 'Is it Futile to Try and Be Useful? Historical Archaeology and the African-American Experience', *Northeast Historical Archaeology* 23, 1–7.

Moore, J. and Scott, E. (ed.) (1997) *Invisible People and Processes: Writing Gender and Childhood into European Archaeology*. London: Leicester University Press.

*Oakland Tribune* (1910) 'Cornerstone is Laid for New Zeta Psi Chapter House', February 6, 1910, 21.

Potter, P. (1991) 'What is the Use of Plantation Archaeology?', *Historical Archaeology* 25, 3: 94–107.

—— (1993) *Public Archaeology in Annapolis: A Critical Approach to History in Maryland's Ancient City*. Washington, D.C.: Smithsonian Institution Press.

Sofaer-Derevenski, J. (1994) 'Where are the Children? Accessing Children in the Past', *Archaeological Review from Cambridge* 13, 2: 8–20.

Upton, D. (1996) 'Ethnicity, Authenticity and Invented Traditions', *Historical Archaeology* 30, 2: 1–7.

Wilkie, L. A. (1994) 'Childhood in the Quarters: Playtime at Oakley and Riverlake Plantations', *Louisiana Folklife* Vol. XVIII: 13–20.

—— (1998) 'The Other Gender: The Archaeology of an Early 20th Century Fraternity', *Proceedings of the Society for California Archaeology* 11, 7–11.

—— (forthcoming) 'Archaeology and Material Culture of Zeta Psi: Constructions and Consumptions of Fraternity Identity and History', *Journal of Material Culture*.

Wright, R. P. (ed.) (1996) *Gender and Archaeology*, Philadelphia: University of Pennsylvania Press.

Zeta Psi Archive (1909) November 17th Letter from New House Finance Committee to Alumni. Berkeley: Zeta Psi Fraternity.

# Part III

# Disappearance and disclosure

# Chapter 10

# Bodies of evidence

*Victor Buchli and Gavin Lucas*

In 1849, the academic world of Harvard was thrown into turmoil by the murder of a prominent physician and benefactor George Parkman; as the case unravelled it appeared that a Professor Webster at Harvard Medical school had owed Parkman large sums of money and consequently Webster's laboratory was searched, although it revealed nothing. Finally, a curious janitor broke into the lab's privy where he found parts of a dismembered body and a subsequent police search of a small incinerator found the burnt fragments of skull and dentures. The whole weight of the medical school including Oliver Wendell Holmes was convened to study the remains and eventually, Webster was convicted and hanged the following year (Snow 1982: 102–5). This case has been ventured as one of the first instances of forensic anthropology, but it also serves to illustrate the key element in forensics: the *corpus delicti*, the body of the crime, whether this is an actual body or the traces of a crime.

Throughout the nineteenth century and most of the earlier part of this century, the material evidence and particularly the testimony of material evidence took second place to eyewitness or confessional information – despite the allure of Sherlock Holmes (Snow 1982: 109). Forensic evidence was largely supplemental and the development of forensic science, while it has a long pedigree, did not take on a major role until this century (Snow 1982; Iscan 1988; Hunter 1994, 1996). The change in the States came after the 1950s as a result of Supreme Court constraints on the use of confessions and eyewitness testimony forcing the police and FBI to rely more on material evidence. Further enhanced by the recovery and need to identify the Korean War dead, the whole status of material evidence, the *corpus delicti*, was transformed so that today, it can often overturn eyewitness or confessional information.

According to Laquer, the *corpus delicti* has gained particular prominence in the twentieth century corresponding with the phenomenon of subjects who are increasingly individuated, with unique identities, papers, records and bureaucratic subjectivities retained in state documents (Lacquer 1999). While in the previous section the personal and the collective were often in conflict in processes of remembering and forgetting, here we see the production of the personal and the articulation of identity through Foucauldian technologies of self and the collective production of subjectivities. Justice and concepts of genocide that characterise modern experience and define modern collectives require a victim, a *corpus delicti*; the individuated subject provides the material basis for the articulation of collective identities and injustices. In this light, the identity of victims (the repressed, the disappeared) – and perpetrators – takes on an increased resonance in forensic work which is usually absent in most archaeological work. The Serb action of destroying all written documentation of Kosovar Albanians is an interesting case in point; the systematic policy to erase all documents, physical and electronic, that can testify to the existence of an ethnic group while correspondingly the work of forensic anthropologists is reclaiming that identity, highlights the importance of this phenomenon.

Namelessness and lack of individuation are quite rare in late twentieth-century societies and to entirely eliminate someone or a people is a very hard thing to do (as Serbian and other military and police authorities know too well). The elimination of the body by murder and its secret burial always leaves its trace, if only in the gap left by its absence, an absence as physical as any presence. But not only can forensics help to recover lost identities, it can equally help to target perpetrators of crime. We know the bullet entered the back of the head at this angle by an experienced marksman of a particular height, standing exactly there. The forensic evidence can indicate a certain style of execution. The perpetrators of genocide have unique signatures and identities, they are not nameless 'genocides' (Thomas Osorio, Operations Officer, International Criminal Tribunal for the former Yugoslovia, personal communication). They can be individuated, given personalities, even a 'style', thus working back in a complementary fashion from the evidence of the body to not only constitute the individuality and identity of the victim, the object of mourning, but also the anonymous killer, who becomes individuated and the focus of retributive justice.

Forensic science however is not simply confined to the body inscribed by violent crime – it can also extend to other 'crimes', especially those of social iniquity. The ravages of industry or pollution and the consequences of poor diet and poverty are equally revealed in the autopsy. The physical anthropologist is well versed in the ways these social processes are physically inscribed by the examination of bone wear and deformation. The art of the autopsy reveals as much about the way our bodies are shaped by social processes, about how we live as much as how we die. Indeed, there are other victims, living victims who are socially marginal, but the conditions of their disenfranchisement are obscure and unconstituted. Being among us, they frequently leave no dramatic traces, and pass us by on the street unnoticed. In many respects such individuals are not constituted as subjects either, they escape Lacquer's process of individuation and are socially outcast or marginal. Where is their body of evidence? This is the subject of investigation in our study of the disenfranchised single mother who disappeared without a trace to her neighbours and local government. An individual clearly seen as being in need and deserving of care who ceased to be an object of care, either by her neighbours, her local community or the state. She is in effect the object of systematic indifference. The archaeological act in this instance catches the traces of her existence just as it is about to disappear and finally exit the discursive realm as a result of this bureaucratic and social indifference.

Forensic anthropology of course has a popular appeal as Cox discusses in her contribution. The public fascination with the violence of murder and equally with the way in which forensic anthropology in turn re-constitutes the murder. A certain obscene spectacle is generated by the forensic anthropologist who manages in gruesome and physical detail to elaborate on the horror, thereby feeding a public fascination with extreme violence. This spectacularisation in a way serves, it might be argued, as a means of coming to terms with the spectres of violence, in a sense to domesticate or, paradoxical as it sounds, *sanitise* it. If we take Mary Douglas's notion of purity and danger, the decomposing body represents a particular threatening element in modern experiences from the medical to the social (Douglas 1984). These are things that happen but should not be seen and become, on a number of levels, obscene. At a visceral level they elicit responses of nausea, disgust and repulsion. At a personal extreme, we may even deny them because such images do not correspond with our experience – consider a mother in the former Yugoslavia who refuses to acknowledge the material evidence of her son's remains because the only identifiable artefact found on the body is a key ring with a key that fits into her home but the key ring is not one she associated with him so it cannot constitute her massacred son, thus keeping the obscene death of her son at bay (Thomas Osorio, personal communication).

The constituting effects of forensics and other works dealing with situations of horror are inevitably forced into this domestication – for to reproduce the horror without such sanitation would be equivalent to repeating the act itself, repeating the horror. This was a central issue in the last section when the problem of dealing with the Holocaust was raised – how to keep the memory of the horror alive but without preventing the wounds of that horror from healing. For example, the Holocaust by the photographer Lee Miller at Buchenwald followed aesthetic photographic conventions, not simply as the professional response of a photographer, but as a means of translating a scene of horror into light, shadow, lines and composition (McLernon 1998). This aestheticisation sanitises the images (we cannot smell the putrefying flesh and feel the nausea in our stomachs), and domesticates them. To do otherwise would mean responding to the directness of the sight and the event, leaving the observer incapable of establishing and objectivising distance with which to represent the horror.

The necessity of uncovering mass graves, doing autopsies and recording this in the name of justice is traversed by feelings of voyeurism and the fetishisation of violence. It is precisely these feelings that contend with and demand the response of sanitisation. On the one hand therefore, an archaeology that deals with crime is involved in processes of uncovering or disclosing truth, but on the

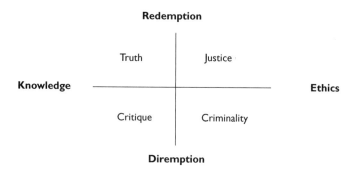

*Figure 10.1* Disappearance and disclosure.

other is also implicated in acts of voyeurism. This voyeurism stands precariously, equivocating between disgust and curiosity.

In Figure 10.1 two axes cross each other, that of knowledge/ethics and redemption/diremption. A redemptive knowledge is in search of truth, a diremptive one, critique, while a redemptive ethics is after justice, a diremptive one, criminality. Legendre's contribution on the missing bodies of a World War II bomber is most certainly an example of redemptive archaeology, a search for the truth and what happened. Cox and Fondebrider and Doretti in their contributions also discuss primarily the redemptive axis, but go further to deal with the problems of articulating between truth and justice and how they can conflict. In forensic work, justice and truth become twinned pursuits and archaeologists find themselves working side by side with policemen, courts, and war tribunals. But at the same time the issues of justice and humanitarian aid are also often in conflict. For example, when dealing with the atrocities associated with ethnic cleansing, the material evidence required by the International Criminal Tribunal for the former Yugoslavia is very different from the material evidence required by the families of victims and local communities (see the ICTY website: http://www.un.org/icty). Archaeology plays a new social role mediating these conflicts. This is a significant problem in the work of Clive Snow (Joyce and Stover: 1993) and other forensic anthropologists such as Fondebrider and Doretti (see the Argentine Forensics Team website: http://www.eaaf.org.ar) and Cox.

Our study of an abandoned flat looks more to diremptive issues, in particular the mediation between critique and crime – what is criminal, what is complicitous in light of Cox's observation regarding the criminality of silence? Not just murder but social injustice. When is it acceptable to invade someone's privacy, to do what we did, and how does this compare to investigating other 'scenes of crime', such as mass graves? Our work is clearly a critique but it also addresses the problematic ambiguities involved in a diremptive approach to the experiences of the recent past, which might be perceived as criminal or a legitimate social critique as it ambiguously straddles the areas of critique or crime along the lower axis of our figure. The common theme to all the chapters in this section are the critical and ambiguous tensions generated along this redemptive/diremptive axis – between voyeurism and silence or turning away and the axis of knowledge/ethics – the curiosity to know and see and the obscenity of knowing and seeing.

## References

Douglas, Mary (1984) *Purity and Danger: An Analysis of the Concepts of Pollution and Taboo*, London: ARK Paperbacks.

Hunter, J. (1994) 'Forensic Archaeology in Britain', *Antiquity* 68: 758–69.

Hunter, J. (1996) 'A Background to Forensic Archaeology'. In J. Hunter, C. Roberts, A. Martin (eds), *Studies in Crime: An Introduction to Forensic Archaeology*, London: Batsford.

Iscan, M.Y. (1988) 'Rise of Forensic Anthropology', *Yearbook of Physical Anthropology* 31: 203–330.

Joyce, Christopher and Eric Stover (eds) (1993) *Witness from the Grave*, London: Crafton.

Lacquer, Thomas W. (1999) 'The Dead Body and Human Rights', unpublished manuscript.

McLernon, Pat (1998) 'A Response to Adorno: the Necessity of Form in Visual Representations of the Holocaust'. Paper delivered at Heritage that Hurts, Third Annual Cambridge Heritage Seminar, Cambridge University.

Snow, C.P. (1982) 'Forensic Anthropology', *Annual Review of Anthropology* 11: 97–191.

# Chapter 11

# Archaeology of World War 2

## The Lancaster bomber of Fléville (Meurthe-et-Moselle, France)

*Jean-Pierre Legendre*

France represented one of the main theatres of operations during the conflicts in both World War 1 and World War 2. Even so, relevant archaeology in this country is still in an embryonic stage. The excavations carried out in Saint-Rémy-la-Calonne (Meuse), concerning a 1914 burial site that notably led to the exhumation of the body of the famous writer Alain-Fournier, is a particularly interesting example of the potential of this type of study (Adam, Boura, Duday 1992). Yet it remains an isolated case, just when the round-table discussion of Péronne in 1997 proved all the interest that historians of the period could find through the archaeological approach of vestiges of war (Schnapp 1999). In such a context, the recent investigations in Lorraine concerning the wreck of a World War 2 bomber is an interesting contribution to a field that is still, unfortunately, too often considered by French archaeologists as purely anecdotal.

On 23 July 1997, in the area of Fléville-devant-Nancy (Meurthe-et-Moselle), metal particles were discovered by workers while digging the foundations for a new access road to a domestic waste incinerator factory. Since it is quite frequent in Lorraine to find explosive devices, the civil engineering firm decided to stop work and notify the police as a precautionary safety measure. Bomb disposal experts arrived on the following day, but because of the particularly small particle size of the excavated metal it was impossible to identify anything precisely. Subsequently, a metal detector was used and the on-site prospecting revealed that many other metal particles were buried over a surface of some 70 to 80 square metres. The local inhabitants, who were present at the site that day, gave abundant but contradictory information. Some said that an American bomber had crashed there during World War 2. Other inhabitants were sure that it was, on the contrary, a German plane. According to some others, the debris could also be that of a V1 rocket! This information provoked the Town Council of Fléville to get in touch with the Aeronautical Museum of Nancy-Essey and the Regional Department of Archaeology of Lorraine. Consequently, a meeting of the relevant contributors was called who subsequently made a decision to excavate the site under the supervision of the author and of the Aeronautical Museum's curator, Mr Moreau. The mandate was to try to uncover certain elements that would make it possible to identify whatever was buried there. If it was discovered that it was in fact the remaining debris of a war plane, then the object of the operation should be to determine its type and nationality as well as the circumstances leading up to its final destination.

The metal scraps that were discovered were situated in a damp area located on very clayey ground. Just about the centre of the zone, there were traces of a dried-up pond. The surface of the pond presented organic black sediment emitting a strong smell of oil. The archaeological excavation revealed the presence of four engines, two on each side of the pond, which in fact proved to be a subcircular pit full of silt and metal debris. There was also a large amount of other metal debris scattered around the pit. The engines were completely disintegrated and were discovered at a depth of about 4 metres, together with distorted propeller blades. These engines were later identified as Rolls-Royce Merlin V12s. Near the engines were two large rubber tyres from the wheels that formed part of the undercarriage. The subcircular pit located in the centre of the area of the scattered scraps was 4 to 5 metres in diameter and about 2 metres deep. It was full of blackish silt in which there were many other pieces and fragments of the plane. It became manifestly clear that this pit was in fact the crater created by the fuselage when the plane crashed, and that all the excavated parts belonged to this structure and to the equipment and the armaments of the plane. But it was also clear that none of the parts found in the crater were *in situ*, because of the mixed arrangement in which they were found.

Notable items that were discovered included the following:

- Fragments (mostly of small dimensions) of the fuselage frame and cladding. On one of the pieces of cladding were two identification plates, each bearing a type number (683) and a factory number (78001), whereas on another piece of cladding, the letters RA (. . .) were painted in red on a black background. Those letters appeared to represent the beginning of a serial number.
- A complete rear tail wheel.
- Pieces of steel armour plating.
- Pieces of insulating material.
- Various electric cables.
- A dozen steel gas bottles, among which one bearing the word 'Nitrogen' written in black letters.
- Aluminium foil strip ('window') used to confuse height seeking radar equipment for the ground ack-ack gunners.
- Six 7.62 mm (.303 Imperial calibre) Browning machine-guns and about 200 cartridges.

In addition to the above-mentioned items there were also several items of personal equipment:

- Two parachutes. On one of those parachutes, two snap-hooks were still attached to the cords.

- A piece from an oxygen face mask.
- The sole from a flying boot.
- A pair of gloves used by air gunners.
- A fragment of a blue-grey material, presumably from a flying suit made of woollen cloth with its pocket still intact. In the pocket was a first-aid kit containing first-aid plaster dressings and two self-injectable morphine vials. Also a silk map of eastern France including part of Belgium and Germany.

From the evidence of the four Rolls-Royce Merlin engines and the Browning machine-guns it was almost certain that this was indeed an English heavy bomber of the World War 2 period. The discovery of the plates bearing the type number (683) and a factory number (78001) made it possible to be more precise about the model and the dating of the plane, 683 being the number relating to the Lancaster type. This plane was built during World War 2 by Avro. Existing in several versions, the Lancaster was a heavy bomber with a range of 2,700 km and a cruising speed of 338 km/h (max. speed: 462 km/h). The Lancaster was a relatively large aircraft of its time. Its length was 21 m with a wingspan of 31 m and its overall height was 6 m. The maximum bomb load was in the region of 10,000 kg (22,000 lbs) depending on flying time, where bomb load was dependent on the amount of fuel to be carried. The Lancaster was basically a night-flying bomber although it did operate frequently during daylight hours. Its armament consisted of eight Browning machine-guns, four in the rear turret, two in the mid-upper and forward turrets.

The Avro Lancaster aircraft represented the backbone of the Royal Air Force Bomber Command and completed more than 156,000 sorties and delivered well in excess of 600,000 tons of bombs and incendiaries on enemy targets (Gunston 1980). Among the Lancaster's greatest achievements were the destruction of the Ruhr valley hydroelectric dams by the famous 'Dambusters' of 617 Squadron, in May 1943. Although the factory number (78001) and the accompanying type number (683) provided an indication of the type and model of the aircraft, it was the piece of cladding bearing the letters RA (...) that led to the true identity of the aircraft and its origin.

The actual identification was performed by two historians who are specialists in the field of research concerned with the identification of British Royal Air Force airplanes that had crashed on French soil during World War 2. They were John Paul Basset and Patrick Baumann. They rapidly identified the letters RA (...) as being the prefix given to a series of 121 Mark I Lancasters built under licence by Metropolitan Vickers for the Royal Air Force between 1944 and April 1945 (Basset 1997). Among these planes, only one could correspond to the wreck that was discovered in Fléville. It was in fact RA 502. This aircraft proved to be from 550 Squadron based at North Killingholme in Lincolnshire, England and was reported by the RAF Records Office as having crashed 'near Flaville [sic] or Flavigny' during the night of 1 to 2 February 1945. The initial route of RA 502 proceeded north of Nancy, via Pont-à-Mousson and Château-Salins, presumably a considerable distance from the point of discovery. Yet this apparent anomaly is easy enough to explain if one considers the circumstances under which the plane crashed.

If one should match up the information given by the Records Office (and above all by the station narrative compiled at the Squadron base of the bomber after the crash) with the account of the survivors, the circumstances of the accident are quite clear. RA 502, identified under the call sign letter of Z for Zebra, took off on 1 February 1945 from 550 Squadron base at North Killingholme in Lincolnshire. Its mission was to bomb railway marshalling yards at Ludwigshafen, in the Ruhr valley. The bomb load of RA 502 comprised a 1,800 kg (4,000 lb) bomb called a 'Cookie', which gained its reputation from the surface devastation it caused in built-up areas. It was followed by another 1,620 small incendiary bombs of 1.8 kg making some 3,242 kg (7,332 lb) of incendiaries, the total bomb load being in the order of 5,042 kg (11,132 lb).

The Crew Members of RA 502 Z-Zebra were: F/O Aubrey Lohrey, pilot and captain; Sergeant Edward (Eddie) Westhorpe, navigator; Sergeant William (Bill) Anderson, bomb aimer; Sergeant Vincent (Vic) Cassapi, flight engineer; Sergeant Norman Tinsley, wireless operator; Sergeant Andrew (Andy) James, mid-upper gunner; Sergeant Allan Jarnell, rear gunner.

After dropping the bomb load, RA 502 turned for home without lights in order to escape German night fighters. The moonless night was particularly dark and this lack of visibility probably goes some way to explain the following events. Allan Jarnell, the rear gunner, reported seeing a twin-engine night fighter he had identified as a Messerschmitt Me 410 'Hornet'. Allan Jarnell did not take any action because he reported that this night fighter had not shown any inclination to attack. It was only a matter of minutes later, however, that Andrew James reported another aircraft crossing RA 502's beam from directly below and at that same instant the collision occurred. Retrospectively the cause of the collision was assumed that another Lancaster bomber on the same flight path had seen this marauding night fighter and was in the act of taking evasive action but in doing so, failed to observe the plane flying directly above. It was later established that this was indeed Lancaster NG202 from 170 Squadron of RAF, also returning from the same target at Ludwigshafen. Tragically, the rear gunner, Sergeant Virgil Linquist of NG 202, was killed instantaneously when the propellers of RA 502 sliced through the tail section. Even though the vertical fins were seriously damaged the pilot of NG 202 succeeded in bringing his plane back to England. RA 502 was, however, more seriously damaged with both the engines on the starboard side shut down and one or more of the engines on the port side possibly malfunctioning. Consequently since it was not possible for the pilot to maintain straight and level flight without the imminent danger of losing control completely, he reluctantly gave the order to abandon the aircraft.

On receiving the order to abandon the aircraft the rear gunner (Allan Jarnell) reported he could not turn his turret in order to bail out. In retrospect this dilemma should not have been unexpected because the shutting down of both starboard engines could possibly result in hydraulic pump failure of the system that drives that gun turret. Fortunately, Bill Anderson who was at that time standing by near the navigator's position immediately volunteered to assist by manually winding the turret around to a position where Allan Jarnell could be extricated from it, then both he and Bill Anderson could escape via the rear exit door.

Having managed to reach the rear exit door, where the wireless operator and the mid-upper gunner were standing by, they immediately abandoned the aircraft and had no cause to suspect that both Andrew James and Norman Tinsley would not follow directly afterwards. The flight engineer and the navigator escaped via the forward emergency exit, followed soon after by the pilot. The aircraft was then at a height of only 1,500 metres. After landing, the airmen were ultimately given all assistance by American Forces who were at that time stationed near Nancy. After a brief interval of time under the care of these American Forces, the crew were repatriated via Paris by train and then on 7 February 1945 by air to Croydon in the UK.

The news that both Sergeants Tinsley and James were reported missing did not cause too much consternation in the first instance. This was because no one had any cause to suspect they had not bailed out with the remainder of the crew. And it was not until some days later that it became a real possibility they had indeed been killed. Their bodies were never found and consequently they were officially reported missing, with a strong probability that they had been killed during the crash. Their names are now inscribed on the memorial of reported missing airmen of the RAF of Runnymede, near London. The discovery and subsequent excavation of the wreck made it possible to provide new elements concerning the aircraft and the death of the two aircrew members. The presence of the two parachutes and the evidence of particles of clothing give a reliable indication that they did not leave the aircraft immediately following the bomb aimer and the rear gunner. One can only assume that if they had (for whatever reason) delayed their exit until after the pilot had left, then the plane would have almost certainly dived out of control, thus making any attempt to bail out then virtually impossible.

From the position of the engines and the crater formed by the fuselage, the trajectory of the plane on impact clearly shows that the aircraft plunged almost vertically into the ground. It would appear therefore, that after the aircraft was abandoned it nose-dived and crashed to earth with extreme violence. This violent impact explains why the engines were buried at a depth of some four metres, although it should be noted that the soil in that area was clayey and compact.

With regard to the reported missing airmen, the presence of the two parachutes, the items of a piece of flying suit and the sole of a flying boot leads us to consider the fact that they were still in the aircraft when it crashed. This fact is strengthened by the presence of snap-hooks still attached to one of the parachutes. Those snap-hooks are parts of the parachute harness that was worn at

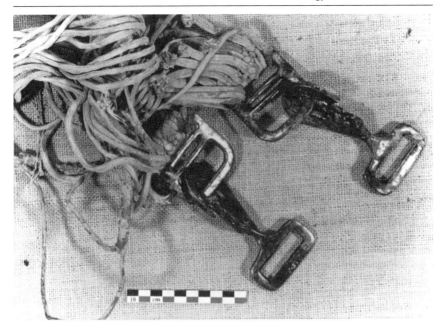

*Figure 11.1*  Detail of one of the parachutes, with two snap-hooks still attached to the cords. The presence of those snap-hooks clearly shows that the airman had hooked his parachute, but that he finally did not use it. (Photograph by Véronique Brunet.)

all times during flight by the airmen of RAF bombers (Figure 11.1). It should be noted, with the exception of the pilot and rear gunner, the remainder of the crew did not wear parachutes during the flight. Their parachutes were stored at convenient locations dispersed along the fuselage. Therefore, the presence of the snap-hooks still attached to the parachute cords clearly shows that the airman had hooked his parachute and was ready to use it, but that he finally could not.

During the intensive search carried out at the crash site, no sign of human remains among the debris of the aircraft was uncovered. A local inhabitant of Fléville did offer an account in which he talked of the discovery at the time of the crash, of a flying boot still containing human shreds. These meagre remains would have been buried somewhere in the graveyard of the village, but unfortunately, the exact place could not be precisely located. Except for this story, the disappearance of the bodies could possibly be explained by the fact that most of the debris belonging to the fuselage found in the crater represented only the neglected pieces left there after the wreck had been salvaged by scrap merchants, a plausible reason why nothing was found *in situ* in the crater. The excavated items, such as the armour-plate, the oxygen bottles and other material had no or little market value, whereas the aluminium, most needed at that time, was obviously highly salvageable. Consequently, even though it represents the most commonly used material of the whole structure of an aircraft, there were only small fragments of this metal remaining on the site. This salvage operation was but a supposition during the excavations; it was however confirmed later by the accounts of the inhabitants present at the time. These inhabitants indicated that scrap merchants had very quickly intervened and dismantled the aircraft before the owners of the fields could dispose of the remainder. With regard to the bodies of Sergeant James and Sergeant Tinsley, if they really were among the debris of the aircraft, it is not possible to imagine how the scrap merchants did not find them. Yet there is no mention of bodies (identified or not) in the local French records. If the first 'metal hunters' who arrived discovered the bodies soon after the crash, they may have buried them near the wreck and they are still lying there today. The reason for this behaviour remains unclear, but it may be linked to the fact that the scrap merchants were afraid of being caught by the local police while in the act of plundering the wreck and the presence of two bodies would have worsened their case.

The French Air Force Historical Department (Service Historique de l'Armée de l'Air) put forward the suggestion that the two bodies could still be on the crash site, but in a part of the aircraft that had not been excavated, and consequently they still lay there undiscovered (Rohrbacher 1997). Though this hypothesis is tempting, we can set it aside for at least four reasons:

1    The main argument backing up this theory lies in the fact that only the rear part of the aircraft would have been found. Yet, the discovery of various parts of the plane, from the motors to the rear wheel, shows that most of it has been found. Only the front part of the cockpit is missing, but this would have been pulverised by the enormous impact forces of the crash. Indeed the aircraft almost certainly plunged vertically into the ground and therefore the cockpit suffered the greater part of these impact forces.
2    The prospecting of the area of the crash with a metal detector did not reveal the presence of another metal structure.
3    It is highly unlikely that the plane may have created two craters when it crashed. This could have been the case if the plane had broken into two parts during the collision, but it is clear it did not happen that way and furthermore, after exhaustive investigations only one crater was found.
4    Even if the plane had broken into two parts when it hit the ground, it is hard to imagine that Sergeant James and Sergeant Tinsley could have been in one part of the aircraft and their parachutes and fragments of their uniform in another. Moreover, if there had been another section of the fuselage near the first one, the scrap merchants would have seen it and they may well have found the bodies.

Therefore, the question remains: why did not Andrew James and Norman Tinsley abandon the aircraft immediately after their comrades? All the accounts tally and indicate that they were perfectly able to do so, they were certainly not wounded. Andrew James and Norman Tinsley were stationed in the aircraft at positions closest to the emergency exit. They opened the rear emergency door and should have bailed out before Bill Anderson and Allan Jarnell. Bill Anderson reported that both the missing airmen stood next to him when he bailed out, and that nothing could cause him to think that they would not follow immediately afterwards. A possible clue could be construed from the station narrative which states that there was a short time in the event that the pilot would not be able to remain in intercommunication with anyone during the actual time he was about to make preparations for his own escape. However, right up to that moment he was continuing his orders to abandon the aircraft in order to ensure everyone had sufficient time to evacuate. In all probability, neither Andrew James nor Norman Tinsley would have plugged into an intercom socket while standing by the open escape exit door. Why should they? Consequently, after receiving no further response from his crew, the pilot may have abandoned the aircraft while they were still inside. Any neglect of responsibility by Aubrey Lohrey is of course not in question, for he abandoned the aircraft because there was nothing else to do, and only after making sure everybody had presumably bailed out. He had indeed called his comrades continuously and having received no answer, he took the only course of action open to him.

One might argue they may have misunderstood the order to bail out, if it had not been for the fact that both Bill Anderson and Allan Jarnell had bailed before their eyes. One might argue that they deliberately delayed their exit a matter of moments too long. One might argue also that some fear or dread of the predicament may have overcome them and they froze rigidly and so, were unable to take the necessary action that could have saved their lives. It should be noted that this was the first time any of the crew had bailed out. Vic Cassapi told us that the training concerning the use of parachutes had been limited to theory with some simple practice on landings (this had taken place using a special drill apparatus situated in a hangar). In any case, a change of mind would be both futile and fatal once the aircraft had spun out of control.

Once the pilot had left, the crippled aircraft probably plunged rapidly (see above archaeological observations concerning the impact) and consequently, it was much too late to try to bail out. Though totally innocent of the death of these two young men, Aubrey Lohrey may possibly have developed a feeling of guilt on that subject. Once back on the Squadron, he became more and more uncommunicative and appeared to retreat inwardly within himself (Cassapi 1999a). The tragedy certainly undermined his confidence as a pilot and captain. He subsequently carried out only one more mission with the remainder of his crew whereupon he was called before a medical board of health and thereafter he received a justifiable honourable discharge and was later repatriated to New Zealand. Aubrey Lohrey is undoubtedly one of the heroes of this event; his presence of mind, skill and leadership enabled four of his crew to survive the tragedy. Vic Cassapi, who actually bailed out with his intercom still plugged in, can testify to the fact that he had managed to gain precious altitude immediately after the crash, that he had managed to maintain control of his aircraft for as long as he did, and that he continuously called out to the crew over the intercom 'Bail out! Everyone out! Bail out!'

Another deed of heroism was performed by the bomb aimer, Bill Anderson, who, on his own initiative, went to the assistance of the rear gunner Allan Jarnell who was trapped in his turret and unable to move in any direction. Without thought of the peril he was placing himself in, he unselfishly set about the task to extricate Allan from his turret. Without his providential intervention which was all the more courageous when considering the already hopeless situation RA 502 was in, Allan Jarnell would have been trapped in the aircraft and with certainty, he would have perished in the crash also.

Even if, as we see, the confrontation of historical and archaeological sources leads to a quite precise reconstruction of the events, it is however interesting to notice that some questions still remain unanswered:

- How can the crash of a relatively large four-engine bomber leave so few traces in the French records? Although the crash occurred in a densely populated area, near the town of Nancy, there is no trace of this event to be found in the local police records (Rohrbacher 1997) or in the local newspaper *L'est républicain*.
- Why did the scrap merchants who dismantled the wreck leave among the scrap two parachutes in white silk, even though their value was considerable at a time when this kind of material was much sought after?
- What happened to the bodies of Sergeant James and Sergeant Tinsley and where are they buried?

These questions point at the limits of the archaeological and historical approach even when, as is the case here, we have in addition records of the time and the accounts of the survivors at our disposal. Moreover, Vic Cassapi explained in a very interesting document that the station narrative kept in the army records in Britain presented certain inconsistencies, even though it had been written on the spot (Cassapi 1999b). For example, this report came to the conclusion that the starboard main spar was damaged during the collision with Lancaster NG 202, although there is no evidence of this theory. The report stated also that the starboard inner engine could not be feathered; in fact, this was the first of the starboard engines to be feathered, followed shortly afterwards by the starboard outer engine. Last but not least, the report mentioned a fire in one of the engines, and there was no such fire.

The epilogue to these events took place in Fléville-Devant-Nancy on 23 October 1998, when three survivors (Bill Anderson, Vic Cassapi and Allan Jarnell) came back 53 years after the crash to unveil a commemorative monument erected at the very place where the bomber crashed. This monument consists of a granite facier which is adorned with a bent propeller blade recovered from the wreck in order to symbolise the accident (Figure 11. 2).

This ceremony undoubtedly constituted for us one of the key moments of the operation, since it was the occasion to meet the survivors. It is quite an uncommon

*Figure 11.2* Fléville-Devant-Nancy, 23 October 1998. Three survivors (from left to right: Vic Cassapi, Bill Anderson and Allan Jarnell) are examining the commemorative monument erected at the very place where the bomber crashed. (Photograph by Jean-Pierre Legendre.)

experience for an archaeologist who, in theory, has not the opportunity to communicate with the people who once used the artefacts he discovers. It is easy to guess the emotion prevailing over the ceremony, all the more as the veterans had not returned since the accident. Little by little, the human aspect of these events became more palpable, which again is not frequent if we consider the impersonal nature of most archaeological studies. After the conversations we had then and the exchange of letters that came next, the past has actually re-emerged more intensely for us than if it had only been considered through some objects and reports. That is not only due to the fact that an event is obviously more striking when it is directly told by the person who lived it, but also because you can find in such an account what you generally lack in an archaeological study. The two departed airmen, recalled to us by their comrade Vic Cassapi, are no longer only names in a report or on a monument, they now have a personality. For example, Andrew James has been described as 'a happy-go-lucky geordie with always something to say' whereas Norman Tinsley was a quiet serious man but with an uncontrollable passion for the song 'Beautiful Dreamer'. He would sing, hum or whistle this tune incessantly, and his comrades had to listen to his sultry tones through the intercom on every mission! (See Figure 11.3.)

Moreover, our knowledge concerning these tragic events makes it totally impossible for the archaeologist to consider, with the detachment usually linked

*Figure 11.3* The crew members of RA 502 Z-Zebra, from left to right: F/O Aubrey
          Lohrey (pilot and captain), Sergeant Edward 'Eddie' Westhorpe (navigator),
          Sergeant William 'Bill' Anderson (bomb aimer), Sergeant Vincent 'Vic'
          Cassapi (flight engineer), Sergeant Norman Tinsley (wireless operator),
          Sergeant Andrew 'Andy' James (mid-upper gunner), Sergeant Allan Jarnell
          (rear gunner). (Photograph: Collection of Vic Cassapi.)

to scientific studies, the parachutes that the two airmen did not have time to use
or the shred of flying suit in the pocket of which there still was, pathetically
enough, a small first-aid kit. The power of evocation and the emotional
dimension contained in these objects are considerable, as is the case for the
excavated propeller blade with which the monument is adorned. Furthermore,
this monument seems to us much more evocative of the events than most war
memorials. We can reproach some memorials with being too smooth or sweet.
We have the feeling that this bent piece of metal, as well as all the debris we
found on the crash site, conveys much better than most memorials the sacrifice
and death of these two young people who, like so many of their comrades of the
RAF, gave their lives for the freedom of Europe.

## Acknowledgements

Very special thanks should go to Vic Cassapi, whose help was invaluable to us.
We also would like to thank Bill Anderson and Allan Jarnell for the information
they provided.

# References

Adam, F., Boura, F. and Duday H. (1992) 'La fouille de Saint-Rémy-La-Calonne: une opération d'archéologie funéraire expérimentale, ou l'anthropologie de terrain en quête de ses références', *Les Nouvelles de l'Archéologie*, 48–9, 1992: 59–61.

Basset, J. P. (1997) *Identification d'un avion tombé à Fléville-devant-Nancy (Meurthe-et-Moselle)*, unpublished document.

Cassapi, V. (1999a) *Fléville-Devant-Nancy – 23 October 1998 – the pilgrimage*, unpublished document.

Cassapi, V. (1999b) *A report on the air collision of Z-Zebra*, unpublished document.

Gunston, B. (1980) *An illustrated guide to bombers of World War II*, London: Salamander.

Rohrbacher, G. D. (1997) *Découverte et identification d'un avion tombé à Fléville-devant-Nancy*, Vincennes: Service Historique de l'Armée de l'Air.

Schnapp, A. (1999) 'Une archéologie de la Grande Guerre est-elle possible?', *14–18 aujourd'hui*, 2, 1999: 19–27.

Chapter 12

# Science and human rights*

## Truth, justice, reparation and reconciliation, a long way in Third World countries

*Mercedes Doretti and Luis Fondebrider*

## Introduction

From the 1960s onwards, a number of different revolutionary movements developed in the so called Third World. In response, many governments embarked on a systematic repression of the groups involved. But to a large extent, civilians not involved in any of the parties in conflict became the main victims. So it was that a new era of violence began, in which the kidnapping, torture and assassination as well as the disappearance of thousands of people became a political strategy for a number of governments. In the countries that suffered such repression, the consequences have been profound and long term, not only within those families directly affected, but throughout society.

The precise patterns of repression varied from one region to another. They ranged from summary assassinations to the more refined system of illegal detention centres (a sort of updating of the concentration camps established during the Second World War).

With these various forms of repression, a new language emerged as the international media searched for ways to describe the methods used. There were 'death squads' in Brazil, Peru and Central America, 'scorched land policies' in El Salvador and Guatemala, 'famine as a weapon of war' in Mengistu's Ethiopia, and 'forced disappearance of persons' in Central and South America, including Argentina.

In Latin America, atrocities of this type were mainly perpetrated by military and dictatorship regimes, in the regions and against the sectors of society where guerrillas were more active. In Central America, the poorest population in the countryside, mostly indigenous peoples and the peasantry were the most affected. However, in Argentina, Chile and Brazil, repression was more directed at the urban working and middle classes.

By the mid 1980s, many of the countries that had suffered severe violations of human rights began to develop democratic processes. This in turn brought about a need to review the past, to determine the truth about what had happened, to try those responsible for the acts of violence, and to find a way of reconciling society with its recent history. In particular, the search, recovery and analysis of

* This chapter is dedicated to Dr Clyde C. Snow, PhD.

the remains of the disappeared and massacred people became a major humanitarian and legal issue. Reviews of the past were carried out in a number of different ways, predominantly through the creation of special commissions of inquiry, known as Truth Commissions[1] (government-run in the cases of Argentina, Philippines, Chile, Haiti, and South Africa; UN-run in the cases of El Salvador and Guatemala) and through the trials by national courts (in Argentina, Ethiopia and Bolivia) or international courts (for the former-Yugoslavia and Rwanda). Paradoxically, just as these mechanisms were being established, the same governments often passed laws preventing or limiting the indictment of those responsible for past violations of human rights and in more than one case, general amnesties were declared for such offenses.

Nevertheless, since the 1980s, the scientific documentation of these human rights violations, mostly by using forensic archaeology and anthropology, has become a valuable instrument for the analysis and understanding of the recent past in nations that have undergone periods of political violence.

## The Argentine case

One of the first countries to face this problem was Argentina. It was there that forensic anthropology was first used directly in the legal investigations of massive human rights violations. Between 1976 and 1983, the military government caused the 'disappearance' of approximately 9,000 individuals. Typically 'disappearance' occurred with the kidnapping of a victim by security forces, followed by torture in a clandestine detention centre and finally assassination. The victims were then buried, unidentified, in cemeteries, or dropped from airplanes into the sea.[2] The government denied the existence of disappeared people and the families were never informed about their fate.

With the restoration of democracy in 1983, the relatives of thousands of disappeared people demanded to be told what had happened to their loved ones, and this demand formed an integral part of the restoration of the democracy. In response, the State attempted to provide answers in a variety of ways – through the creation of a truth commission,[3] known as the CONADEP, and by putting those mainly responsible for 'disappearances' on trial. But from the outset, it became clear that truth, justice and reparations were hard to achieve within a weak democracy. Despite the fact that leading 'junta' members were condemned to life in prison and other sentences, the trials could not pursue those further down the line of command. After several military uprisings, the government passed laws limiting and finally ending further trials on human rights violations

1 P. Hayner, 'Fifteen Truth Commissions – 1974 to 1994: a Comparative Study', *Human Rights Quarterly*, The Johns Hopkins University Press, 1994, vol. 16, pp. 597–655.
2 Although there is strong evidence revealing that the latter procedure was also applied to living persons.
3 Specifically, in Argentina, the CONADEP (Comisión Nacional sobre la Desaparición de Personas).

from the previous military regime. In 1989, another democratic government, gave a final presidential pardon releasing from prison those previously condemned.

## The use of science

It was within this context, that forensic archaeology and anthropology began its collaboration in the pursuit of justice in Argentina. It was a collaboration that centred around the search for and identification of the bodies of the missing, who in many cases lay buried anonymously in cemeteries.

At the beginning of democracy, judicial authorities searching the remains of disappeared people employed existing forensic services. Unfortunately, in practice, this meant that neither archaeologists nor anthropologists[4] were involved in exhumations, which were instead carried out by gravediggers and firemen with no special training. Similarly, the studies of the human remains were carried out by forensic scientists lacking experience in the analysis of skeletons. As a result, remains were destroyed, evidence lost and only a very small number of victims were identified.

It became clear that greater rigor was required and working methods would have to change. The CONADEP and the GrandMothers of Plaza de Mayo, a local human rights organisation, requested help from the Science and Human Rights program of the American Association for the Advancement of Sciences – based in Washington DC – which, in 1984, sent a group of seven forensic scientists to Argentina. Among them was Dr Clyde Snow, an eminent forensic anthropologist who in the 1970s began to employ archaeologists in the recovery of skeletal remains.

## Forensic anthropology and human rights investigations

Forensic anthropology is the application of the physical anthropologist's knowledge of human variability to medico-legal problems.[5]

The United States pioneered this collaboration between physical anthropologists, archaeologists and law enforcement agencies. In 1939, US physical anthropologist W. Krogman published the 'Guide for the Identification of Skeletal Remains' in the Federal Bureau of Investigation bulletin. Shortly after the Second World War, forensic anthropology techniques were used on a mass scale to identify remains of soldiers killed in action. Later, they were used to single out American soldiers killed in the Korean and Vietnam wars. However, there were very few precedents for these techniques for systematic investigations

4  It must be said that archaeologists and anthropologists, in most cases, while knowing it was an exceptional situation, did not offer their help. Consequently, in Argentina as in many other countries, poor results were obtained at first.

5  C.C. Snow, 'Forensic Anthropology', *Annual Reviews Anthropology*, 1992, vol. 11, pp. 97–131.

of contemporary cases of massive human rights violations. In this sense, Dr Snow's work in Argentina was truly pioneering.

When he first arrived in 1984, Dr Snow called for a halt to all non-scientific exhumations and requested archaeologists from the Argentinian Anthropological Association.[6] But the Argentine archaeological community was not prepared for the challenge of this kind of work. With few exceptions, archaeologists did not participate in this effort, despite the fact that the country has a number of internationally known archaeologists. Several reasons could be raised to explain this, such as fear, being emotionally too close to the people killed, and non-scientific interest. But we have to accept that the digging up of graves containing the remains of people killed by the premeditated actions of the State raised numerous reservations, even more so when such violence had been carried out by the same State to which the archaeologists belonged.

The few, mostly student, Argentine anthropologists and archaeologists who started to take part in these investigations under the guidance of Dr Snow found themselves operating in a totally new world. This involved working alongside judges, policemen, gravediggers and, most importantly, the relatives of the victims.

First, archaeologists had to persuade various members of the judicial system – from judges to forensic scientists and policemen that the same scientists they sometimes saw on television excavating archaeological sites thousands of years old, could also play a role in these investigations. Secondly, by placing their trust in the scientists, the relatives of the victims introduced them to the daily reality and emotional trauma of those families whose loved ones have been forcibly 'disappeared'. Finally, the very objects of study assumed a new dimension, they ceased to be skeletons with cranial deformations related to cultural practices, or wounds produced by arrowheads. Instead, they were individuals with the same habits and customs as those of the archaeologists, often of the same or similar age, whose bodies frequently showed gunshot wounds to the head. Moreover, they were people the scientists might have known, directly or indirectly, by sharing the same social group, education and even political ideology.

Another significant factor for archaeologists beginning such work was that in most cases, those people indicted for perpetrating the crimes under investigation were still at liberty. This made the context of their work even more complex.

Forensic anthropologists worked together with archaeologists to carry out the exhumation of human remains and associated evidence. Their excavation techniques basically coincide with those of traditional archaeology, but are aimed instead at the recent past in a legal context. In some countries this application is considered a sub-discipline called Forensic Archaeology. It is actually an interdisciplinary approach as pathologists, radiologists, odontologists and geneticists are often part of these investigations.

As a result of these circumstances, first in Argentina and later in other Latin American countries, forensic anthropology has developed a new profile through

6  Colegio de Graduados de Antropologica.

its application to a different field of inquiry to that which it had been applied before. Currently, forensic anthropology is used in human rights investigations in almost all Latin American countries as well in Eastern Europe and some Asian and African countries.

## The different worlds of forensic anthropology

In the United States and Western Europe, where recent history has not been characterised by widespread political violence, the practice of forensic anthropology and archaeology is quite different. Archaeologists or anthropologists with forensic skills, usually work within the academic world and are occasionally asked by law enforcement agencies to carry out the search and recovery of a body. Afterwards, they analyse the remains and complete a report before returning to their usual activities. They do not receive many cases in a year and rarely – if ever – find a common grave containing several bodies. Also, their work is related to ordinary criminal cases resulting from the action of one or more individuals without political motivation.

By contrast, in the investigation of human rights abuses, forensic anthropologists act as independent expert witnesses for the judiciary. Often they carry out the technical details of the job and participate in other aspects of the case. This entails interviewing relatives of the victims and possible witnesses, studying judicial, police and military files, cemetery and hospital records, and ultimately reaching a hypothesis on the probable location of the person sought. In this context, the relationship with the victim's relatives becomes close by virtue of its day-to-day nature, and more important because it is based on mutual trust.

The role that the scientists assume in investigations of this kind results in part from a reversal of the usual relationship between victims' families and the State authorities on whom they would rely to conduct an investigation in normal circumstances. The relatives in question, in general, totally distrust State institutions, precisely because in most cases it was the State, albeit in a previous incarnation, that was responsible for the disappearance of their loved ones. Instead they rely on the support of human rights organisations and the work of independent scientists, which they hope will help them recover the remains of their loved ones.

## Forced disappearance and relatives of victims

In the course of sixteen years of work in over twenty countries[7] which have experienced periods of political violence, we have noticed that the impact of a

---

7  The EAAF has worked in the following countries: Bolivia, Brazil, Chile, Colombia, Peru, Uruguay, Haiti, El Salvador, Guatemala, Honduras, Panama, Croatia, Bosnia, Kosovo, Iraqi Kurdistan, Romania, East Timor, South Africa, Ethiopia, The Democratic Republic of Congo, Philippines and French Polynesia.

disappearance on a family shares similarities regardless of cultural, ideological or religious differences. The relatives of a detained disappeared first of all suffers the sudden kidnapping of a child, sibling or spouse, whom they never see alive again. They have no news of the victim and are left in total ignorance of the fate of their loved ones, not knowing if they are dead or alive, simply because the authorities responsible for the disappearance refuse to give them an answer. Moreover, the justice system does not investigate their cases and so for years they live in a state of limbo. Even in countries where the relatives know that most likely their loved ones have been assassinated, they still cling to the hope they may return alive. So long as there are no corpses, or concrete information about their death, there can be no funeral rites and no final answers. Thus, affliction, fear and deep fractures in family life are found in almost every case, and with it a desperate need to recover remains so that loved-ones may be properly buried and thereby close, if only partially, the circle of uncertainty.

During excavations, relatives often ask to be present throughout the entire process, and in some places such as Iraqi Kurdistan and Ethiopia – have even worked together with us, because they say that it helps fulfil their need to do something more for their loved ones. Archaeologists are mindful of the strict issues raised by their work, but they are also functioning within a much broader – if we may say – human landscape, because in many cases they become emotionally involved with the relatives and their stories. An environment of this kind has other side effects. Often, the forensic work becomes more transparent and understandable for the relatives of the victims when they are able to observe and ask questions of the forensic team.

## Conclusions

There is a sharp incongruence between the needs of truth and justice – as sought by victims' relatives and the more progressive sectors of society – and the imperatives of post-dictatorship governments. In most of the countries where we work, human rights abuses have affected large sections of society. To deal with these massive violations, Truth Commissions, and/or tribunals have been established by new governments to investigate them. Official investigations, however, are often closed once these commissions or tribunals finish their work. In most cases, these institutions exist for a very short period – one or two years – to investigate an enormous number of human rights violations. They are understaffed and underfunded and in many cases, must limit their investigation to a reduced yet representative number of cases. Also, these commissions exist within conditions strongly affected by the political pressures of weak transitional democracies. In some countries, investigations have led to the conviction of those responsible; in others, despite investigations and prosecutions, various amnesty laws have allowed the responsible parties to avoid conviction. Reconciliation without justice is being sought in many cases – an impossible alchemy in which the shadows of the past will stay, unresolved, in the background. Moreover, many of the families of the victims are left with their cases unresolved.

We believe that investigations need to be carried on despite amnesty laws and beyond the mandates of *ad hoc* commissions and tribunals. If these investigations are to have a preventive effect or improve our societies in any way, it is by being able to find and analyse the different parts of truth of past atrocities, and thus, increase the level of knowledge and reflection on our present and future circumstances.

Forensic anthropologists, in this respect, in countries such as Argentina, Guatemala, Chile and elsewhere are allowed to continue working despite amnesty laws or/and after the mandate of special commissions of inquiry. The evidence collected in forensic investigations sometimes represents the possibility of moving from a matter of opinion to a matter of fact. It may not have the same effect as when these investigations are framed within the context of a truth commission or a tribunal, but on a smaller scale, it shares some of their positive historical and ethical goals: to help the families of victims and to help society set the record straight.

## Acknowledgement

We would like to express our gratitude to Jorge Fondebrider, Paulette Farsides and Gerardo Gambolini for their help with the text and Vivian Scheinsohn for her initial call.

## Bibliography

Alex Boraine, Janet Levy and Ronel Scheffer (eds) (1994) *Dealing With the Past, Truth and Reconciliation in South Africa*, Cape Town: IDASA.

W. M. Krogman and Mehmet Yasar Iscan (1986) *The Human Skeleton in Forensic Medicine*, 2nd edition, Illinois: Charles C Thomas.

# Chapter 13

# Forensic archaeology in the UK

## Questions of socio-intellectual context and socio-political responsibility

*Margaret Cox*

## Introduction

In 1996, when discussing forensic archaeology, Charles Thomas questioned whether some archaeologists were perhaps guilty of selling themselves short, and whether we might apply our skills in outer space! He considered that the ability of many to 'hypothesise inferences from visible, tangible evidence' (Thomas 1996: 14) was a skill that should be confidently deployed, not only in archaeology but in any context, and that most of our techniques, both field and scientific, have much wider potential than we realise. He effectively reminded archaeologists that our approaches and expertise have relevance outside of traditional archaeological frameworks, and questioned the frequently encountered impression of a precious and exclusive discipline, one with little social relevance and one not fit to face up to the challenges of 'final frontiers' (ibid. 14).

While perhaps not living up to Thomas's expectations, there is little doubt that forensic archaeologists are working, if not at final frontiers, at least in a new arena: an arena providing new challenges and also research opportunities which may ultimately feed back into and inform archaeological sciences (Cox and Bell 1999), geophysical techniques and recording systems. The past decade has seen the rapid development of forensic archaeology within the United Kingdom (UK). A type of forensic archaeology that has not solely been practised within the UK but also in a wider geographical context is the investigation of violations to human rights, for example in the location and excavation of mass graves in the former Yugoslavia and in Guatemala. The development and application of archaeological principles and methods to the investigation of serious crime have followed a different course in the United States (US) where it emerged earlier this century as a sub-discipline of forensic anthropology. In the US, forensic archaeology is limited in its application to providing a secure contextual framework for recovered human remains. In the UK it has a much wider application including the search and location of buried remains, their recovery, recording, facilitating other forensic sciences, and following the Criminal Procedures and Investigations Act (1996), the passive conservation and storage of a wide range of exhibits. There is a general lack of appreciation of the significance and value of forensic archaeology within some elements of the discipline (Faulkner 1997), and it is not recognised as a sub-discipline of archaeology in the Research Assessment Exercise (both 1996 and 2001). However, there can be little doubt that the subject has been established and will continue to develop.

It is not the purpose of this chapter to further describe the role, parameters and benefits of the forensic archaeologist working within the British criminal justice system or in the investigation of human rights violations. Such matters are discussed fully elsewhere (Hunter *et al.* 1996 and Hunter 1999). Instead, my purpose is to examine and question the socially constructed and professional context of the development of the subject of forensic archaeology in the UK. While raising more questions than I will attempt to answer, I am also seeking to begin the debate about the extent of the responsibilities of the forensic archaeologists.

Aside from benefits to the Courts, why are an increasing number of archaeologists (and others) keen to utilise archaeological principles and expertise in the resolution of serious crime? Why here? Why now? The obvious, but overly simplistic, response is that by deploying the principles and techniques with which we are familiar, we are responding to a perceived need within the judicial system for the enhancement of criminal investigative procedures. That is undisputed. But is it the whole, or even part of the explanation? Given the apparent lack of support for the subject within the discipline of archaeology, archaeologists who apply themselves to forensic contexts are risking alienation within their peer group. This is in two respects. Firstly they undertake work that is perceived as irrelevant to archaeology. Specifically, there is no output in terms of contributing to the development of a public or shared past or history. Forensic archaeology provides output only in terms of a private or restricted history and this must be set against the increased prevalence of relativist views of the past. Secondly, many observers consider that forensic archaeologists are undertaking work that can be considered to be 'macabre' in character. In light of these factors, I am suggesting that the apparent readiness of increasing numbers of archaeologists to take this risk are driven by motives other than the obvious.

This chapter will examine three areas of possible relevance. All reflect that we are products of, and representative of, our place and time. We share concerns and preconceptions common to the British populace as we enter the new millennium. The first area reflects our relationship with, and responses to an increasing awareness of criminal and threatening aspects of society. This is inextricably entwined with the second area, the role of media reporting and popular culture in biasing and defining perceptions of reality (McNeely 1995). The third is that for some practitioners, archaeology not only lacks any immediate relevance to 'life' in its broadest sense, but also to the furtherance of archaeology as a discipline as it has traditionally been defined. That is not to say that other issues do not play a role but they will not provide a focus for discussion here.

## *Is forensic archaeology a craze?*

There are several models that could be applied to the rise and development of a new subject area, but I will focus here on the craze model. That forensic archaeology is attracting interest both in the UK and elsewhere is beyond question. More and more archaeologists are calling themselves forensic archaeologists, possibly attracted by an image that engenders a *frisson* of immediacy and risk to the uninitiated. However, few have any real understanding of the full implications of working within the criminal justice system (Cox 1999), neither is it always possible to predict the outcome and consequences of a course of action at the outset. This interest is matched by a burgeoning number of programmes of study at different levels within UK universities, one of which is regularly enrolling over twenty masters students each year, students drawn from almost every continent.

When a new concept becomes important in the life of a community, in this case that of both archaeologists and law enforcers, it can be called a craze. Some crazes are magnifications or extensions of the normal life of a community and therefore endemic; all reflect opportunities. Arguably, forensic archaeology is an extension of both archaeology and law enforcement. Crazes progress through such phases as latency, expansion, saturation and resolution (Penrose 1952) as well as redundancy, replacement or substitution. If forensic archaeology is a craze, it can be currently described as being in the expansion phase. A common psychological response to being involved in the development of a new concept or craze is a feeling of power (ibid.) and control. In respect of a craze that plays a significant role in criminal investigation, it is likely that such involvement is accompanied by a sense of lessened impotence when dealing with the consequences of irrational acts and a significant measure of control and comfort.

## The archaeologist in a criminalistic society

Examination of crime statistics demonstrates that the incidence of reported crime is increasing in Western society. This is particularly the case for the crime that most often engages the forensic archaeologist: murder (an emotive term used to describe homicide and illegal killing) and the associated concealment of evidence. The term 'murder', mixes contradictory impulses in most people. It conflates evil and innocence, frenzy and restraint, passion and deliberation (Taylor 1998); it also reinforces ideas about civil society where reason and law underline its essential stability.

Fortunately, most individuals and most archaeologists never have to confront the reality or consequences of such serious crime at close quarters. Nor do they have any 'real' or first-hand appreciation of the processes of criminal investigation and the trial of alleged perpetrators in the courts. Consequently, our perception of homicide is inevitably influenced, biased and arguably defined, to greater or lesser degrees, by media reporting of cases and their depiction in popular culture. These two entities merit separate consideration in this context.

### Forensic journalism, homicide and the body

It is recognised that many members of the media audience exercise selectivity in their reading and viewing, that they have their own interpretative creativity, and fashion definitions of reality based on their own perspectives and experiences (Sanders and Lyon 1995). That aside, the output of forensic journalism is as close as many archaeologists come to understand the socially constructed context of the serious crime they might be asked to engage with in an investigative capacity. Media messages are an important factor in the determination of public perception of criminal behaviour and the investigation of crime. As Sanders and Lyon (ibid.: 25) observe, 'the messages and information we receive through the media have extensive impact, from influencing our choice of deodorant to ... affecting our understanding and treatment of crime ...'. It should also be considered that they are utilised '... both subtly and overtly to serve the interests of powerful ... structures that determine the form and content of messages and the larger apparatus of social control ...' (ibid.). They cultivate a belief that the larger social environment is dangerous and frightening; routine portrayals of violence and crime enhance the power of those with a vested interest in maintaining the status quo. Portrayals of deviance can contribute to the audience collectively accepting presentations of reality with some kinds of deviance being attributed to the regnant mass media (Winick 1978: 7). Further, the media can be construed as censors involved in the generation or suppression of moral panics by constructing stereotypical images of social issues (Sanders and Lyon 1995), for example, the decline of the family and single parenting.

Forensic journalism reports the details of victims, perpetrators, the crime scene and the courts but often fails to place its descriptions within adequate and objective discussion of the social structural contexts in which they are embedded (Bailey and Hale 1998). Consequently, many consumers of such reporting fail to fully appreciate, or consider, the wider social context of such crime. The tone and content of some reporting dwells on the horror of the case without addressing why such crimes take place in the first place. This trend is both complicated and compounded by the increasing tendency for such journalism to be peppered with forensic detail and mention of scientific analysis which arguably gives their reporting an extra edge of legitimacy (ibid.: 126). This should be a matter of concern to a profession that seeks to identify the social contexts of the material it studies. Such trends in homicide cases as sexual asymmetry in perpetrator–victim relationships, and familial relationships are generally ignored.[1] Further, the murder, or genocide, of non-Britons is considered to be dealt with indifferently by the UK media when compared to that of Britons (Taylor 1998), thus imbuing compassion for humanity with an unhealthy

---

1  A recent US study has shown that most (93 per cent) of homicides are carried out by males (Bailey and Hale 1998: 129) and most (79.1 per cent) by a familial relation (ibid. 127). The same trend exists in the UK.

nationalistic bias. By default, forensic journalism plays a role in shaping the parameters within which many of their readers, including archaeologists, actively make sense of the world of civil and war crime, its investigation and resolution. Few surveys of the impact of media reporting of crime on public perception have been undertaken. An exception is the work of O'Keefe and Reid-Nash (1987) which indicates that attention to television news appeared to be more influential in increasing levels of fear and concern than crime reporting in newspapers.

By analogy with media reporting, should forensic archaeologists also consider what, if any, moral responsibility their involvement in criminal investigation brings with it? There is a moral responsibility attached to both publishing and suppressing text and images of victims of violent crime, whether civil or in the context of war, the main parameter being the definition of what is appropriate and what is relevant to specific audiences. Although there are regulatory bodies monitoring the output of the press, it is perceived that journalism works within largely self-defined and self-imposed limits that exclude the most horrific detail. This was the case in the trial of Rosemary West in 1995. Such censorship is, however, accompanied by a moral responsibility that accompanies the '*moral sleep* and *historical amnesia*' that exists when such verbal or pictorial imagery goes unseen (Taylor 1998: 6). Martin Bell (1997: 16) reinforces this: 'in a world where genocide has returned in three continents [now four] we should remind ourselves that this crime against humanity requires accomplices – not only the hatred that makes it happen, but the indifference that lets it happen'. Journalism that provides a visual 'architecture of death' (Bailey and Hale 1998: 134) without a clearly defined socially constructed and value-laden context is fostering the consequences of social indifference to power politics. If this point is accepted, where does it leave archaeologists involving themselves in criminal investigation?

In theory, they must be unbiased participants, operating within an ordered and structured process. Clearly, to comment on any aspect of a case one is involved in while it is *sub judice* would be illegal, inappropriate and unprofessional; to do so after the event might be prejudicial against further employment. However, as Tilley reminds us (1998: 306): 'Living in Western society of the 1980s is to be involved with, and in part, responsible for prevailing social conditions.' Taking this one step further, do we have a responsibility to use forensic archaeology to empower the present? Should we consider if we have a legitimate voice in the debate about the political, religious, economic, socially structured and gendered context of crime against both society and humanity? To accept the sense of glamour, risk, excitement and importance that can accompany forensic archaeology without commenting on the background to such crime is arguably immoral. Or, are we to line up with other forensic scientists, whose training and sole purpose is to provide data and evidence for the courts? I think not. To quote Tilley again: 'Archaeology ... is a system of social relationships in the present within which the production of meanings takes place' (1998: 308). Forensic archaeologists have, thus far, restrained from engagement with analysis of the wider context within which they are employed. The dilemma we face is akin to that facing the photojournalist when deciding which images of horror to publish or repress. Taylor's expression (1998: 196) of this dilemma is appropriate and cannot be bettered: 'If prurience is ugly, what then is discretion in the face of barbarism?'

In the UK there are about 800 homicides annually. Yet few attract the attention of the media in any detail. Those that do reflect as much about social values as do those that are largely ignored. The forensic archaeologist is exposed to the full range of homicides, many of which do not involve the middle-class white and blonde women and children the press focuses on. They all too frequently involve illegal drugs, organised crime, sadism, sado-masochism, jealousy, rejection and corruption. Equally, we are exposed to the murder of those of non-Caucasoid ancestry, the poor, the illiterate and prostitutes, which are often only afforded limited and short-lived media attention at best.[2] I clearly remember my involvement in a case which, for the first time, exposed me to the world of 'gang-masters'. The implications of the very existence of individuals responsible for organising gangs of immigrant labour in a manner all too reminiscent of the exploitation underpinning the slave trade were both shocking and harrowing to engage with. There can be no doubt that exposure to aspects of homicide, sub-cultures and 'life' outside those with which the press make us familiar, arguably desensitising us, is extremely difficult to engage with. But, if we choose not to expose the inhumanity of such crimes and do not comment on the political and biased silence accompanying them (at an appropriate point in time), are we guilty of collaboration in the artifice created by the mass media? If archaeologists have a responsibility to empower the past, should we not do the same for the present? Should our role in commodifying the past be different in forensic contexts than in those of traditional archaeology? Alternatively, should we deny our social consciences and simply deliver data for the processes of criminal investigation? Is our silence in the context of forensic work akin to the mystification and self-legitimisation that is arguably prevalent in any archaeology? If so, it is equally as unacceptable.

Like most people with no direct experience of murder, many archaeologists have a side of their personality that is (to varying degrees and in varying ways) fascinated by the horror and inhumanity, misery and viscera, that murder represents. During the trial of Rosemary West in 1995, Jeremy Paxman commented: 'It says something about all of us that they [the press] believe we want to share Fred and Rosemary's fantasies' (cited in Taylor 1998: 122). As voyeurs observing such horrors, experience of murder through press coverage not only titillates readers through salacious descriptions bordering on pornography, it also reinforces ideas about civil society and, as aberrations against social values,

---

2  Reporting of *home* murders takes precedence over affairs of state and international incidents (Taylor 1998).

reinforces ideas and ideals about that society (ibid.). Archaeologists (as others), observing media-moderated and -mediated serious crime, are also comforted by the expected outcome in the battle between good and evil that is represented when it is investigated and resolved. Our faith in humanity, having been shaken, is restored, and a feeling of safety returns, however transiently. With crime statistics indicating an increased threat to individual and group safety, a means of actively participating in the process of maintaining social order and values arguably provides a sense of comfort and power.

A further issue to consider is that forensic archaeologists rarely participate in criminal investigation without knowledge of at least some of the facts of a case. Such scenarios inevitably move us from a limited and mediated context for crime into actuality and engagement at often unexpected levels. Unlike many aspects of law enforcement and the forensic sciences, archaeological education and professional development does not provide training designed to remove us from the context of our engagement with the past. Consequently, it is difficult, if not impossible, not to engage with the perceived context and implications of criminal investigation.

During the first forensic case I was involved in 1992–93, I recall the qualms I felt when I realised some of the immediate implications of my involvement in the resolution of the 25-year-old inquiry. This extended far beyond traditional issues of justice in the sense of resolving crime and punishing perpetrators. In this case, if locating the victim contributed to the conviction of the accused (her husband), the consequences for their three children (then adults), and their families, were likely to be devastating. It would mean that contrary to their long-held beliefs (fostered by their father), their mother had not abandoned them during their early childhood. They had, in fact, been misled by their father. Inevitably, they would have to come to terms with the fact that their father had in fact murdered their mother and concealed her body in the garden in which they played as children. Set that against an opposing but equally legitimate interest: the victim's mother longed to be able to bury her missing daughter and absolve her from the crime of abandoning her husband and young family. Consequently, I was left wondering whose 'justice' we were working towards and empowering.

The old adage that professionals should disassociate themselves from such matters is easy to say but far less easy to practise, particularly without an appropriate educational and professional background. John Hunter experienced similarly complex emotions in his very public involvement in 1997–98, with the search for the remains of a missing marine in the Falkland Islands:

> The feeling of not succeeding and letting people down … marries with not finding Alan Addis in the Falklands when his mother was waiting at every turn. Somehow I felt it was my fault. When you engage with a victim's family you move from the media portrayal of events into actuality; you become part of their world whether you like it or not.
>
> (Hunter: pers. comm.)

### Forensic science and popular culture

In 1996, Arthur wrote: 'As subtly as the tide, forensic science has come to pervade our culture. Go to a film, turn on the television, pick up a book, and you will almost surely come across an example of the craft.' Since the 1970s, such programmes as *The Expert* and the long-running *Quincy* have been gracing our television screens with images of eccentric but case-solving forensic scientists. McCrery, creator of *Silent Witness* (1996: 50), observed that as the methods used to solve crimes become more sophisticated, forensic science is becoming the new detective, that consumers '. . . follow the experts like a favourite football team', often seeking the comfort and reassurance discussed above. Fiction based on crime and punishment captures the imagination and, arguably, social reality begins in the imagination (Bailey and Hale 1998). Our construction of beliefs about crime are mediated by the social context of diffusion which emanates not only from the media and popular culture, but also such organisations as the police, central government and the Church.

Crime writing began with the Biblical story of Cain and Abel, and the use of forensic anthropology with the Biblical account of Jezebel (Martin: pers. comm.), whose remains were identified from a few surviving skeletal elements. A fascination with murder and its resolution is evident in all early folklore, in fairy tales and ballads (ibid.: 5). Consider, for example, the fairy tale of *Little Red Riding Hood*. The nineteenth century saw an explosion of crime-related genres, exemplified by such masters as Dickens, which has continued into the twentieth century. The late 1960s saw the strong male protector of social order in a context of unemployment and escalating violence. That the sub-genre of 'woman in jeopardy' permeates much twentieth-century crime literature (ibid.: 11) and still persists is an unfortunate reflection of socially constructed gender values, as is that of the *femme fatale*. The 'vigilante cop' made *his* first appearance in the 1970s and persists as a genre, also reflecting gender politics and society's loss of confidence in traditional resolution of crime. Cornwall's 1990s character, Kay Scarpetta, reflects the reality of female involvement in the forensic sciences and in this capacity, if no other, is to be welcomed.

There can be no doubt that the current obsession with the forensic sciences reflected in popular culture in the 1990s represents a real and interesting phenomenon. Despite an extensive literature in the 1980s on crime fiction and popular culture, at the time of writing, there is surprisingly little discussion in the sociological and popular-culture literature of the current fascination with forensic science. Nevertheless, in the UK, the 1990s has witnessed the advent and immense popularity of such television programmes as *Cracker* (forensic psychiatry), *Silent Witness* and *McCullum* (forensic pathology) with *Quincy* still continuing to be repeated. At the same time, more traditional genres of police-based dramas are including an increased forensic science content (e.g. *Dangerfield*, *The Bill*). McNeely (1995: 6) reported that in the US, crime and law enforcement programmes on prime-time television are extremely popular with high ratings. More than 25% of all prime-time shows from the 1960s to 1992 focused on themes of criminal justice and this is the largest single subject matter on US television today. No doubt the trend in the UK is similar. Cinema films that include comment about the relationship between forensic scientists, society and serial killers also abound. They include such 'classics' as Anthony Hopkins's suave performance in 1991 as cannibal Hannibal Lector in Thomas Harris's *Silence of the Lambs*, and Oliver Stone's *Natural Born Killers* and John Water's *Serial Mom*, both of which were first screened in 1994.

The crime novel has also seen a similar trend towards the increased involvement of forensic science in solving crime as exemplified by the work of such authors as P.D. James and Ruth Rendell. The creations of such authors as Patricia Cornwall represent a change of emphasis and genre away from traditional policing to increased reliance on forensic science and forensic scientists. Kathy Reichs' recent novels (1997 and 1999), in which the heroine is a forensic anthropologist, mark an increased acceptance of less frequently used forensic sciences and it can only be a matter of time before the hero/ine of a such a novel will be a forensic archaeologist. Discussion of the extent to which popular culture reflects changes in society and to what extent it shapes it, is outside the expertise of this author and scope of this chapter, but has been explored elsewhere. Cawelti, for example (1976: 77 cited in Bailey and Hale 1998: 6), considers that literary crime can serve as 'an ambiguous mirror of social values'.

'True-crime' books are also increasingly popular, a trend traceable to the early 1990s (Weiner 1993); many are authored by experienced crime journalists. Examples based on the West case abound (e.g. Sounes 1995; Burn 1998). Such works juxtapose scenes of happy families with those of the crime. Perpetrators are pictured in contradictory ways and life as respected citizens sits uncomfortably alongside often brutal documentation about the crime and subsequent trial. Shock value is maximised and the reader's subsequent anxiety reduced by images of law enforcement systems representing the restoration of order. Information is often displaced by a contrived imbalance with horror. What such books have in common is that they are imposed on the reader's perception of crime and its investigation (Weiner 1993). They juxtapose ideal lives with nightmarish experience and embody contradictions that they frequently do little to resolve.

Is the development of forensic archaeology simply a part of the UK population's fascination with all things forensic? In its application are we simply part of a wider socially constructed phenomenon? A sub-group seeking comfort from the legitimacy, and illusionary safety, of applying scientific principles and methods (i.e. supposedly objective knowledge), to acts against humanity. If so, it would be prudent to remember that science itself cannot give evidence in court, it relies upon a third party, the expert, to decide which method to employ, to apply that methodology, to interpret the results and to give it voice. Archaeology may employ science, but most archaeologists became involved in the subject because they wanted to become part of, and contribute to, a developing humanistic discipline. The need for such engagement may itself, in part, underlie our involvement in the judicial process.

## Forensic archaeology as a search for social significance

Forensic archaeology is only ever likely to approximate to a full-time career for a small number of those electing to work with such organisations as the International Criminal Tribunal for the former Yugoslavia (ICTY: http:// www.un.org/icty). For most UK archaeologists, it is only ever going to be an adjunct to other employment. This reflects the fact that, fortunately, we have lower homicide rates than many other countries, and reflecting urbanisation, rural topography and climate, few of these victims end their days in clandestine graves. Yet, despite the minimal career opportunities, large numbers of applications continue to arrive on course leaders' desks from graduates wishing to read forensic archaeology at post-graduate level. This clearly cannot simply reflect traditional career aspirations and may have a significance beyond the influence of the media; what does it reflect?

The 1990s have seen a change of balance in the rationale underlying assessment, evaluation and excavation in UK archaeology. This reflects a number of variables including the adoption of regulations such as Planning Policy Guidance Note Number 16 (PPG 16) in 1990, acceptance of values such as the Precautionary Principle, and adoption of US-style cultural resource management. Consequently, the privilege of engaging with archaeology on a traditional intellectual level is one shared by a decreasing proportion of practising archaeologists. That is not to say that archaeology within the planning framework is devoid of intellectual engagement but such engagement is more a matter of assessment and evaluation of individual sites proposed for development than the traditional research-orientated career determined by involvement within archaeological research agendas. For many archaeologists practising within the UK, job descriptions focus on curation, desk-based assessment and field evaluations.

Many field archaeologists spend much of their time evaluating one site after another, some of which are either devoid of archaeology or have minimal interest. Such field-work is then the basis of a report, the production of which can be a mechanical process when they lack discussion of any significant archaeology. Such changes as the advent of PPG 16 have undoubtedly enhanced the recovery, recording and conservation of archaeology in the development scenario, and led to an increase in desk-based and field-based employment opportunities (if not security or terms of employment: Turner 1998). However, the nature of career opportunities for many is at the level of information provider for local planning authorities. While this role is crucial in safeguarding archaeology it can, at present, be lacking in an obvious focus in terms of the advancement of archaeology as a subject.

Couple this perceived level of dissatisfaction with the fact that most archaeologists are thinking and caring members of society, a society with increasing and highly visible socio-economic deprivation and challenges, and the meaning and social significance of a career in archaeology is increasingly challenged. From 1995 to 1996, as an experienced archaeological consultant, I was fortunate enough to be involved in planning for an unusual archaeological scheme. The charity, Centrepoint, proposed to redevelop the crypt, and adjacent church gardens, beneath St Pancras (New) Church, Euston Road, London. The plan was to create a centre for homeless youngsters arriving at the nearby main-line railways stations of Euston, St Pancras and King's Cross, all of which are only a few minutes' walk away. Figures available at the time indicated that if teenage girls were not given proper advice within 45 minutes of arrival they were likely to be picked up by pimps. The prospects for teenage boys were even worse; most were picked up within 30 minutes of arrival. Without immediate and appropriate help, the future for such youngsters includes the horrors of homelessness, drug addiction, prostitution and such associated health risks as tuberculosis, hepatitis A, B and C and AIDS. Combined with this was the fact that the project had immense scientific potential. Once knowledge of this scheme spread amongst the archaeological community, I was inundated with letters and *curriculum vitae* from archaeologists (and forensic specialists) who wanted to be involved. Some were offering their services for no more than expenses. It was clear from these letters that for many, the scientific aspects of the scheme were only a small part of the attraction. The benefits of the project to archaeology were magnified by the sense of contributing to the provision of essential services for the needy in an unjust social context relative to which we would all be considered to be both privileged and fortunate. This scheme did not proceed due to the fact that the client found alternative premises. The disappointment that reverberated through those closely involved was profound and akin to bereavement. There was little doubt that this grief did not reflect the loss of scientific potential but rather the loss of an opportunity to be immediately socially relevant in a context of social hardship and injustice.

As professional archaeologists, particularly those operating within a university environment, we are incredibly privileged to at least occasionally have the opportunity to engage in what Thomas (1996: 14) calls 'theoretical navel-gazing', but the question arises – is it enough? As an archaeologist, the experience and the questions that arose from the involvement described above, led to an increased striving towards an involvement in a socially immediate and valuable archaeology. Unfortunately, few such opportunities are available to us – apart from leaving the discipline altogether.

Operating on an entirely different level, the arrival of television archaeology presents opportunities to engage within a wider social context and public at the level of providing entertainment and education. The warmth and relish with which such programmes as *Time Team* and *Meet the Ancestors* have been received by the public at large demonstrates the value of giving an archaeology back to the public. Despite the pontificating television archaeology generates amongst some professional archaeologists (see BRITARCH after every episode of *Time Team* or *Meet the Ancestors*), engagement with society's needs, even at this level, can be rewarding.

## Conclusion

I would suggest that, just as the perception by archaeologists of both serious crime and its investigation is mediated by journalism and popular culture, so too is our need to be involved in a 'sexy' subject – forensic science. Equally, as architects of, or commentators on, social processes and relationships in the past, we cannot be impervious to social inequalities, injustices and problems confronting our present. If our chosen career is not providing a sense of social relevance in an unjust world, or empowering the present in a significant and valuable way, then we will seek that satisfaction where we may. Increasingly, many of us are seeking to engage with society and socially devised and divisive problems within society at first hand. To contribute actively to the process of justice offers a means of achieving that. It has obvious social relevance and a sense of control and comfort in dealing with threats against us as individuals and within a wider society. This is enhanced by the knowledge that the relevance of forensic applications to the discipline of archaeology are beginning to be realised and published and will increasingly be so with experience and time.

Involvement with criminal investigation undoubtedly brings multifaceted rewards. However, I would suggest that such involvement brings with it responsibilities above and beyond the requirements of the criminal justice system. At present we are passive, unquestioning players contributing to the institutionalised silence that surrounds public perception of the social and political context of serious crime and injustice. As academics used to discerning the social and cultural significance of material culture, not to apply our intellectual skills in this context may ultimately be to our detriment in terms of both academic credibility and commitment to humanity.

## Acknowledgements

I am grateful to Gavin Lucas and Victor Buchli for inviting me to contribute this chapter. The exercise has proved both thought provoking and cathartic. Several colleagues have taken the trouble to comment on the contents and are thanked for their responses and suggestions. They are: Timothy Darvill, John Hunter and Paul Cheetham. Ultimately, however, the content and approach are mine and I take full responsibility for both. I am particularly grateful to John Hunter for permission to quote from recent correspondence between us and to Anthony Martin for information from his unpublished research. Finally, Denise McGinley is thanked for being a competent and willing research assistant.

# References

Bailey, F. Y. and Hale, D. C. (1998) *Popular Culture, Crime and Justice*, New York: West/Wadsworth Publishing Company.

Bell, M. (1997) 'TV News: how far should we go?' *British Journalism Review* 8, 1: 7–6.

Burn, G. (1998) *Happy like Murderers*, London: Faber and Faber Ltd.

Cox, M. J. (1999) 'Criminal concerns: a plethora of forensic archaeologists', *The Archaeologist* No. 33: 21–2.

Cox, M. J. and Bell, L. S. (1999) 'Recovery of human skeletal elements from a recent UK murder inquiry: preservational signatures', *Journal of Forensic Sciences* 44: (5) 945–50.

Faulkner, N. (1997 February) 'Wrong winner', *British Archaeology* No. 21: 10.

Hunter, J., Roberts, C. and Martin, A. (1996) *Studies in Crime: An Introduction to Forensic Archaeology*, London: Batsford.

Hunter, J. R. (1999) 'The excavation of modern murder', in *The Loved Body's Corruption*, ed. J. Downes and T. Pollard, Glasgow: Cruinthe Press. pp. 209–20.

McCrery, N. (1996) 'Murder most fascinating', *New Scientist* 151, 2040: 50.

McNeely, C. L. (1995) 'Perceptions of the criminal justice system: television imagery and public knowledge in the United States', *Journal of Criminal Justice and Popular Culture* 3, 1: 1–20.

O'Keefe, G. J. and Reid-Nash, K. (1987) 'Crime news and real-world blues: the effects of the media on social reality', *Communication Research* 14, 2: 147–63.

Penrose, L. S. (1952) *On the Objective Study of Crowd Behaviour*, London: H. K. Lewis & Co. Ltd.

Reichs, K. (1997) *Déjà Dead*, London: Random House.

Reichs, K. (1999) *Death du Jour*, London: Heinemann.

Sanders, C. R. and Lyon, E. (1995) 'Repetitive retribution: media images and the cultural construction of criminal justice', in *Cultural Criminology*, ed. J. Ferrell and C. R. Sanders, Boston: Northeastern University Press, pp. 25–44.

Sounes, H. (1995) *Fred and Rose: 25 Cromwell Street*, London: Little, Brown and Company.

Taylor, J. (1998) *Body Horror: Photojournalism, Catastrophe and War*, Manchester: Manchester University Press.

Tilley, C. (1998) 'Archaeology as socio-economic action in the present', in *Reader in Archaeological Theory: Post-processual and Cognitive Approaches*, ed. D. Whitley, London: Routledge, pp. 301–14.

Thomas, C. (1996) 'Digging at the final frontier', *British Archaeology* No. 11: 14.

Turner, R. (1998) 'Jobs in British archaeology', *The Archaeologist* No. 31: 12–14.

Weiner, S. (1993) 'True crime: fact, fiction and Law', *The Legal Studies Forum* XVII, 3: 275–90.

Winick, C. (1978) *Deviance and Mass Media*, London: Sage Publications.

# Chapter 14

# The archaeology of alienation
## A late twentieth-century British council house

*Victor Buchli and Gavin Lucas*

## Part I: The excavation

In July of 1997 we were allowed two days' access to a recently abandoned council house; the project started from an idea of exploring the theme of alienation from a dual perspective of the material culture of a marginalised and socially disenfranchised person or family in the late twentieth century and the process of marginalisation and alienation that we, as archaeologists, effect on the people we study – whether now or two thousand years ago. This latter issue will not be directly addressed, but it is inherent in everything we will discuss, as we both were constantly provoked into thinking about our presence in that house, and what our reactions were to the material culture in which we were immersed. We hope something of this will come out in our discussion, however obliquely.

The project was conducted as if it were a normal archaeological site. In short, the 'excavation' involved the usual processes – starting with base planning of all the rooms and photography of all the 'deposits' prior to disturbance by us. Following that, we proceeded room by room to record all the contents and their position within the room using a simple database, inputting straight onto a laptop. In addition, sampling of micro-deposition on floors and a record of the sequence of decorative schemes on walls and woodwork were taken through random spot samples.

Each item was categorised loosely on broad consumption divisions, such as one might find in a department store or the different shops on a high street or in a mall. Where appropriate, age and sex attributes were also assigned to an object – this was based not on supposed use but commercial identification so that, for example, an item of clothing defined as male is based purely on the fact that it may be labelled as a man's garment and come from a male clothing store. In the analyses that we will present therefore, one must bear in mind that some of the patterns may not show the true picture, especially as, for example, items of clothing can be used by either sex, either because the item in question displays minimal sexual differentiation (such as T-shirt) or it is being actively used to subvert stereotyped sexual identities.

What characterises this study above all, is the archaeological context in which the work was done; there were no informants – just like an archaeological site, the people had left, leaving only their material culture behind. As such, the event of abandonment pervades the interpretation of the house, and forms an important part of how the material culture will be studied and will have particular resonance when we discuss the wider context of abandonment in relation to issues of housing and homelessness.

## The house

The property we entered was a two-bedroom 1960s house with a ground and first floor, front drive and back garden. On the ground floor, as you come in, there is a small hall and staircase leading up to the first floor; straight ahead is the living room while moving to the right one enters another living room or dining room and then into the kitchen. Going upstairs onto the landing, a small bathroom lies ahead and to the right, two bedrooms (Figure 14.1). We want to ask two questions through the material culture we encountered in the house – who lived there and why did they leave?

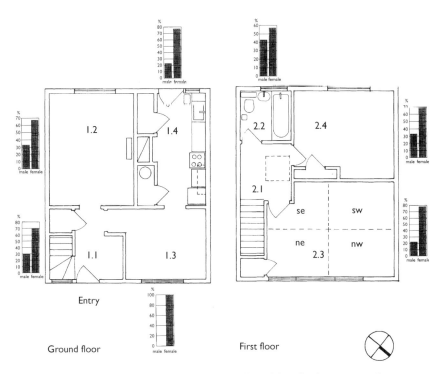

*Figure 14.1* Plan of house with proportions of male and female objects according to room. (Courtesy: Victor Buchli and Gavin Lucas.)

### Who lived there?

There was a kind of dual process going on in the way we explored these questions – one was through our own familiarity with the material culture and our everyday ability to read it, the other a more conventional application of archaeological methodology where understanding comes, ironically, by almost de-familiarising the house in terms of our everyday perception, and re-constructing it as an archaeological site, making it familiar under another guise. In what follows, the interpretations are very much a product of this dual process and we will not attempt to try to pull them apart although at times it might appear that one approach is taking precedence.

Over the two days we spent in the house it seemed fairly obvious that it was occupied by a family unit of some sort; a child or children were present and a male and female adult. This much we gleaned from the kinds of objects we found – toys, adults' and children's clothing, a bedroom decorated with Flintstones wallpaper, and so on. A statistical breakdown of one category of material culture, clothing, corroborates this. A rather too neat picture of the archetypal nuclear family perhaps. But is it? If we look again at this breakdown, it does not just show woman, man, girl and boy; why do women's clothes account for half the total and twice as much as the man's who in turn is represented twice as much as either child? Are there two women living there or does it say something about consumption of clothing? There are many questions raised by this one figure which lead on to examining the material in other ways, which in turn can raise new questions. Thus in looking at the consistency in the size and style of the clothing and shoes, it seems most likely that only a single woman is represented, but this also revealed that the boy was probably older than the girl. We do not think we need to labour this point, suffice to say that so far, we still do not really know *anything* of who lived at the house, beyond an approximate body count. How do we go further and investigate some of the dynamics of the family that lived there? To try to take this a little further we want briefly to focus on two relationships within the family; that between the children and the adults and that between the two adults.

### The children

Taking a very broad breakdown of those objects that can be defined as adult or child room by room, we get a picture of ubiquitous child presence across the house. However, the converse cannot be said; adult objects are common in all rooms except one: the back bedroom of the upper floor, which was also clearly the children's bedroom. This shows quite an interesting picture of the children's position in the home, in that it was deemed quite important for them to have their own space – that while they could occupy any room of the house, they also had their own exclusive sphere, in contrast to the adults who appear to have no exclusive space – not even their bedroom, which with the living room, contains the next highest number of child-associated objects.

The importance attached to the children and the value in which childhood is held, are further emphasised through the quality of children's clothing compared to the adults'; it was noticeable, for example, that while the children's shoes were often of leather and the clothing in natural fibres, the adult's shoes were more commonly PVC and the clothing in synthetic fibres. Such patterns of consumption suggest a very giving and loving relationship between the adult or adults and children. What can we say though, about the relationship between the adults?

### The adults

Using the same coarse breakdown by room as for adult/child objects, the ratio of adult male to adult female objects shows that female objects dominate in all the rooms – in fact male presence is very minimal, including the adult bedroom and the main living room which further builds on the idea of a single-parent household. Indeed, the two rooms that show anything of a greater presence of male objects, are the two rooms that are perhaps most associated with someone who comes and goes – the hall and the bathroom. In the hall this consists of coats, in the bathroom, toiletries. It suggests a picture of a man not permanently living there but whose presence is ephemeral and perhaps temporary. What, then was the relationship of the man to the woman?

While the presence of toiletries indicates overnight visits, there are lots of more explicit material references to sexual activity in the house – condom wrappers, K-Y jelly, a lovers' guide video and several items of erotic underwear, all pointing to the relationship being a sexual one. Certain documentary details collated from within the house seemed to confirm that the man was the father of the children; subsequent discoveries of methadone prescribed to the partner and father of the children lent weight to the suspicion that the man was also a heroin addict.

Taken together, examination of these two themes in the dynamics of the family inhabiting the house points to a single mother raising two children with a non-co-habiting father who is however still in a sexual relationship with the mother and probably a paternal relationship to the children. The question now remains, was this state of affairs the norm, or was it a recent development within the family; in other words, how does this pattern relate to the ultimate abandonment of the house? Why did they leave?

### Why did they leave?

Examination of the quantities of material from room to room, shows quite a varying pattern, some being packed, others quite empty. However, to put this into some kind of context, it was immediately apparent upon entering the house that the material in the living room was stacked up in preparation for removal while that in the kitchen and main bedroom, as well as all the other rooms, had been already either sorted through or simply left as it was. What this provides is quite a crucial insight into the valorisation of material culture by the occupants, that a process of selection was conducted in terms of what was deemed most important to take and what to abandon.

Part of this process is obscured by the fact that we do not know what was already removed, although we can guess; certainly some things were notable by their absence (e.g. beds) and the intention at least was to return and pick up the rest which had been gathered together in the living room. For whatever reason, this material was not collected, but this fact does suggest some urgency of abandonment and a reluctance to return to the house afterwards. In looking at the material then, we can use the distinction of the rooms to shed light on what was valued and desired to be kept and what was not.

The kinds of things selected for removal which occur in the living room include certain items of clothing and furnishings, as well as tablewares, memorabilia, books and videos. Almost all of the latter in fact were found in the living room with few examples elsewhere in the house. Conversely, a large selection of clothing and furnishings as well as toiletries, household goods, foodstuffs and kitchenwares were abandoned. Again, most of the latter occurred in the kitchen or bathroom with few examples in the living room. Just from this, one gets a certain sense of what items are regarded as more valuable and in many ways the choices are perhaps unsurprising. However, to try to provide a more personal dimension which may also help in understanding the cause of abandonment, we want to look at two of the classes in more detail, clothing and furnishings.

> *Clothing* – the clothing that was selected for removal included a coat, several jackets, a dress, a two-piece woman's suit and a few other items. In contrast, the clothing left behind was mostly jumpers and T-shirts as well as all the underwear of which almost all was of the erotic kind mentioned earlier.

> *Furnishings* – the furnishings selected for removal were predominantly household decorative items – curtains, vases and figurines, while those left were mostly Christmas decorations.

The intention to remove much of the more personal domestic items such as the interior furnishings, books, tableware etc., suggests a need to take the home out of the house as it were; clearly the sense of the house as a home is very strong with a lot of care and investment given to its creation. Conversely however, many personal items, particularly of clothing, were left and in this respect the abandonment of the material references to sexual activities such as erotic underwear along with the binning of the lovers' guide video might suggest a breakdown of the sexual relationship, and this may well be closely implicated in the event of abandonment.

Why they left is, of course, almost impossible to know in all its details, as are the special dynamics that operated between the four people we have been discussing; however, we can place their lives and the house in a broader social context which adds another, and still personal dimension to the material culture we encountered.

## Part 2: Context

Later on we went to the housing authority to find out more about the house we had just excavated. The authority could only say that the house had been occupied since 1991 by a single 25-year-old mother of two children aged 4 and 6. She moved into the house just after giving birth to her first child. She was on full income support and housing benefit. The fact that the unit was suddenly abandoned caught the housing authority by surprise. The household was not in arrears, there was nothing to indicate that there might be any trouble that would result in abandonment and the creation of what the authority called a 'void property'.

Typically, single mothers on income support are probably among the most vulnerable members of British society as are single elderly women. In terms of being housed, they are also the most problematic for a number of complex reasons. Unmarried women are the most reliant on state housing. Forty-nine per cent of divorced and separated women depend on state housing as opposed to 33% of men in the same situation (Sexty 1990: 29). Households headed by women are twice as likely as households headed by men to be found in council homes (42% compared to 21%) (Sexty 1990: 30). The unmarried and young are particularly in need. By the age of 23, two-thirds of young men and women move away from their natal homes needing to be housed when they can least afford it.

Despite these figures, housing policy is geared to assist established heterosexual married couples. This continues despite the fact that married couples represent the smallest group of council tenants (Sexty 1990: 30). Otherwise, priority is usually given to the 'vulnerable', usually defined as people who become homeless as a result of catastrophe, mental or physical disability or when escaping documented and strictly defined domestic abuse in addition to single mothers with dependent children and single expectant mothers like the young woman of this abandoned household.

Thus young unmarried women are particularly vulnerable in securing housing and under greater threat of becoming homeless. The primary cause for women's vulnerability to homelessness according to studies conducted in the past ten years is what observers term as 'relationship breakdown' between the woman in question and her family or her partner. In the last quarter of 1989 17% of all homeless households were made homeless as a result of 'relationship breakdown' (Sexty 1990: 54).

Ideally, the state strives to ensure that young women are not lost to social services and made homeless as a consequence of 'relationship breakdown'. Before the 1985 Housing Act, individual housing authorities were not guided by any regulations as to how to cope with such a situation. Housing authorities dealt with the problem on an *ad hoc* basis. This meant an uneven and haphazard response to the situation which was highly inflected by local concerns, and social mores particularly regarding domestic violence. Though unrationalised, some recourse was possible on an individual basis and vulnerable women in that position might be able to be re-housed and enjoy continued support.

The 1985 Housing Act changed all that. It was worded in such a way as to explicitly protect heterosexual married women in nuclear families experiencing documented, violent and physical abuse, typically at the hands of their husbands with whom they shared a house. In attempting to rationalise the procedure with which the housing needs of such women were assessed, a specific norm was invoked that meant that women who did not fit into that category were not catered to by housing authorities. There were no longer *ad hoc* procedures which might respond to individual situations and needs. Rather there is now a bureaucratic procedure enshrined by an act of Parliament that ensures that only women who fit a very specific profile can enjoy any assistance in housing following a 'relationship breakdown'. However, women in these situations are protected only in terms of a specific definition as wives and mothers, they are not protected in terms of their status as women in general. Single women, unmarried women co-habiting with opposite-sex partners, lesbians and the elderly all lose out according to the 1985 Housing Act's constitution of women as only wives and mothers.

Under part III of the 1985 Housing Act, housing authorities are obliged to accept women escaping domestic violence as officially homeless. But there is the problem of evidence of that violence usually involving physical proof in the form of police reports and documented injuries before a housing authority might act. Some authorities would only recognise a woman leaving an abusive situation as 'legally homeless' after she has exhausted all possible legal remedies such as going through the lengthy and daunting procedure of getting an exclusion order, or initiating divorce proceedings (Charles and Jones 1993: 10). One report found that a London council would wait until it was taken to court before acknowledging its duty to rehouse (Charles and Jones 1993: 10). Almost all local authorities would not accept a woman as legally 'homeless' with priority for alternative housing if she has 'only' suffered mental or emotional abuse (Charles and Jones 1993: 10).

Proposed new guidelines have called for a re-assessment and expansion of these criteria in order to catch those women who fall through, who are the most vulnerable and in need of housing assistance. As it stands now a woman would only be considered for alternative housing in the case of 'relationship breakdown' if she was violently abused by a live-in husband and had legal and medical proof of that violence. In the case where the woman is single or lesbian, many housing authorities would not recognise an abusive partner residing elsewhere. If the woman has children, that is when she is defined as a mother, where the legal concern is not so much for her as for the safety of the children, then she can only be re-housed in cases where there is documented physical abuse particularly towards the children. British law and housing authorities have been very slow in recognising other forms of abuse, both physical and psychological. Only in 1991 was rape within marriage acknowledged and considered prosecutable, let alone any psychological abuse a woman might suffer at the hands of her unmarried partner.

Considering these difficulties women are often reluctant to leave or apply to local housing authorities for help. They are caught in an impossible dilemma. Unless the reasons for relationship breakdown can be shown to accord with the rather strict definitions of abuse recognised by the Housing Act, where a woman is protected only in terms of her identity as a wife and mother, then there is little recourse and assistance. There are refuges, but they are crowded and only temporary; women often return to the old households they are fleeing from because there is no other place to go. The national re-housing scheme, which re-houses women fleeing abusive partners to other parts of the country, usually has to assert a 'local connection' before re-housing a woman in a particular community. An abusive partner would often know that 'local connection' and follow the woman there.

When a woman goes to a refuge for temporary housing, having been declared legally homeless, she is usually there for several months until which time she is given one chance of alternative housing (Sexty 1990; Charles and Jones 1993: 11). It is her only chance. If she does not accept she is considered to have made herself 'intentionally homeless' and no longer qualifies for assistance. Often the housing offered is of the worst quality, with few provisions for the improvement of the space to make a comforting and soothing environment after the ordeal of fleeing an abusive domestic situation and several weeks and months in a refuge. Some commentators have noted that this disregard for providing a suitable home that could provide a modicum of shelter, flaunts the ambivalent and conflicted attitudes women often have of the home, as source of pride, place of pain and conflict and shelter from the difficulties of the outside world. Many local authorities have removed 'decorating grants' so that women could at least turn sub-standard housing into something more habitable. Critics view this as insensitive to the needs of comfort and safety beyond just the provision of a roof over the heads of such women. As one woman in a study reported, 'I just want my own place, just for me and my son, you know, just to shut the front door and that will be it' (Charles and Jones 1993: 104).

Added to that, the privatisation of council housing during the Thatcher years has resulted in an exceptionally diminished housing stock available to house and re-house women who have become homeless as a result of relationship breakdown. Housing authorities' reluctance to house adequately arises from the authorities' need to ration the scarce resources of a diminishing housing fund, therefore they interpret their duties under current legislation as narrowly as possible thus exacerbating the situation of those women who are not accounted for in legislation even further (Charles and Jones 1993: 12). Critics point out that the only way to alleviate the situation is to sell off less council housing stock and build more public-sector housing that is geared to the majority of women in need of assistance. To date there is little evidence to suggest such a turn in housing policy to alleviate the situation.

Studies have shown that because many women fear retaliation and stalking by abusive partners they simply stay in abusive situations and try as hard as possible to maintain the household, particularly when there are children involved. However, when services are not available and restrictively used, women either continue to endure an extremely bad situation leading to further abuse and injury, or attempt to flee, with the result that many women are lost to social services and end up homeless. Usually a woman would not be visible administratively as having a potential problem. Studies have observed that a woman is highly unlikely wilfully to accumulate arrears if she is planning on leaving a council flat, because she knows the accumulation of arrears would cause problems for any subsequent search for housing in the public sector (Davis 1993).

Additionally, a woman would often only leave an existing tenancy when she has secured an alternative one. This is very difficult as she would have to pay for the old tenancy while the new one is being finalised: a burden that many women already in a vulnerable position cannot afford. If a woman cancels her existing tenancy to live elsewhere, many authorities will view that as making herself 'intentionally homeless', and not house her again. In such cases the authority will have advised the woman to get an injunction against her abusive partner before they will re-house her. If she has children she must also take her children with her as well, otherwise it would be very difficult for her to get them back if she leaves them with her partner.

## Conclusion

What we have described here is what is known about the context of an abandoned household (Figure 14.2). The woman who abandoned the site has, according to existing parliamentary legislation and housing policy, made herself 'intentionally homeless' for whatever reason and is not therefore eligible for aid any more if she asked to be re-housed, which she has not. She has entirely lost her local housing benefit and support from social services. She is very much on her own with two children when previously she was clearly in need, having had access to full benefits and housing support. There is nothing to indicate that she found an alternative means towards independent living. What we have recorded at the house and discussed suggests very strongly that we have recorded the remains of an abandoned household of a single mother in the wake of relationship breakdown.

The reasons for breakdown are unknowable. However, we know she left very suddenly. Her relationship with the father of her two children was tenuous. He

*Figure 14.2* Abandoned bedroom floor. (Photograph by Victor Buchli and Gavin Lucas.)

lived on the other side of town. He seemed to have visited regularly, keeping a supply of toiletries, clothes and methadone to help him overcome his heroin addiction. Seeing that his methadone supply was due to be renewed as late as May 5, just a little over a month before the house was reported abandoned by neighbours, suggests that this guarded, but ostensibly caring relationship was still being maintained just a few weeks before the woman decided to leave everything and take her two children with her. Coming upon the abandoned traces of this household it would seem to us that the pressure of maintaining the relationship with the father of their two children and the strained and tenuous family they created while coping with heroin addiction was too much to bear. Being legally single, young, able-bodied, resourceful, but poor, like many women who are compelled to leave their homes as a consequence of relationship breakdown, she would probably have known that there were no state resources to help her. Taking her chances, scrupulously never having accumulated any arrears, whilst still packing, she suddenly got up and left.

## References

Charles, Nickie and Anne Jones (1993), *The Housing Needs of Women and Children Escaping Domestic Violence*, Swansea: Housing for Wales.

Davis, Cathy (1993), *Women and Violence at Home: Policy and Procedure Guidelines for Housing Associations*, London: National Federation of Housing Associations.

Sexty, Carol (1990), *Women Losing Out: Access to Housing in Britain Today*, London: Shelter.

# Conclusions

# Chapter 15

# Presencing absence

*Victor Buchli and Gavin Lucas*

Numerous themes criss-cross the various presentations of this volume. They all focus, however, upon the critical consequences of presencing absence in the recent past – bringing forward or indeed materialising that which is excessive, forgotten or concealed. As a result this body of archaeological work begins to appear qualitatively different from more conventional archaeological projects and other disciplines working on the recent past. Communities and individuals are more directly involved and implicated in the creation of vital pasts with the help of archaeologists, as we have seen in many of the contributions to this volume. Moreover, at a more direct and individual level, archaeologists can help mediate the experience of individuals in a manner that can only be described as therapeutic, whether it concerns work on mass graves, World War Two bombers or issues of national heritage. In such contexts, the archaeological act and its particularly well-suited methodologies permit the (re-)constitution of individual experience and thereby provide a much needed social relevance to groups and individuals who would not otherwise have the possibility to engage recent pasts and experiences.

There is, however, a problem endemic to any such enterprise, and that is the tension that arises between uncovering truths, such as those required for the collective needs of justice, and the humanitarian and therapeutic needs of individuals or disenfranchised groups, where different truths serve conflicting ends. In such a situation, where does the cessation of striving for knowledge end and the suppression of information begin? Framing the issue in these terms of knowledge claims or epistemology can provide no answer for it is above all an ethical issue. Therapeutic value supersedes truth value and in fact is often at odds with it. However, once we accept the problem as ethical, we are faced with yet another one: the constitution of narratives of modern experience at times hints at a certain voyeurism because of the immediacy of the people, events and circumstances under discussion – those things hidden from view and otherwise 'forgotten'. Margaret Cox in this volume discusses this voyeurism facilitated by the archaeology of the contemporary past and contrasts it with the complicities resulting from social indifference, 'moral sleep' and 'historical amnesia'. As she relates quoting Taylor: 'if prurience is ugly, what is discretion in the face of barbarism?' How are obscenity and voyeurism reconciled with complicities that materialise 'moral sleep' and 'historical amnesia' through the absences and exclusions they generate?

The concern with the contingent values of different truth claims, forces us to consider the effectiveness of such claims as coping strategies; that is who gets hurt and who does not by the pursuit of these therapeutic strategies (Rorty 1987) and what the relative costs are about relating truths (in the Foucauldian sense, see Butler 1993: 93) in connection to the conflicted and painful experiences of recent memory. Consensus is in fact very difficult to achieve and we would argue with Butler (1993: 221) that such a consensus is undesirable except in a highly contingent, construed and argued manner that takes into account the inevitably conflicted and contradictory needs of individuals and communities, a course that many of the contributions in this volume attempt to steer.

## Critical empiricism

This therapeutic encounter, which we witness in so many of the works in this volume, is facilitated by what we would call a critical empiricism. This critical empiricism provides a means of disentangling the superfluity of information we encounter in the present using the methodological tools archaeology has traditionally used to address the dearth of information in the more remote past. This is not, however, a call for a new realism, or the revival of some foundationalist project – a 'strategic essentialism' even – that would form the basis of a consensus. Rather it is the very creative act of constituting irreconcilable elements of social life, those Durkheimian social 'facts', which even though they are the products of our own creativity, have very real impacts on the way people experience the world; how they respond to it and in turn how they shape it (Durkheim 1966: 1–13). As William Rathje has insisted in this volume: '… material traces are not a simple mirror; they are a critical component which plays a leading role in the direction of behavioural change' (see page 69). If then, as a result, such actions by archaeologists of the contemporary past serve to alleviate these tensions, then this contingent 'agreement' would serve as a consensus merely in the sense of an 'honorific' (Rorty 1980: 335) or term of approbation to signify a momentarily satisfactory and effective coping device (Rorty 1991: 101 and Rorty 1982). As Rorty suggests, such an 'honorific' should be discarded as soon as other issues, identities and conflicts appear outside the bounds of discourse that our archaeological interventions and materialisations re-establish (Rorty 1991: 17). Butler argues further along these lines with Rorty that such boundaries should be generated precisely because of this defining momentary consensus – with an eye towards the generation of new inclusions and new subjectivities that the contingencies of our changing experience demand (Butler 1993: 221–2 and Rorty 1991: 19).

Such critical empiricism works to constitute and individuate experience that is lost or alienated such as we have seen in most of the contributions in this volume. It works effectively to both facilitate necessary forgetting as well as obstruct it. In short it is a very powerful therapeutic tool, albeit one that can work for or against individuals or groups despite the best of our intentions as muted by a number of the contributions in this volume. This critical empiricism is the result of ever increasing technologies (both social and methodological) with which to constitute information, individuate experiences and subjectivities as discussed by Walter Lacquer (Lacquer 1999) and Michel Foucault (Foucault 1995). Such constitutive practices arise from engagements with those marginal, unarticulable elements that are outside dominant discourses: the 'stubborn chunks' described by Homi Bhabha. Through the reconstitution, regeneration or redemption of these 'chunks', that is through the various 'composting actions' as described by Mary Douglas, the presencing of absence is facilitated by this critical empirical work (Bhabha 1994 and Douglas 1993).

Conversely though, as in the case of forensic archaeology, it can be seen as a means of control over irrationality and perceived threats to collective security – an almost neurotic attempt to gain control over ever more uncontrollable and alienating circumstances. Such a coping mechanism is by no means secure from abuse, and indeed any foreclosure or grounding would be complicitous with such abuse. Nevertheless, an archaeology of the contemporary past offers a possibility for materialised security in a society characterised by the speedy immateriality of the spectacle (de Bord 1995) and the simulacrum (Baudrillard 1982) where none was previously possible – or where dominant powers such as nation states foreclose the possibility of any materialisation of an alternate authenticity. The 'Past' has been replaced by the 'Truth' as the archaeology of the contemporary past seems to provides a modicum of security to experience – a certain grounding, a coping device – where there was none before. This is certainly the case when one considers the work of the Ludlow Collective, or the Argentine Forensic Team and more generally from human rights abuses to insurance claims and criminal justice. What are the social and political implications of purveying such a materialised 'security' that cuts through the plethora of images, texts and discourses? What in its turn, becomes excessive, forgotten or hidden to realise these new subjectivities; what is *their* social cost? This would seem to add a greater burden to the work of the archaeologist of the contemporary past. As we know from war crime tribunals, collective 'truths' can be at odds with individual humanitarian and therapeutic goals. Such a critical empiricism offers no guarantees and should force us to be extremely vigilant as to the social purposes towards which such claims for materialised security are put; how effective are they as coping strategies, what are their social costs or at whose expense and finally what new forms of exclusion and absence would arise and then challenge the new discourses that we materialise?

## The creativity of the archaeological act

The presencing of absence, that is its materialisation through the archaeological act, makes things 'matter' in the sense Judith Butler uses, that is bringing absence into being materially and enfranchising it as an object of social discourse (Butler 1993). Its materialising function suggests, as has Stevenson in this volume, that 'the role of the archaeologist is that of the designer, in that we "design" social relationships …' (see page 61), a pointed suggested by Cox, Doretti and Fondebrider as well. This creative materialising or 'mattering' works against dominant assumptions about physicality whether it is through 'performativity' as in Butler's work or the very 'immaterial' monuments in South Africa such as Mandela's sidewalk or the site of the plane crash that killed Samora Machel. This critique of physicality is achieved by the ever increasingly sophisticated methodological and social 'technologies' of the archaeological act used towards the presencing of absence. These creative interventions effectively challenge the effects both socially and materially of these privileged assumptions of physicality and serve to 'design', challenge and literally refigure the present.

The contributions of this volume suggest new ethical and socially creative aspects of various archaeologies of the contemporary past which in turn suggest new directions and a re-evaluation of the social significance of archaeological work in the twenty-first century. By moving away from an ontology of 'discovery' to that of materialisation and the problems of physicality, the archaeological act facilitates a more critical disciplinary practice with more pronounced yet contingent social purpose. This volume represents an attempt to reclaim socially vital and creative archaeologies from the margin (whether they be nutritional studies, sustainability, design histories, or forensic science), thereby re-incorporating those practices left outside (upon the insistence of our disciplinary boundaries and hierarchies) which have been 'wasted' – so to speak – and the complicities they have served both willingly and not, with an eye towards re-incorporating them back into the discipline, reviving it and the social work it does.

## References

Baudrillard, Jean (1982) *Simulations*, New York: Semiotext(e), Inc.
Bhabha, Homhi (1994) *The Location of Culture*, London: Routledge.
Butler, Judith (1993) *Bodies that Matter*, London: Routledge.
de Bord, Guy (1995) *The Society of the Spectacle*, New York: Zone Books.
Douglas, Mary (1993) *Purity and Danger*, London: Routledge.
Durkheim, Emile (1966) *The Rules of Sociological Method*, New York: Free Press.
Foucault, Michel (1995) *Discipline and Punish*, London: Vintage Books.
Lacquer, Thomas W. (1999), *The Dead Body and Human Rights*, unpublished manuscript.
Rorty, Richard (1980) *Philosophy and the Mirror of Nature*, Oxford: Basil Blackwell.
Rorty, R. (1982) *Consequences of Pragmatism*, Minneapolis: The Harvester Press.
Rorty, R. (1987) 'Thugs and Theorists', in *Political Theory*, vol. 15, no. 4, November.
Rorty, R. (1991) *Essays on Heidegger and Others*, Cambridge: Cambridge University Press.

# Chapter 16

# The archaeology of the contemporary past

*Laurent Olivier* (translated by Vérène Grieshaber)

Difficile à reconnaître, mais c'était ici.
Ici, on brûlait les gens.
Beaucoup de gens ont été brûlés ici.
Oui, c'est le lieu (…)
On ne peut pas raconter ça.
Personne ne peut se représenter ce qui s'est passé ici.
(…) Et personne ne peut comprendre cela.
Et moi-même aujourd'hui … je ne crois pas que je suis ici.
(Simon Srebnik, in Lanzmann, C. 1985: *Shoa*. Paris, Fayard)

Can we envisage an archaeology of the contemporary past? And if so, in what context? To consider the limits of the archaeological field is to ask, in fact, what is the specificity of the discipline: what is archaeology's project and on what kind of materials and information is it based? Such an approach calls into question established situations, on which the conventional practice of the discipline depends, without overturning presuppositions that have established their authority. For what constitutes the specificity of an archaeology interested in the vestiges of a past still near to us is the relation of proximity maintained regarding places, objects, ways of life or practices that are still ours and still nourish our collective identity. In these conditions, where are the limits to be fixed; where does archaeology begin and end? And to what extent does the archaeological approach to places and things of the present affect our relation to them? Finally, must we approach these remains of the recent past in the same way that we would approach more ancient vestiges of our collective history? Or is it necessary to imagine something else, to conceive of another archaeology and another approach to the remains of the past, one that would take account of the particular situation of the remains of the contemporary past? These are some of the questions to which we should attempt some kind of an answer and which we shall try to grasp as they occur in concrete examples: the mass graves of Argentina or Croatia, the restoring of Auschwitz and, in France, the preservation of the ruins of Oradour-sur-Glane.

## Recent vestiges and archaeological remains

Can the remains of the contemporary past be considered as entirely distinct archaeological vestiges? The European Convention for the Protection of the Archaeological Heritage (also known as the Malta Convention) answers the question unambiguously 'yes', by giving a definition of the notion of archaeological heritage that is both accepted Europe-wide and incorporates as a matter of course vestiges of the contemporary period. This text notes particularly the 'archaeological heritage as a source of the European collective memory and as an instrument for historical and scientific study', and as a consequence specifies in its first article that: 'shall be considered to be elements of the archaeological heritage all remains and objects and any other traces of mankind from past epochs, the preservation and study of which help to retrace the history of mankind and its relation with the natural environment; [. . .] The archaeological heritage shall include structures, constructions, groups of buildings, developed sites, moveable objects, monuments of other kinds as well as their context, whether situated on land or under water.'

Hence, any buried or submerged remains, so long as they provide information on 'the history of mankind and its relation with the natural environment' – and that whatever their chronological date – can thus be properly considered a part of the archaeological heritage. It is thus necessary to envisage the existence, following on chronologically from the archaeology of the medieval and modern periods, an archaeology of the contemporary period: this new field in the discipline stretches to the chronological limits established by history, i.e., globally, from the beginning of the twentieth century to the present day.

## From the 'house of horror' to the mass graves of Bosnia

Beyond these basic definitions, the situation of the remains of the contemporary past is a complex one, for they are immersed in our present. Hence, though archaeologists are in general little concerned with the study of the contemporary period, they are not the only ones to be investigating the material remains of the present in search of information on the recent past. The police, notably, are one of the principal professional groups situated outside of archaeology who conduct painstaking excavations in order to reconstruct certain events of the recent past. These investigations often use the same field techniques as archaeology. Radar similar to that used in the geophysical prospecting of archaeological sites is used for detecting where the earth has been disturbed, to find shallow graves where the remains of victims might be found. Recently, several techniques borrowed from archaeology were applied by the English police in examining 25 Cromwell Street, better known in the press as the Gloucester 'house of horror'. These analyses, leading to the extensive excavation of the floors and foundations of the Wests' house, helped uncover the remains of ten or so female victims, kidnapped and killed by the couple. These investigations helped expose the criminals through the reconstitution of the sequence in which the bodies had decomposed, having been cut up and buried over several years in different parts of the bathroom, the cellar and the garden.

In these circumstances, where the remains of the near past are analysed using methods shared with archaeology, should we consider these police operations as researches of an archaeological kind? In this instance, the answer is likely to be no, since these investigations do not aim explicitly to deepen our archaeological knowledge of the contemporary period, whatever they contribute indirectly to that end. On the other hand, in situations where the discovery and identification of murder victims concerns entire populations and touches on events that, by their scale, take on genuinely historical significance, the status of such investigations in relation to archaeology becomes rather more ambiguous. In Argentina, for example, teams of legal anthropologists have been working since 1985 on the identification of victims of the dictatorship of 1976–1983, using the excavation of skeletons from mass graves (see Chapter 12). The number of these *desapacidoss* (or disappeared) is estimated at 30,000. This figure confers upon these acts of violence the status of major event in the recent history of the Argentine nation. In this instance, the work of legal anthropologists, restoring case by case a long covered up historical truth, is not in the end much different from the work of historians. Like historians of the contemporary period, these specialists help survivors at an individual level complete the labour of mourning, and help with the collective acceptance of the existence of this trauma in the country's past.

Further, the experience gained at the end of the Second World War in the work of identifying victims from various types of mass grave has contributed, in the post-war period, to the constitution of a new domain within the archaeological field, known as forensic archaeology. This new approach, specific to the archaeology of the contemporary period, is concerned with the 'taphonomy' of mass graves and with the changes in condition of human remains within these particular environments. Originally, this research sought above all to measure the extent to which physical transformations might affect the establishment of the circumstances of death, or on the other hand to establish how long a body had been in the ground. Certainly, the research protocols developed over the last ten years in the examination of mass graves in South America have provided experience that is very useful today in analysing events of a similar nature: in fact Argentinian anthropologists have been called to Croatia to work on the study of mass graves produced by 'ethnic cleansing'. The former Yugoslavia is no doubt the first case where the anthropological study of mass graves has been applied systematically, after pressure from the International Penal Tribunal: in Bosnia, where 24,000 people are reported missing, the mass graves around Srebenica have been subject to systematic excavations since January 1996, after satellite photographs, revealing evidence of the concentration of populations, were published by the Americans in the summer of 1995. Entrusted to experts mandated by the IPT, these investigations aim to establish responsibility for massacres in order to bring their perpetrators before a court of international justice. They are becoming more and more systematised, as was seen after the mass exterminations in Rwanda. Like archaeologists who work traditionally on more ancient periods, specialists in recent mass graves base their expertise on the study of artefacts found around these burial places that might help establish the identity of bodies, and on the study of marks preserved on the human remains that enable eventually to establish the circumstances of death.

So, the closer we come to the archaeological remains of the present, the more indistinct everything appears; non-archaeologists excavate to research recent micro-events, using archaeological techniques; and anthropologists are involved in field work whose objective is not archaeological, when it is not archaeologists themselves who take on the work of exhumation. The discussion might never end if we sought to fix the point where archaeology begins and ends in such activities, since these operations are actually to be seen as hybrid constructions, or as what the sociologist of science Bruno Latour calls 'quasi-objects' (Latour 1991): these exhumations are as much interventions of an archaeological kind as they are anything else. Indeed, as soon as there is study of the physical transformations effected by human activity, there is the practice of archaeology. On the other hand, for archaeology to exist as an autonomous approach, it must base itself on the data preserved in a field that is specific to it, which it can make the basis of its proofs. It is not certain that, from the excavation of First World War battlefields, still less so from the mass graves of Croatia and Rwanda, something specifically archaeological can be learnt about the contemporary period. On the contrary, the information to be derived from human remains in these instances – about traumas, about the condition of teeth or bones – acquire meaning only when they can be cross-referenced with testimony or sources of a historical nature, which are, precisely, not inscribed in the terrain.

## Towards an archaeology of the short term

This archaeology that draws from the terrain nothing more than the confirmation of information derived from elsewhere looks very much like the first archaeology, as developed in Europe between the middle of the eighteenth century and the last third of the nineteenth. In both instances, archaeological materials are seen as testimony to, or illustration of, a historical reality that exists in its own terms, separately and independently of archaeology. From this point of view, the archaeological approach, as a field practice, can only with difficulty claim to be anything other than the undertaking to bring to light or uncover remains that are unknown, but which belong to a past that is known. In short, there is little observation, there is largely exhumation, because we do not see what kind of new information can be derived from the remains of periods with which we are familiar. In this situation, the reason that archaeology cannot manage to exist in its own terms is not that it lacks materials to investigate, it is in fact because it is too well informed. This is the whole question concerning the existence of an archaeology of the contemporary period. If archaeology is constituted as a self-sufficient discipline as soon as it bases itself on the investigation of that part of the past that is unknown, where are we to find this hidden mass within are own present?

We seem to be confronted with a problem concerning temporal scale, determining the nature of our relation with this immediate past, which has not yet truly emerged from our present. The historian Fernand Braudel shows well, in his work on the Mediterranean area, how history, as a problematic, develops in the articulation of long-term cycles, on a millennial scale, and the dynamics of short periods, associated with the immediate events of the present (Braudel 1969). In fact, the Braudelian perspective on history opens two interesting avenues for our concerns here. It shows, on the one hand, that there is a diversity of dynamics, developed on every timescale, whose trajectories cross over, in some sense, the different periods studied by history. In other words, the process at issue in each of the sequences studied within historical disciplines develops beyond the actual duration of these phases therefore these phases can be approached from a diversity of temporal and spatial scales, all of which constitute meaning. These dynamics vary from the microscopic scale of punctual, localised events, to the macroscopic scale of global evolutions developed over the long term. But, on the other hand, the existence, within these historical processes, of this superimposition of dynamics of differing scale leads to a different kind of implication; it suggests that the position that we occupy in time and space in relation to these phenomena is not without its bearing on our apprehension of the past. From this point of view, evolutions that have occurred since these particular periods of the past studied by history or archaeology count just as much as those that preceded them and which made them what they are.

We are singularly lacking in distance if we envisage approaching the archaeology of the contemporary past in the same way as we would that of the deeper periods of our history. The remains of our immediate historical environment are no less bearers of archaeological information than those of more ancient periods, but, since we are not yet able to grasp the medium and long-term dynamics into which these remains will be inscribed, we cannot apprehend such information. In this sense, if it is legitimate to demand that henceforward the existence of an autonomous archaeology of the contemporary past be recognised, it would be a manifest mistake to want to pour it into the traditional mould of the archaeology of more classical periods. On the contrary, we should envisage an archaeology of the short term. This particular approach should, on the one hand, take account of the specific investigations linked to our temporal proximity to this near past but it should also, on the other, develop problematics adapted to historical dynamics of very short scale, varying from a few hours to a few generations. For the most part, this new archaeological domain has yet to be engendered.

## The collective fabrication of the past

The preceding remarks are profoundly troubling, since they lead us to call into question the traditional separation established between the subject and object of archaeology, or, in other words, between the point of observation that would identify the present and the field of observation that would constitute the past. For to envisage the existence of an archaeology of the contemporary past is to push the discipline's procedures to the limit, and to question archaeology's relation to its object, the remains of the past. Yet more profoundly, the particular configuration of this contemporary archaeology challenges the status of expertise on the past conventionally accorded to specialists who study its remains: confronted with the remains of the contemporary past, in effect, we are not, in the manner of external observers, separate from the object of archaeology. On the contrary, we cannot help but add to the constitution of archaeological remains. We are situated, both as actors in the present and as observers of the past, at the heart of the production of archaeological materials.

We should no doubt remind ourselves once more that archaeology does not properly speaking work on the remains of the past. The imperatives of the administrative management of archaeology have certainly accustomed us to speaking of the archaeological 'heritage' – in the sense of an ensemble of cultural and scientific assets inherited from the past, for which we in the present are responsible – but in reality, things are not so simple. If archaeology is concerned with fossilised remains from the past, they are nonetheless preserved in the present, and it is effectively in our present that they are manifest to us. Firstly, the nature of the information to be extracted from them depends on their state of preservation at the moment when they are studied. Secondly, the way these remains are investigated, interpreted, represented depends on the particular research preoccupations of the present day. In this sense, archaeological remains are inseparable from our present, and it is they who need us if they are to exist. More deeply still, we are ourselves producers of archaeological materials, and when we practise the discipline, we do little more than add a new archaeological episode to the existence of places and things that have often already known a long series of functions and uses. In other words, we add new strata of information and interpretation to object themselves characterised by considerable stratifications of meaning over time. This implies, in these circumstances, that an objective management of the archaeological 'heritage' is not possible; nor is a neutral 'treatment' of archaeological remains. We have not, as archaeologists or 'managers' of the past, withdrawn outside the places and things that constitute the object of archaeology; on the contrary, we live with them, among them.

What should we do with the archaeological remains of the 'recent past', and how should we account for them? Here, the specificity of the archaeology of the contemporary past resides in the proximity of the remains, resisting a univocal representation of the past, unlike the vestiges of more ancient periods, usually deprived of narrativity, indeed even of identity. From this viewpoint, the case of such sites as Auschwitz, in Poland, and Oradour-sur-Glane, in the Limousin, show very similar experiences regarding the conservation and presentation of remains, while at the same time underlining the impossible distanciation of the past that is required by any undertaking of restoration and preservation.

## Auschwitz and Oradour-sur-Glane: the impossible representation of the past

There is no need to recall the considerable importance that attaches to the site of Auschwitz-Birkenau in the history and consciousness of the twentieth century. The ruins of the concentration camp are on UNESCO's list of world heritage monuments. The site has been preserved and opened to the public since the end of the Second World War, both to bear witness to the horrors of the Nazi system, and to commemorate the victims of the Holocaust. The memorial museum at Auschwitz was created in 1947, and its running entrusted to a survivor of the camp, Tadeusz Szymansky. In its present form, the museum, occupying several of the camp's wooden huts, dates from 1955. The whole domain, created in April 1940 on Himmler's orders, originally covered a vast area of 42 square kilometres. Auschwitz II (Birkenau) has been razed to the ground and the site left abandoned; only Auschwitz I has been partially preserved. This secondary camp covering 174 hectares contained more than 600 brick and wooden huts, of which only 200 remain standing today. The museum features objects or personal effects that belonged to deportees, such as immense piles of luggage, or shoes piled up at the entrance to the gas chambers. Human remains are also preserved, such as the masses of hair taken from victims, intended for industrial recycling.

In its conception, this centre for extermination on an industrial scale was not built to last, but to answer immediate objectives, liable to change over time. More than half a century after the conflict, this ensemble of buildings, of a more or less temporary nature, is badly threatened by erosion. So, at the beginning of the 1990s, an international committee for the preservation of the Auschwitz-Birkenau site was established, on the initiative of a former US ambassador, Ronald Lauder. The threat of destruction concerns not only the buildings but also the remains featured in the museum. In winter, snow has often been seen falling onto the piles of human hair, because of leaks in the roof. All the elements on display require immediate restoration and need to benefit from exhibition conditions of a museographical kind.

The financial requirements are estimated at more than 40 million dollars. A first allocation has enabled the installation of a heating system in the camp huts, in order to maintain the remains on display at a constant temperature; in these wooden and brick constructions, the temperature can vary between minus 20 degrees in winter to more than plus 30 degrees in summer. The work to be done also includes the restoration of a series of huts, as well as the establishing of new routes to and entrances into the camp, in order to make visiting easier. A new museographic project is also being considered: 'We would also like visitors to grasp the trauma suffered by the victims of Auschwitz-Birkenau, thanks to a new presentation, in which individual stories can be traced', says Franciszek Piper, one of those responsible for the project. However, the Polish conservators of the Auschwitz Museum remain cautious about a project for the more complete restoration of the camp's remains. If we restore too much, they insist, we are necessarily providing neo-Nazis and revisionists with the argument they need to claim that Auschwitz is a hoax.

Should Auschwitz be restored and, if so, how far should we go with the museographical standardisation of a site that is not a museum, of remains that are not properly speaking a collection? Should Auschwitz be represented to make it accessible to generations who have not known the Holocaust and, again, if so, how far should we go with what has to be called a 'mise-en-scène'? These questions, that call into doubt the very identity of the site and of its commemoration, have been asked in similar terms at Oradour-sur-Glane, in the Limousin (Farmer, 1994). There, on 10 June 1944, a battalion of the 'Das Reich' SS Division exterminated almost the entire population of the town, before setting fire to it. As at Auschwitz, the idea of preserving the site as a monument came early; Oradour was classified a historical national monument in 1946. By means of a special law, the ruins of the town were to be preserved in order to be shown to the public, while a new Oradour was built nearby. Again as at Auschwitz, the preservation of the site meets a desire to bear witness, by the presentation of the place where Nazi atrocities were committed, in conjunction with an exhibition of the remains that constitute its traces.

The problem of how to restore and present the ruins of Oradour was first posed in 1945, where a development programme was entrusted to Pierre Paquet, Chief Architect and Inspector of Historical Monuments. At the beginning, this programme consisted only in operations to maintain and clean up the ruins. At the time it was envisaged basically to leave the site as it was, while protecting the church from the effects of weather – it is there that the principal testimony to the massacre of women and children is preserved – as well as cleaning and shoring up the walls in the main street that were in danger of collapsing. However, from 1946 onwards this minimal conservation plan was to be extended, to take in, notably, the upkeep of the town's gardens. Though the intention was that Oradour be visited as a kind of national cemetery, it was important that these gardens not be left to become wasteland, giving visitors the impression they had been abandoned. So, the Oradour conservation project went from an initial programme of strict preservation of the ruins as they were in June 1944, to a programme for the site's valorisation. By this means, the state authorities attempted to produce an image of the site in harmony with a political and ideological message addressed to the public. General De Gaulle, Head of the Provisional Government of the Republic, stated on his official visit to the site in 1945: 'Oradour is the symbol of what has happened to the country itself. To restore and conserve memory, we must stay together, as we are at this moment. A site such as this remains something common to us all. Never again should such a thing happen anywhere in France.'

A parallel slippage is revealed with the work for the preservation of the ruins. The first attempts at consolidation occurred less than a year after the event, in spring 1945. Though all that had been envisaged was basic maintenance, here again it is a genuine labour of restoration and valorisation that was initiated. The rubble and fallen masonry were cleared away from the streets; the wooden lintels of the doorways were replaced with reinforced concrete, to withstand bad weather. Similarly, the increase over the years in the work of stabilisation and restoration of the ruins led to a change in the conception of how the programme for maintaining the site was organised, leading to its professionalisation. It had been thought, at the outset, that these works would consist essentially in basic maintenance that could be entrusted to guides recruited on site, and could be carried out periodically outside of visiting times. But, from the 1950s onwards, the acceleration in the ruins' degradation, combined with the general level of erosion of the site, necessitated the passing of this increasingly difficult task on to specialised companies.

At Oradour as at Auschwitz, the preservation in its original condition of a site whose memory is to be preserved is an undertaking first envisaged as a simple procedure, but destined to encounter in time problems that are increasingly difficult to manage. Restoration rapidly becomes distortion, because what is required for the preservation of the remains in question leads not only to their 'reconstruction' or 'reconstitution', but also to the fabrication of hybrid constructions that belong as much to the present as to the past, and in which the surviving portion of the past progressively diminishes. For reasons of conservation, heating is installed at Auschwitz and a bus shuttle service is introduced; at Oradour, for the same reasons, year on year, a park is being created out of ruins reinforced with concrete and surrounded by lawns. Like the present, the past cannot be reduced to a single point in time, because both relate us back to a multiplicity of temporalities. To conserve Auschwitz or Oradour is to try to fix the physical evolution of these sites at the moment in time from which they are supposed to derive their meaning.

This undertaking is not without its difficulties, since it is terribly restricted, not least by the very sites that it seeks to preserve. At Oradour, to classify the site goes hand in hand with the exclusion of the town's inhabitants who still own houses there, or who still cultivate their gardens there, and to whom access to the site is forbidden. Similarly, it appears necessary to close off the houses, blocking their entrances with iron bars, and to isolate the ruins, shut off within an enclosure. Faced with the remains of the recent past, restoration necessarily devitalises, because it requires the fixing of sites and things at an ideal – i.e. fictive – moment of the past. In doing so, it condemns itself, paradoxically, to tamper more and more with remains that it would seek to maintain in an unreal integrity. We can say, in fact, that what constitutes the remains of the past is their degradation and loss, for these remains are, like we who observe them, plunged in the movement of time. To replace the rotten timbers of the huts at Auschwitz, to reinforce with concrete the ruins of Oradour, may be to render the site more readable, but it is above all, intrinsically, to change its nature and to divert its evolution. The archaeology of the recent past reminds us that we cannot keep separate from us the remains of the past by casting them into a past that is no more, since these remains only exist in the temporal relations that they maintain with our own present. In these circumstances, to try to fix the remains of the past in this ideal state of the past is effectively to destroy those very remains; to clear away the rubble of Oradour is to clear away materials conditioned by the past, marked by the present and destined to be shaped by the future of the site itself. To restore, to preserve, is to destroy the present or future history that that would have been known by the sites or remains we wish to preserve; it is to replace them with a present and future that is not theirs, but is ours, rather. By preserving the remains of the past in an artificial state of the past we make them undergo new physical transformations, we incorporate new materials; we make them into composite objects, in which the past, the present and the image we have of the future are inextricably mixed. These are new archaeological objects to which we give life, whose modifications bear witness, physically, to the new interpretations that have been imposed upon them and which, thereafter, sustain their identity.

## When the vestiges invent history

We would like to think that these sites, because they have been the scenes of exceptional or tragic events, intrinsically preserve the memory of those events. In fact, neither places nor things say anything whatsoever in themselves, unless it is to those who have memories of them. 'The countryside, there, for you is empty, says Pierre Nivromort to his grandchildren during his return journey to Auschwitz, but for me it is full of people: here I see women in rags digging a trench; I can smell burnt flesh' (interview in *Liberation*, 3 October 1996). What do we do when faced with these sites that are empty of meaning? To bear witness to this incommunicable past, it becomes necessary to tell stories; that is, to invent a history that could be told by the remains, or by the traces of past events. This is, essentially, the museum's role.

At Oradour, the first project for the museification of the site was born only several months after the massacre, in October 1944. Its purpose was twofold, firstly, to transform the ruins of the town into a kind of 'sanctuary' and to organise visits around several particular places, where the drama unfurled (the church where the women and children were massacred, the barns where the men were shot, or the cemetery where the victims are buried). It was also intended to have an emotional impact, by presenting the places as they were just after the event. 'The visitor will remember all the better by sensing the invisible presence of the inhabitants', say the minutes of a meeting of the Commemoration

Committee, dated 21 October 1944. 'An object found in its place, for example a cooking-pot in the fireplace [. . .] will often create the strongest impression.' Entirely similar concerns inform the presentation of sites and remains at Auschwitz. And, as with the museum at Auschwitz, the ambitions of the museographic programme at Oradour depend on the exploitation of objects from everyday life, exhibited to underline dramatically the sacrifice of victims brutally torn from the lives they led. To this end, the presentation *in situ* of objects, or more generally the preservation in their place of remains and traces, conforms to the construction of a narrative discourse to be read into the space of the site. So it is striking to note how much, from the outset, the presentation of remains is associated with their 'mise-en-scène'. At Oradour in particular, the presentation of objects in their place, if it is to generate the intended emotional charge, must necessarily be accompanied by a development of the space. As was decided at the meeting of the Commemoration Committee in October 1944:

> In several dwellings where moveable objects have been destroyed, our action should be confined to the conservation of the walls; but in many others, in particular certain garages, where cars, lorries, bicycles, metal objects that have survived the fire can still be found, it is appropriate, unless in their upheaval they present a particular striking effect, to free the vehicles from the debris accumulated around them and to present them, and the other objects, in the place they used to occupy, in order to show piously and faithfully the sites as they were at the time of the fire.

The Oradour project thus aims to create, in some sense, the image of a new Pompeii of the recent past, where the objects of everyday life will bear witness to the cataclysm that brought time to a halt on 10 June 1944. But, in every case, this false Pompeii has to be fabricated, like a cinema decor in which would be found all the necessary accessories for the representation of a history that, with the distance of time, takes on more and more the form of myth. For if time effectively stopped at the moment of the drama for the families of the victims, if the commemoration of this event merges into the recognition of a collective identity, the site itself carries on its slow transformation, by a gradual process of disintegration, along its own trajectory.

The case of Dr Desourteaux's car, abandoned for over fifty years in the town square of Oradour, is an interesting example of this phenomenon of transference, whereby certain objects are invested with a role as symbolic representation, and reveals the growing discrepancy between the remains and the history they are burdened with. On arriving at Oradour on Saturday 10 June 1944, Dr Desourteaux was stopped by the SS and forced to park his car in the town square, where the male population had been assembled. From there, he was led with the others into one of the barns at Oradour, and was killed. In fact, the car in the town square at Oradour is not his; after the massacre, the doctor's brother came to fetch the car to bring it home, where it remained. The car that was to become 'Dr Desourteaux's car' was the wine-seller's car; when the fire services arrived, it was blocking the access, so it was moved into the square, from where it has not moved. Abandoned for more than half a century to the weather, 'Dr Desourteaux's car' has lost all its paint, the seat coverings, its interior fittings, and its tyres have literally dissolved into the ground. This carcass, looking strangely like the fossil of a car, was in 1992 scrubbed clean, made stable and covered with a protective varnish. The car appears all the more incongruous in this decor of blackened ruins, evoking some improbable lost civilisation of the 1930s.

## Perspectives: for a 'multi-vocal' archaeology

On 5 December 1996, the dome of Hiroshima was placed by UNESCO on its list of humanity's world heritage sites, to bear witness to the atomic explosion on 6 August 1945. The classification of this ruin, asked for by Japan, provoked strong opposition from the United States, who pointed out that sites related to the last war are 'by their nature matters of controversy and it would probably be better not to include them on the list'. All sites of the contemporary past are effectively, by their nature, matters of controversy, not so much because these sites sustain individually some particular polemic, but because they are inseparable from the debates and issues of our present. In this sense, this particular category of archaeological remains seems to be situated within what Bruno Latour defines as a space of mediation. The identity of these remains, or the signification that they take on, are not given them in advance by some process of inheritance; on the contrary, they are the provisional result of a negotiation, by which diverse and sometimes rival interest groups come together or oppose each other. Thus, the archaeological remains buried, with the remains of lost soldiers, in the battlefields of the Meuse or the Somme concern not only the military history of France, or the French department for ex-servicemen. Their fate also concerns the various nations who took part in the conflict, the families of the soldiers, the ethnic or cultural communities, lost or surviving, to which the dead of the Great War belonged, the population of the regions where this supra-national heritage is preserved, as well as the enterprises, public or private, that exploit the land in which these remains are preserved. The same can be said for sites that bear witness to the Holocaust or to Nazi persecutions, the recognition of which brings out the play of divergent interests: the families of the victims want the memory of the disappeared to be preserved; the State tends to absorb these sites into a monument-apparatus designed to sustain an ideological discourse; the inhabitants of the region, lastly, would like to live normally with this troublesome heritage, too heavy for them to bear alone. Time itself helps to modify these networks of alliance, the stakes involved, and to maintain the unstable dynamic whereby representations of the past are constructed, by ceaselessly adding new adaptations to ancient interpretations.

The particular situation of contemporary archaeology, the situation of the historical discipline as a whole, has three principal implications regarding the conduct of the discipline. These implications bear upon methodology, upon theory, and upon ethics. From the methodological viewpoint, the archaeology of the remains of the contemporary period cannot be reduced to a univocal enterprise, confined just to specialists in the analysis of the material remains of the past, the archaeologists or scientists usually associated with those remains. By the very nature of the materials to be dealt with, the archaeology of the near past can only be an undertaking realised 'by several voices', one in which different professional or political groups are involved, along with the diverse social or cultural communities who have an interest in what these remains become, and in the meaning given to the history that they bear witness to.

This multi-vocal archaeology, whereby the collective memory or the testimony of individuals enjoys an authority normally only accorded to specialists of the past, requires that, on a theoretical level, we reconsider the question of the construction of archaeological interpretation. The archaeology of the contemporary past is in effect directly faced with the problem of the present signification of the past's remains, and with the diversity of interpretations, according to the perspectives and approaches at issue. The study of the internal functioning and of the place occupied by archaeology and archaeologists, in each situation, within this network of interrelations, constitutes an essential aspect of the discipline's interpretative procedure.

Finally, from the ethical viewpoint, the stakes involved in the archaeology of the contemporary past require us to think differently the interpretation of the past and the role played, to differing but complementary degrees by the individuals and collectivities engaged in the process of constructing history. Hence, the functioning of the archaeology of the contemporary past is not centralised or pyramid-like, in the manner of traditionally organised knowledge-production and diffusion. On the contrary, in the new configuration of contemporary archaeology, information circulates in a network, and is exchanged at every level of the structure, without a pre-defined hierarchy constricting its exploitation. In this sense, contemporary archaeology is part of the development of new forms of citizenship, within which the problems of the collectivity are laid bare and discussed by groupings of individuals at every level, from the simplest to the most extended; while solutions to these problems are investigated through the permanent inter-relation of these different scales of collective organisation.

Let us recall, once again, that there can be no chronological limits beyond which the remains of the past would lose their identity as archaeological vestiges to constitute the environment of the present time; the present, made up as it is of a diversity of past temporalities, constitutes of itself, and in its entirety, archaeology's field of study. Similarly, all manifestations that bear witness, physically, to human activity are, by their nature, concerned with archaeology. The archaeology of the contemporary period has a legitimate existence, then, but a frame in which it can find its proper place remains to be discovered. A vast field of research opens up before us, enriching the traditional archaeological heritage with a substantial ensemble of new remains that we must henceforward study, protect, and valorise.

## Acknowledgements

My deepest thanks go to Dr V. Buchli and Dr G. Lucas, who invited me to contribute this chapter on the archaeology of the contemporary past. I am indebted to discussions and exchanges with them for several of the ideas developed here.

## References

Braudel, F. (1969) 'La longue durée', in *Ecrits sur l'histoire*. Paris, Flammarion.
Farmer, S. (1994) *Oradour. Arrêt sur mémoire*. Paris, Calmann-Levy.
Latour, B. (1991) *Nous n'avons jamais été modernes. Essai d'anthropologie symétrique*. Paris, La Découverte.

# Chapter 17

# Epilogue

*Ian Hodder*

We have grown accustomed to the idea that as archaeologists we work not only with the past but with the present. Our engagement with the present involves not only ethnoarchaeology and experimental archaeology, but also the varied politics of the past. Archaeologists in many parts of the world have been confronted by issues of reburial, repatriation, land claims, indigenous rights and competing perspectives.

Historians too have recognised that each age writes its own history, and that the writing of history is part of a political process. But to many, the writing of history can be seen as a disconnected intellectual pursuit. It is less easy to ignore archaeology as a contemporary social process because objects survive into a public present. Their materiality forces a contemporary engagement. Archaeology is very much 'in your face' as contract archaeologists are called in to deal with the destruction of sites, as monuments decay and need conserving, or as objects are looted for material gain. In this volume both the Ludlow Collective and Laurie Wilkie provide examples of the media interest that surrounds many archaeological field projects. The presentation of the past often becomes contested and complex in these very public and highly charged contexts.

So all archaeology deals with the contemporary past. But this book goes further and explores the boundaries of the idea that archaeology is about the past. A focus on the archaeology of the present challenges the very definition and existence of the discipline. By probing the boundaries of the discipline these authors create an undisciplined moment at which new vistas and new definitions are opened up.

Definitional problems are already implied by the emergence of a strong field of modern material culture studies. Here the bridge between archaeology and other disciplines is created by the focus on material culture. But since material culture has long been of interest, however marginally, in anthropology and cultural studies, and since its study can be accomplished using ethnographic and social science techniques, this particular bridging or displacement only minimally challenges the separate identity of archaeology as the study of the material remains of the past. But when archaeology is used to excavate the present we see that the discipline need not be confined to a preoccupation with the past but that it can be defined as a particular mode of inquiry into the present.

Archaeology redefined as the systematic recording of material traces, or as the study of objects in relation to contexts, or simply as 'digging beneath the surface of things', creates new types of bridges with other disciplines. What remains distinctive is the method – a particular mode of inquiry. But it immediately becomes clear when the method is applied to contemporary behaviour by the authors in this volume that the interpretative framework within which the archaeological technique is used must merge with other disciplines. Thus, Rathje argues that the study of contemporary garbage necessitates inclusion of a wide range of perspectives including psychology. The excavation of a contemporary council house by Buchli and Lucas produces results that require a full sociological perspective. Wilkie and others in this volume show the need for dialogue and participation with a diversity of contemporary groups.

The archaeology of contemporary life involves a full engagement with contemporary theorisation of identity, commodification, class, gender and so on. It involves dealing with social and ethical issues from garbage disposal to ethnic cleansing and human rights. Archaeology provides the techniques but interpretation must immediately engage with a broader literature.

This stretching and redefinition of the discipline in relation to contemporary life leads to a reflection on archaeology as a whole. As already noted, archaeology is always partly about the present, even if the past in the present can be dated back to 1 million years. So, again, archaeology provides the techniques, but interpretation engages quickly with the social and cultural disciplines in the humanities and social sciences. Study of the archaeological past must always be embedded within an understanding of why the material past is of fascination to us. In this volume it would have been possible to explore more fully the ways in which archaeology resonates with a wider contemporary cultural engagement with decay, fragmentation and putrefaction. The possibility of such linkages underlines the close ties between archaeology, cultural studies, the study of popular culture, the social sciences, and social and cultural anthropology generally.

This encroachment of archaeology into wider domains occurs because of the material presence of the past in contemporary life, but also because of an increasing recognition that an archaeological methodology offers a particular perspective on the world around us. As Rathje's work has repeatedly shown, material and verbal evidence often give different perspectives. The excavation by Buchli and Lucas of a council house allows one to see into the details of the life of a nameless mother of two, dealing with a heroin-addicted partner, and suddenly just taking up and leaving. The archaeological approach gives a sense of the life struggle behind the statistics of single mothers and state support.

The archaeological focus on the deed rather than on the word allows exploration of the movement of the mass as opposed to the elite history of the few. This claim has long been made by archaeologists in their struggles with history, but a contemporary relevance is given by the chapters in this volume. Stevenson shows that focus on the design of middle-of-the-range earthenware tells us much more about life of masses of people, and their aspirations, in the inter-war period, than do accounts of 'high artists' of that time. Wilkie provides a fine account of archaeological evidence indicating African-American use of wild food and education in order to forge a path to freedom. She argues that the Civil Rights movement began in these homes prior to the period after World War II when it is more normally thought to have begun. Examination of daily practices of masses of people may often provide an alternative picture of social and cultural change, as is clearly shown by the Ludlow Collective.

But within the mass, archaeology also allows an insight into the personal, the emotive, the identification of individual death and tragedy. Both chapters dealing in this volume with forensic archaeology point to the deep emotional implications of working with the families of the deceased. Legendre provides a moving account of an aircraft crash and concludes that a twisted, rusted airplane can be a more vivid memorial than a sanitised stone monument.

This book provides a long sequence of moving, powerful chapters that confront and challenge us. They disturb us because they bring archaeology into the social and emotional immediacy of our contemporary lives. In doing so they also confront and challenge archaeology as a discipline devoted to the study of the material traces of the past. Archaeology comes to be more a discipline concerned with the materiality of life. As such, the way is opened for the dispersal of archaeological debate and interpretation into wider domains. The chapters in this volume invite us to consider a redefinition of archaeology as a particular mode of inquiry into social and personal life. Existing techniques include questionnaire surveys, in-depth interviews, participant observation, historical study and so on. But separate and distinct is an archaeological mode of inquiry that relates objects to their material contexts through systematic recording and interpretation. This mode of inquiry can be applied to all stages in the production, use and discarding of artefacts. It involves the idea of excavating to layers below the verbal, conscious, represented. To redefine archaeology in this way would involve a major task, but the authors in this volume can be congratulated for pushing beyond the edges of the discipline and so opening a rather different vision.

# Index